WHEN I START MY BUSINESS, I'LL BE HAPPY

WHEN I START MY BUSINESS, I'LL BE HAPPY

A Practical, No-BS Guide to Successful Online Entrepreneurship

SAM VANDER WIELEN

balance

New York   Boston

Balance
Hachette Book Group
1290 Avenue of the Americas
New York, NY 10104
GCP-Balance.com
@GCPBalance

First Edition: April 2025

Balance is an imprint of Grand Central Publishing. The Balance name and logo are registered trademarks of Hachette Book Group, Inc.

The publisher is not responsible for websites (or their content) that are not owned by the publisher.

The Hachette Speakers Bureau provides a wide range of authors for speaking events. To find out more, go to hachettespeakersbureau.com or email HachetteSpeakers@hbgusa.com.

Balance books may be purchased in bulk for business, educational, or promotional use. For information, please contact your local bookseller or the Hachette Book Group Special Markets Department at special.markets@hbgusa.com.

Library of Congress Cataloging-in-Publication Data

Names: Vander Wielen, Sam, author.
Title: When I start my business, I'll be happy : a practical, no-BS guide
  to successful online entrepreneurship / Sam Vander Wielen.
Other titles: When I start my business, I will be happy
Description: First edition. | New York : Balance, 2025. | Includes index. |
Identifiers: LCCN 2024048224 | ISBN 9781538767382 (hardcover) |
  ISBN 9781538767405 (ebook)
Subjects: LCSH: New business enterprises. | Entrepreneurship. | Electronic
  commerce.
Classification: LCC HD62.5 .V36 2025 | DDC 658.1/1—dc23/eng/20241226
LC record available at https://lccn.loc.gov/2024048224

ISBNs: 9781538767382 (hardcover); 9781538767405 (ebook)

Printed in the United States of America

LSC-C

Printing 1, 2025

For Mom and Dad. I miss you both so much. Dad,
I know you're going to make my book a bestseller in heaven.

To my boys, Ryan and Hudson, who have been the light
I needed in my darkest times. I love you both so much.

Contents

Contents

Introduction

The surly flight attendant had just come around with the boiling-hot cigarette-flavored coffee when, *BAM!* Our plane flying from Amsterdam to my hometown of Philadelphia plummeted thousands of feet through the sky after hitting what must have been the world's worst air speed bump—that's what it felt like at least. In the back of my throat, the burning hot vomit rose up and my heart clenched tightly through my chest as the plane jolted hard to the left and the pilot adjusted our speed and altitude to try, unsuccessfully, to calm things down. (*Note: If you're scared of flying or hate scary stories, this one is over real quick and I swear it has a point. Sometimes pants-crapping moments are the best life lessons, so it's worth it.*)

Through the cries and anxious shifting about in the cabin, I clutched my husband Ryan's sweaty hand, wondering how the hell I had gotten here. Not on the actual plane, of course. That much I knew. I'd gone on my first real "vacation" after becoming a lawyer: a ten-day Baltic Sea adventure around northern Europe. The firm had even given me a "special phone" to make sure I was reachable for all ten days. It's funny how unimportant you can be or feel to a company until they need to reach you while you're on vacation.

In those minutes that felt like hours, I had flashes of everything in my lawyer life up to that point: the bar exam, the sexual harassment I'd experienced at firms, the number of times I'd hid in the bathroom at work, hoping they would forget about me and I could sneak out when the cleaning staff came in for the evening. Or all of the days of inhaling entire bags of Boom Chicka Pop while I sat at my desk, hoping the fullness and pain it caused in my belly would distract me from the pain I felt in my soul. *How did I get here? How did I let it get so bad?* As if my entire miserable life was projected onto a movie screen in what I dramatically thought were my last moments, I saw all the "watercooler" moments I had spent complaining about how awful it was to be a lawyer. How I'd rather do literally anything else. How I couldn't believe this all *happened to me*, like I didn't choose it and couldn't do anything about it. I'd tell anyone who would listen about my sad story of "having" to work as a lawyer and being "forced" to work under such awful circumstances. I couldn't freaking stand the sound of my voice. Not just because I don't like how my voice actually sounds (who does?), but because I saw clearly, for the first time, just how horribly and annoyingly victim-y I had become.

In a moment of clarity during an otherwise terrorizing plane experience, I was able to feel the distance between who I was at that moment in my life and who I felt I really was inside. I'd unintentionally drifted down a life path that wasn't consistent with my values, hopes, or goals. But it probably would have been a good idea to have a clear picture of what those were in the first place.

I was curled up on my mom's couch when she suddenly face-planted into her bowl of hummus after taking a few too many pills. I carefully wiped the hummus out of her hair while I waited for an ambulance to arrive. I knew it was only a matter of time before she would wake up in a fit of rage, angry that I'd called for help and stepped out of my role as the protector of her personal and professional reputation. Even though I was just fourteen, this was far from the first time I'd seen her this way, and sadly it would be far from the last. Although it was the only way I'd ever know my mom, people tell me she wasn't always that way.

My mom had a hard life. She was also incredibly driven despite it. One month after I was born, my parents got divorced. My mom was accepted to medical school at the age of forty while pregnant with me. Newly divorced, she started medical school when I was nine months old. Everyone told her she couldn't do it, except for my dad. Was she the kind of mom who knew when my school assignments were due or who baked cupcakes for PTA fundraisers? No. But she bet on herself when no one else did.

Even though we were so proud of her for chasing her dream, having a mom in medical school and residency until I was nearly eight wasn't easy on me or my sister, Cara. We both needed and wanted comfort and attention from our mom. Looking back, though, during this time in my life without my mom present, I was probably the happiest and the most authentic version of myself. I felt free to be inquisitive, adventurous, and highly independent. I didn't feel as bad as I eventually would around my mom for being sensitive or sassy.

It was after she graduated from medical school and started her own medical practice that Mom began to battle many of her own demons. To put it bluntly and mildly, she put me and Cara through hell until she died last year. We endured an unsafe, unstable, trauma-filled home with very little outside support. As her addictions and mental illness worsened, we shrank ourselves to fit the parentified mold she demanded we fill. Terrified of her next violent episode or suicide attempt, we tiptoed around her, trying as hard as possible to not do anything that could cause another breakdown. As is common among abused children, we stuck by her through all of her breakups, divorces, legal issues, suicide attempts, and overdoses, even though we didn't receive the same support from her. Meanwhile, we were explicitly and implicitly told to keep all of this a secret, as it was "our responsibility" to protect her medical license or else we would "end up on the streets." It was bad enough to experience her repeated, seemingly neverending erratic, violent episodes and addiction, but the responsibility to keep anyone from finding out riddled me with anxiety and hypervigilence that I still feel today.

It's hard to truly know who you are or what you want to do with your life when you don't feel safe enough to ask for help or to honor your own needs. We were too busy trying to keep a ticking time bomb from exploding to even think about ourselves. As college and a future career came closer, I became laser-focused: Pick a secure, financially stable career that gets me as far away from here as I can go, as fast as possible. Maybe I watched too many episodes of *Law & Order* as a child, but I thought becoming a lawyer was the best way to do so.

By the time I was on that plane, I realized I had never taken the time to actually figure out what I wanted to do with my life. I decided to become a lawyer from a place of fear. I saw independence as the fastest track out of my mom's control, and becoming a lawyer was the most independent, solid career track I could think of. I had no sense of self—I couldn't even pick out furniture when my husband and I bought our first home together, because I literally had no preferences or taste. Looking back on it, even though I was a practicing lawyer, wife, and "independent" homeowner, I didn't know who I was or what I wanted. I'd achieved the independence I sought, but I still didn't feel free. On the way home from Europe, I realized that in my pursuit for stability, I never stopped to consider what I wanted my life to look like or what would make me happy. My dreams were never part of the equation. I needed to make a change.

Flying on a plane is the ultimate exercise in letting go of control. Unlike being a passenger in a car, you can't say, "Pull over! I'll take it from here." There's not even an opportunity for backseat driving, and, once you're on the plane, you're on for good. Outside of *Top Gun*, there's no parachute to safety over the Atlantic Ocean. There's something about going through a scary moment in which you have no control that makes you realize where in your life you do. I realized all my whining about my career choice was just that—a choice. Every day I chose to put on one of the black Banana Republic skirt suits I hated, get in the fancy Mercedes I bought to make myself feel better about my miserable career, and go do work that essentially helped insurance companies get richer. I wasn't given the opportunity or safety needed to consider myself or my preferences as a child, but I could now. I couldn't blame anyone or anything for my circumstances. I could hold my mom accountable for what happened to us as children, but also move forward and claim my own future. I needed to take responsibility and choose my own path. In those terrifying moments on the plane, I realized I had options.

Realizing that *you* are the only thing standing between you and all of your pain is truly a transformative experience. There's no one left to blame. No bad boss. No adversaries. Just you. If you've also experienced hardship in your life or job, you're not to blame for what's happened to you. But you can do something about it from here on out. You can change directions, regardless of what's happened to you in the past.

Within days of that terrifying plane ride, I started my own business online. I thought owning my own business would solve all of my problems for good. Wouldn't it be nice if you just made one big life shift at the age of twenty-seven and *yay*! Life problems solved—smooth sailing from here on. It'd be a lot easier, right? But what I didn't know when I left the law and started my own business was that my entire world would soon be turned upside down in both the best and the worst ways possible. Within the first few years of starting my business, I'd have brain surgery, learn my dad had cancer, become his caregiver, lose my dad, and then tragically and shockingly lose my mom within a year of losing my dad.

This isn't a grief book or a book about childhood trauma. It's not a book of sob stories of all the hard shit I've been through. I've got a trilogy for you on that one (or, as my mom desperately wanted for her own life story, a five-part Lifetime movie series). I'm here to show you how, despite everything I've been through, I've managed to build a multi-seven-figure online business that has helped thousands of people around the world, and that allows me the freedom and flexibility I'd sought for all my life. Starting my own business didn't solve all of my problems. In fact, it created several new challenges and obstacles to overcome. Even though I'd built a successful online business, it wasn't smooth sailing—neither on- nor off-line. Thanks to what I've been through and what it pushed me to create, I've got loads of marketing secrets and business-building strategies to pass on to help you do this, too. Not to necessarily fix your life but to help you take ownership of it, find your life's work, and actually enjoy what you do.

———

This book is for you if you want to start your own business, or grow the one you have, and you are:

- excited to get started, but you're not sure what the *right* kind of business is for you, or what to sell;
- a current business owner who's sick of all the ever-changing tips, trends, and pressure to be on social media 24-7;

- curious about how to make sales and revenue even when you're not actively "working," because you've got other stuff going on in your life;
- over the bs, gimmicky digital-marketing culture of gurus trying to sell you a course and would rather learn business strategies and tips from someone with professional experience;
- interested in taking a business you already have online, but feel overwhelmed with where to start;
- eager to create a digital product, course, physical product, or other online offer with a sustainable marketing system, grow an engaged email list that drives consistent sales, and create your own evergreen funnel; and
- hoping to create and maintain a profitable business model that generates consistent cash flow, flexibility, and freedom.

So much of the information you'll find about building a business online is not offered by people with any actual business, legal, or financial background and thus is not as reliable as you might expect. And hearing the same tips again and again from people whose experience consists solely of starting a lifestyle or personal-brand business is not helpful or replicable. You want to build something real that lasts. You want to have an impact on your industry and your clients, and you want to feel proud of the products and content you put out there.

With my years as a corporate lawyer, starting my own health coaching business, and then starting and growing a multi-seven-figure online legal templates business, I have a lot of professional and personal experience to guide you along your own journey. Part of what's helped me to build such a successful online business has been my commitment to doing things differently than others and committing to building a more evergreen business (don't worry, you're going to learn *all* about this throughout the book!). So while I'm not going to teach you the latest TikTok trend or how to hack the algorithm (which is essentially the online business world's version of diet culture—neverending because it doesn't work), I will teach you how to build a viable, sustainable business online that doesn't require twerking, lip-synching, or being glued to your phone 24-7.

Maybe your road to entrepreneurship hasn't been smooth either. Maybe you want to learn from someone who's built a successful business and has been through some shit. *That* I can help you with. Whether you've already hit a few of life's speed bumps or you will in the future (because, life), you can build a business that enables you to navigate life's rough waters. Plus, that business will run a whole lot smoother between the speed bumps, too. Throughout this book, I will share parts of my own story, as well as a few stories from my colleagues, to demonstrate that life's challenges don't just make us stronger; they make our businesses stronger, too.

WHEN I START MY BUSINESS, I'LL BE HAPPY

CHAPTER 1

Goodbye, Briefcase

B ut...you don't even have a briefcase." My dad was confused and skeptical when I told him I was leaving my corporate lawyer career behind to start my own online health coaching business. "I don't need a briefcase," I said, waving my MacBook in the air. "I've got *this!*" In my dad's mind, and in many like his, "real" businesses require briefcases, not laptops and an Instagram account. "But how will your clients know you're...*professional?*" Dad asked. Imagine how surprised he was to find out that I—like my clients—wore hoodies and leggings (hey, it was 2016—leggings were *the* fashionable go-to uniform) in our video meetings, not suits. "Plus," I said as I rolled my eyes, "they can't even see your pants anyway."

Looking back now, I should have known that if my own dad didn't get what I was setting out to do with my business, other people wouldn't either. It wasn't his fault, though. The term "online business" was still relatively new at the time. Just when we had gotten used to bloggers being a thing, the rise of Instagram (and later TikTok) brought us influencers, coaches, and creators. Early on, anytime you told someone you had an "online business" and there was no physical storefront they could see or visit, they would scrunch their eyes and say, "So, basically you're an influencer?!" (Influencers and bloggers have completely valid and difficult careers, by the way. They are significantly different from business owners, however, because they sell or promote other people's products and don't usually sell their own.) These days, any business that maintains an online storefront can be considered an online business. For our purposes, the industry I'm referring to specifically, and the one that my dad was most confused about back then, involves the increasingly popular primarily or exclusively virtual service-based businesses, like coaching, consulting, and online courses and education. There are also online related services such as copywriting and website design, as well as e-commerce entrepreneurs who sell physical goods like handmade items or artwork through online storefronts. These types of businesses use social media, email lists, websites, and other online marketing channels (e.g., YouTube, podcasts, blogging, digital ads, SEO, etc.) to build an online presence, audience, and subsequently—revenue. Instead of selling widgets or baked goods to customers just in their local community, these online businesses sell digital and physical products to people all over the world.

These types of online businesses are growing rapidly and have been for years. In 2023, the online coaching industry alone generated more than $4.564 billion in revenue, which represents a 60 percent increase from 2019.[1] There are an estimated 109,000

---

1. International Coaching Federation, *Global Coaching Study: 2023 Executive Summary,* https://coachingfederation.org/app/uploads/2023/04/2023ICFGlobalCoaching Study_ExecutiveSummary.pdf?utm_source=Website&utm_medium=CTR&utm _campaign=GCS&utm_id=Executive+Summary+.

coaches online worldwide;[2] however, this figure seems ridiculously low. The number of actual coaches is likely hard to quantify because anyone can call themselves a "coach," and there's no one governing body or registration. A search on LinkedIn for anyone with the term "coach" in their job title in the United States yields over 453,000 results. The Instagram hashtag #onlinecoach has generated more than 3.9 million posts, while the hashtag #onlinebusiness has generated 13.5 million.[3] Given these large numbers and the opportunities available to you online, why not strike out on your own? Before you start down the path, let me share a bit about my own journey to online entrepreneurship.

THE EXIT AND REENTRY

The pain in my neck just wouldn't quit, so I finally gave in and made an appointment with Kramer,[4] or as my mom called him, "the torture doctor. But, like, the good kind of torture." With my shoulders hiked up by my ears and my hands tightly balled into fists, I slumped into Kramer's office for a bodywork session.

"I saw that you're coming in today to help you manage your stress. What seems to be causing you so much stress, do you think?" he asked.

"My job is so stressful," I said. "I'm a lawyer and it's just awful. I hate it so much…" I went on and on, telling him my "sob story" of how I was "forced" to go to my awful work to do my awful job for my awful boss every day.

"Mmm, well. It's your choice!" Kramer smirked.

MY CHOICE?! My indignant, entitled insides were raging. "How is this my *choice*? My boss is a jerk. The work is stupid.

---

2. International Coaching Federation, *Global Coaching Study: 2023 Executive Summary.*
3. As of July 13, 2023.
4. Name changed.

They're abusive! No one should have to work in such an awful, negative environment!" Looking back, I cringe at how I said "have to."

Kramer kept his smirk and got to work on my tightly wound shoulders. At the time, I thought he was just another example of someone who didn't get it. Who didn't get *me*. But it turns out, Kramer was right all along.

My exit from the law was made less with a bang, and more like repeatedly stubbing the same toe on the same door over and over, without learning the lesson of not walking into the door anymore. I wish I could tell you there was a honeymoon period where I really loved being a lawyer and that one day we simply fell out of love. In reality, the honeymoon ended the day I got "married" to the law.

With my cheap black leather Aldo heels digging into the backs of my feet, I hobbled into my interior, windowless office on the twenty-something floor of a Philadelphia skyscraper to start my first year as an associate at a fancy law firm. As I sank into my new leather office chair and put my Phillies bobblehead on my L-shaped desk, I felt overwhelmed by dread and regret. It was the first time in years, or possibly my entire life, I wasn't running toward something. In the past, I'd always been focused on achieving something—volleyball wins, college acceptance, law school, passing the bar exam, getting the job. In between all of that, I was trying to survive my mom's dissociative episodes and psychotic breakdowns and manage the near constant flashbacks and fear of her committing suicide. I pushed and pushed and pushed, without ever slowing down to take a look around and see where I was headed. I hadn't even gotten the bar exam results back yet, and I already didn't want to be a lawyer. (Typically, you start working at a law firm before you get your bar exam results back. If you don't pass, you either lose your job or the firm gives you time to retest and try again.) With six figures' worth of student loans coming due any day, I felt the weight of my choices pressing down hard. Not to mention, what would everyone think if I didn't follow through with my lawyer path? My dad had told everyone from his favorite ShopRite cashier to my middle school math teacher that I became a lawyer. Wouldn't I be letting everyone down if I walked away from something they were so proud of me for? Did it matter if I was ever proud of myself for it? "I can't walk away," I thought. "I am *trapped*." Victim mode: activated. Needless to say, I wanted out of the law from the moment my tuchus hit the cheap, cold leather chair. I'd hide in the bathroom and cry, interrupted by my secretary letting me know that the senior partner I worked for needed me for the fifteenth time that day. Working at a law firm felt like my home life growing up. One minute I'd get praise for turning in a fantastic brief or motion, only to accidentally step on an unknown, invisible land mine and get berated and insulted. I never knew what I was walking into when I came to work each day. And just like I had to as a child, I kept it all a secret because the competitive, cutthroat nature of (some) law firms doesn't lend itself to speaking up. Especially as a woman—I was just "lucky to be there." You just had to deal with it. But, stuck as I felt I was, I spent the next several years trying to find my way as an attorney in different law firms. I thought if I just had a different boss, or worked on different types of cases, I'd be happy as a lawyer. No matter what I tried, though, nothing felt like what I was looking for. Every time another firm/boss/area of law didn't work out "for me," it was *their* fault. I acted like I had been punished with a life sentence as a lawyer (honestly though, that could be a thing). I joined complaint sessions with my colleagues where we griped about everything from our pay to our bosses to the perks (or the lack thereof). With time, I began to take notice of the whiny tone in my voice. This was months before the plane incident. I still had a few lessons to learn before I'd be jolted to make a change.

My First Misfire

As little whispers in my gut began to say, "I think I don't want to be a lawyer anymore…," I started exploring more of my personal hobbies, like cooking and fitness. I'd sweat away the stress of my job at the gym every day, and on Sunday I'd spend hours prepping food to take to the office. Even though I made fairly healthy food, I ate beyond fullness to dull the pain of my choices that led me to being a lawyer and how trapped and hopeless I felt. I used my lunch break to take a quick walk, even though I was routinely chastised for doing so—some higher-up people thought taking this kind of break made me look lazy.

In between settling cases, arguing motions in court, and writing endless numbers of briefs, I realized I didn't want to be my colleagues when I "grew up." While I'm glad there are so many incredible, smart, talented lawyers in the world, I could feel in the deepest part of my being that I wasn't one of them. I wasn't sure who I was, exactly, or whom I was meant to help with what. I just knew that the practice of law wasn't it. If you've found your way to this book, you also may have felt that you were supposed to be doing something different, but you didn't know exactly what "different" was. I felt that to my core.

When I realized I didn't want to spend my entire life being a lawyer, I had to come to terms with what that meant for the identity I'd crafted for myself and that had been crafted for me by others. It's possible to allow something we don't enjoy to become our entire life or identity. When you've set out to achieve something specific, or you've had your heart or mind set on a certain life path, it is incredibly difficult, and brave, to choose a different path. People may doubt your choice, or even feel threatened by your bravery to live a life in alignment with your values. They will project their own fears onto you about how "risky" your choices and changes seem to them. They might say, "But I thought you loved [insert your job here]!" If you're as good at hiding your pain as I was, even those closest to you might not know how deeply you crave change. They might not know how badly you need change, or how afraid you are to take the first step. These early realizations began to fissure the life I thought I'd wanted, creating cracks in my perfectly planned fast track to independence. Eventually, those cracks would expand and break my life wide open, but I didn't know how to fix the resulting damage.

I believe that when you feel stuck, taking some messy, unplanned action, no matter how small, is the best place to start. After talking to anyone who would listen about food, I started my food blog, called *Barrister's Beet*, in 2024. On it, I posted grainy, dark photographs of my embarrassingly simple recipes for busy professionals. I still remember bursting out of my office to tell my favorite secretary, Colleen, that I'd gotten my first comment on a steel-cut oatmeal recipe—"*from a stranger on the internet!*" I squealed as we jumped around in celebration.

Starting a food blog taught me my very first business lesson, one I'll repeat a few times for you: *Your hobbies don't have to become your career.* While I love food and cooking in my personal life, maintaining *Barrister's Beet* made me realize food blogging wasn't what I wanted to do as a career. This experimentation phase is perfectly normal. Hardly anyone I know in the online business space is doing today exactly what they started out doing. It's common for new entrepreneurs to begin by making their hobby or life's passion their job. It happens so often because we see others becoming successful doing things we also are passionate about on social media. I'm not here to encourage you to start a business you hate—quite the opposite (in chapter 3, I'll walk you through my strategy of how to build an in-demand business that you actually like). If you love what you do, fantastic! I do too. But turning your hobby into your livelihood isn't always the best move. It's only natural to seek out something completely different if you're currently in a job you hate. But turning a passion into a business, or trying to, can suck out the passion you had for it, too.

All experiences you have in life, good or bad, end up helping you in some way. My fledgling food blog gave me a taste of an entirely new-to-me world, one filled with people exploring their interests in food, fitness, health, cooking, and everything in between. I got a taste of the online business and creator world, too. My logical, type A mind was blown when I saw how creative online business owners were on social media. I watched as they talked about "search engine optimization" and "funnels"—things that sounded like a far cry from the briefs and motions world I was embroiled in. Little did I know, that was the spark that would light a raging fire.

I wanted to be a food blogger because I'd watched so many of my favorite bloggers gain notoriety and live seemingly exciting lives. In reality, being a successful food blogger is a lot of freaking work. Looking back, I wanted to be a food blogger only if I could be one of the top food bloggers. The problem was, I wasn't willing to do any of the things required to actually become successful at it. That's a good way to tell if you really want to do something, or if you just want the outcome of something that looks good. It's okay to dream, but it's important to recognize the difference between dreams and what you're willing to sacrifice and persevere in working toward. Today, I love what I do and I love my business. But my business is not my passion; it's my job, one that allows me to chase my actual passions (like cooking, traveling, and working out) outside of my day-to-day work.

It's okay for your business to be your job. Jobs don't have to suck. We'll talk about this in more depth, but for now, know that this is an important distinction for your sanity and your boundaries. As your business grows, it is important to maintain hobbies and passions you don't get paid for and that no one in your audience ever sees. Make sure you do things that have nothing to do with your business, and that won't bring you likes, followers, or subscribers. I'd be willing to bet it will make you a better entrepreneur in the long run, too.

The Cheeseburger to Freedom

Okay, so food blogging was not going to be my thing. Continuing as a lawyer was certainly not the future I saw for myself either. But I still wanted to build a business, and I wanted that business to have *something* to do with food. That's when I saw the health coaching industry taking off online. I signed up for a six-week online course and couldn't believe that in such a short time, I earned a certificate that not only labeled me as a "certified health coach" ("certified" has a different meaning now than it did in 2016), but that equipped me to guide others on their health and wellness journeys. Still working full-time as an attorney, I got my health coaching business and website up and running on nights and weekends. I started sharing about my new side hustle with friends and family. Almost immediately, a friend reached out asking for health coaching services. And just like that—I had my first paying client. They referred me to a friend who became my second client. And then a small business purchased my first online course for all their employees. All along my journey from *Barrister's Beet* to my health coaching business, I kept my job at the firm, saved cash, and cut down on my expenses. But as the coaching business grew, and after that nightmare flight from Amsterdam, I decided to pull the plug from corporate lawyer life. I wanted to go all in on being a health coach and entrepreneur. I crafted a plan to leave, making sure my husband and I had enough in savings to cover my start-up costs and our household and personal expenses (we'll discuss financial planning in more detail in chapter 4).

When I finally mustered up the courage to tell my boss I was leaving, my secretary nearly had to shove me inside his office to tell him the news.

"I'm putting in my notice to leave the firm. I'm going to start my own health coaching business," I said as sweat coated my upper lip. His reaction was completely different than I expected. I couldn't believe how happy he was for me. He not only congratulated me, but he told me he'd do anything he could to help me build my new business.

I hurried back to my office next door to his, imagining for the first time my life outside of those depressing four walls. I couldn't believe how well my boss had received the news that I was leaving, which was why it hurt so badly when just five minutes later I overheard that same "encouraging" boss tell another colleague, "Did you hear the news? Sam's leaving us to go teach fat people not to eat cheeseburgers." Cue: evil lawyer laughter that you think only happens in movies. I'm not sure what hurt most: the mocking laughter, the fat phobia, or the fact that he played straight into what are normal human worries when deciding whether to take a big life leap. *What will people think of me? Will I be taken seriously? Mocked? Judged for leaving the "serious, safe, and legitimate" corporate world for something less widely recognized and accepted?* Maybe you've felt that way, too. Like the weight of the world—or even of your family members' and friends' eyes—on you was so heavy and scary that it felt safer to stay where you were, no matter how miserable it made you feel. But how long can you choose everyone else's comfort and happiness over your own? How long do you stay committed to a path you set out to take only because you're embarassed or ashamed of having to admit it was the wrong one? At some point, you break and you don't really have a choice.

As much as that cheeseburger moment still stings, I owe everything I've accomplished thus far to it. His words have been in my head at every difficult business turn. I've imagined guys like him in my mind every time I get messages from people telling me how miserable they are in their jobs. As I sit here eight years later and see the ripple effect of how my eventual legal business has helped so many entrepreneurs legally establish and grow their own businesses—businesses that offer services and sell products that help other people—I smile to myself, thinking of him. And every time I've reached some new peak in my business or accomplished something I set my mind to, I thank him for being the catalyst that set me free from any regret. Sometimes life's most painful moments are the fuel you need to take action.

PIVOT

I lasted as a health coach for only about a year, but not for the reason you might think. Looking back, I see how naive and inexperienced I was when I left the law to start that business. I think almost everyone who's ever worked a corporate job has thought they could run the place much better than the higher-ups—without ever having been in their shoes. Getting a coaching certification in six weeks online was not enough to qualify me to help people navigate their own health, let alone to run an online business. What was even more surprising to me then was the fact that I didn't even need that online certificate. I could have called myself a "health coach" anytime I wanted. Truthfully, there was nothing legally stopping me, at that time, from calling myself "certified," even if I wasn't. The online coaching industry was and still is highly unregulated. I learned more during my year as a health coach about what was actually going on online than I did about the art of coaching. Having now worked with incredible coaches myself, coaching is a very difficult skill that takes time, dedication, and education to effectuate actual change and impact. At the time, there were many uncredentialed, inexperienced people jumping into the online space at an alarming rate, and many more starting coaching businesses and labeling themselves an expert, healer, or guru overnight. Though I tried to stay clearly within the scope of practice boundaries of what a "coach" could do, that's not what I saw happening around me. I stepped back and questioned what I was really trying to become a part of. Did I want to add to what I saw as a growing problem? Was there something I could do to help this new industry be better than I found it? Coupled with the same whispers in my gut saying, "I don't think this is quite it either...," I started to see potential in a new business idea I had. And shockingly, it was a legal one.

The idea to start an online business catering to the legal needs of online business owners wasn't spontaneously my own—it was inadvertently sparked by demand (which we'll talk more about in chapter 3). Since the online space was so new and evolving so quickly, and few attorneys had started businesses catering to it (and even fewer practicing attorneys even knew it existed), online business owners didn't know where to turn to find answers to their legal questions. Even though, in the thick of health coaching, I rarely mentioned my former lawyer status, and I certainly wasn't offering legal services or products, I couldn't stop the flood of (very good) questions I received from people all around the world, seeking legal information about their new or existing online businesses:

- Do I need to form an LLC?
- What kind of business insurance do I need?
- What do I do if someone sues me?
- What kind of contract do I need for this type of service or product?

While I wasn't exactly sure why they were asking me, specifically, I leaned into my favorite word—*curiosity*—which led me to wonder why this type of information wasn't available elsewhere. What hole was there in the market, if any? It didn't take long to find it.

Honestly, when the idea for my current business came to me, I was a little taken aback. I thought I'd left everything to do with the law behind when I transitioned out of the firm. But one day, during an acupuncture appointment, I slipped into a dreamlike state. I saw something clearly in my mind's eye: A series of doors flying open—*Whoosh! Whoosh! Whoosh!* One after another, each door flew open, revealing the possibilities that awaited me if I pursued this new legal templates business idea I'd had. Days later, I began putting the pieces together. I registered it as an LLC, got business insurance, set up a business bank account (with $100 cash, nearly all I had left in my health coaching business account), and started building my own website. Within days of setting up my website, hitting "publish" on my ten SEO-optimized blog posts, and putting my legal contract templates up for sale, I sold my first legal template for $347 to a random person who found my website through Google. I knew if I could make one sale that way, I could get others. So, I doubled down, shut down the health coaching business, and gave the legal business all of my love and attention. In the first month, I generated nearly $5,000 in gross revenue—more than I had in any month as a health coach. Although I felt like I was failing yet again by closing down my health coaching business, I knew this pivot was the right move. Who said your first pivot has to be your last? Without my first pivot to become a health coach, I never would have discovered the pivot I was about to make. With self-permission to not give a crap what anyone thought about me or my pivots, I was off to the races as a lawyer-turned-entrepreneur selling legal templates and helping entrepreneurs learn the legal side of online business.

Failing Forward

If you asked me then, I would have told you my health coaching business was an epic failure. All in all, my wellness business lasted nearly a year from start-up to shutdown before I shifted to my current legal templates business. But looking back, I am so appreciative for what I learned from my first "failed" business. Without it, my legal business would never have become the multi-seven-figure company it is now. There are (at least) two lessons you can take away from my journey to make your business-building experience smoother than mine:

First, you have to know that failure, at some level, is part of entrepreneurship. My failed experience with my health coaching business was not unique in many ways. More than 20 percent of businesses fail within their first year, with 30 percent shuttered by the end of year two.[5] Even if your business doesn't fail completely, you may stumble, fall, and need to get back up again in the early days of entrepreneurship. When I started my health coaching business, I made a lot of what I now know were mistakes. At the time, I was experimenting to see what worked—which was exactly what I should have been doing. Some of those "mistakes" included:

- spending too much time, money, and energy to craft the perfect website, without ever focusing on my messaging, SEO, copy, or client avatar;
- focusing too heavily on social media instead of longer-form, searchable, and optimized content on a "discovery" platform like YouTube or a blog;
- mimicking what I saw being done, said, and sold online

---

5. Timothy Carter, ed. Jessica Thomas, "The True Failure Rate of Small Businesses," Entrepreneur, January 3, 2021, https://www.entrepreneur.com/starting-a-business/the-true-failure-rate-of-small-businesses/361350.

around me, instead of finding my own unique voice, niche, and product;

- selling too many products at wildly different price points; and
- being unclear about who my ideal customer was and what kind of product they wanted (rather than what I thought they should want).

If you've started your own business, you're familiar with these mistakes—and plenty of others like them—as well. If you haven't started a business yet, I want you to know about these common pitfalls now so you don't feel any shame or sense of failure if you encounter these mistakes, too. There are inevitable speed bumps on the way to success—no matter how far away success might be or seem right now. The only thing worse than feeling like a failure is feeling like you're the only one failing. And you're certainly not the only one, my friend. At least not here, anyway.

You might hope you'll never make a mistake along your business journey. Or you might even be holding back on taking any steps toward starting or growing your business because you're so afraid to make one. But it's best to make mistakes on a lower-stakes venture or early on in your business when the stakes themselves are lower. Missteps are inevitable. Being open enough to notice them, pivot, and update for the next iteration is a mark of a good businessperson. The best and only way to benefit from mistakes is to commit to being open to learning from them. Every time I make a mistake, which still happens often, I try to be as curious as possible about where it came from, how it happened, what I can learn from it, and what I can do differently moving forward. Learning and evolving are, in my humble opinion, some of the coolest parts of the job—and you should quickly get comfortable with them. My job is to help you avoid some of the mistakes that can be the most costly, painful, and business-deadly so you can instead focus on your business and its future growth.

Another important lesson: Most of your past experiences, failures or not, will become the greatest assets in your life and business. Starting a different business before my current one gave me a dry run at starting and growing an online business. My prior business "failure" directly contributed to the nearly immediate success I had when I pivoted to my legal business. By the time I got my legal business up and running in 2017, I was able to move quickly and more efficiently because of what I learned from my experience and mistakes with my first. Without them, my legal business might have been a failure, too.

Of course, you don't have to start a business and fail at it before you start a successful one. The point is that the business you set out to create might look different in the future. You might set out to do things one way, and end up doing them in a completely different way. This is not a bad thing. But as you embark on this journey, it is important for you to know that if failure *does* happen, it's okay. And maybe for you it wasn't a failed business or a grainy-photo food blog—maybe it was your career, relationship, product, or education that you now think of as a "failure." I hope to convince you that it was anything but. Everything you've been through so far has prepared you for where you are now and what's to come. And if any of it hadn't happened, you wouldn't be here today. So, as you're hurtling through current and past challenges in your life, please have the faith and the strength to know it is all going to be part of your story one day. It might help to remember this: The stories and experiences you've collected over the years are going to be a gold mine when it comes to creating content.

TRANSITIONS

Throughout this book, I'll not only share my story to guide you toward your entrepreneurial dreams, but we'll spend some time with other folks and their unique businesses, backgrounds, and experiences. We'll start with Christina (Chris). Chris took her dream-on-paper advertising job in Silicon Valley and thought she had made it. When it turned out the job wasn't at all what she wanted, she felt crushed. Chris realized that she'd put entirely too much pressure on her career to be the thing that fulfilled her. She also realized she had taken the job only because she didn't know what she really wanted to do, was sick of living in the in-between, and settled on picking something that looked "successful" on paper.

In 2017, Chris left her job in advertising to start her own online career coaching business. Her business generates over six figures in revenue per year, and she has helped more than three hundred people from all over the world find a career path they love. Better yet, Chris works twenty or so hours per week, does her Costco runs midday, and gets to spend loads of flextime with her two beautiful young children.

If most people were offered Chris's life on paper, they'd take it. Yet the traditional business world treats Chris's type of business as less legitimate or labels it a "lifestyle brand." This is a lesson that you can build a business that you love and that supports a life you love even more than your job title—it doesn't matter what anyone calls it or labels it as. It's more about living your life and figuring out how your business fits into it. Not the other way around.

With this in mind, consider this: *What is inspiring you to build your business?* Around the world, many people have spent the last few years collectively questioning their career choices and paths forward in life. During the height of the COVID-19 pandemic, those privileged to have jobs that could easily convert to work-from-home status were compelled to reevaluate their priorities.

Our parents' generation worked, for the most part, at the same job, for the same company, for the majority of their careers. They felt loyal to their employers, bosses, and coworkers, but there's been a generational shift. We don't feel the same sense of loyalty to the entities that sign our paychecks. Employers no longer offer much in the way of job security and safety, which has created a workplace culture that is not built on mutual benefit. But is this reason enough to start your own business? It's important to get clear on what you want and why before taking the first step.

The pandemic might have inspired some to make a change in their employment status, but for many, that choice was made for them. Pandemic aside, we exist in a nation of mass layoffs, corporate bankruptcies, and company collapses that have left people asking "What now?" for the first time in years. Whether someone's job change was by choice or not, this significant shift in the job market was the catalyst that led to a lot of people investigating what it would be like to start their own business instead of working for someone else. People realized their jobs, once thought to be as stable as bedrock, were in reality more like a volcano, ready to burst and disrupt their lives at any moment. Which is what Chris felt. It's what I felt. Perhaps it's what you feel, and it's become your why, too.

Embracing the Catalyst

As someone who had a thriving business *before* a world-changing pandemic hit us in 2020, I can tell you that the online business world was already exploding when COVID-19 came to American shores. In my own company, we were already flooded daily with inquiries from starry-eyed entrepreneurs who were ready to start online businesses. They especially wanted to start something flexible and virtual so they could chase time, money, location, and career freedom. Sometimes you need a major shake-up—like a pandemic—to show you how off course you've gotten. It encourages you to take a step back, reevaluate, and figure out what direction you actually want your life to go in. As the online business industry has grown and welcomed more entrepreneurs in the past decade, there have been more potential customers to draw upon, too. As many people look for alternatives to traditional medicine, law, finance, dating, self-care, career, therapy, and other services, coaches and virtual providers often fit the unique needs of people looking for help outside of the traditional pathways. And as online tools and software have made it even easier to start a website, set up an e-commerce shop, and sell products, makers, artists, and shop owners have been able to move their businesses online, too.

Nicole,[6] a dietitian, was sick and tired of waiting weeks to get into her ob-gyn while she was having difficulty conceiving. Even when she could get an appointment, she was given only minutes before she felt rushed out the door with few if any answers. Online, she found an endless supply of both credentialed and noncredentialed coaches offering IVF and infertility coaching services. She was able to get the one-on-one care and attention she was looking for from a licensed professional who offered coaching services, but who was located thousands of miles away from her home in Florida. Instead of in-office visits, she has weekly Zoom check-ins. And like many online coaches, her IVF specialist communicated with Nicole regularly about any issues that popped up along the way. It's a level of hands-on service and support that's not feasible in our current medical system, but one that can easily be found online. The nature of online businesses is now empowered—with access to a computer and a strong Wi-Fi

---

6.　Name changed.

Wait, Is That Legal?

We'll talk about this in detail later on, but not all online services being offered are being done so legally. In many cases, people offering services online are doing so outside of their scope of practice. I'm not encouraging or condoning entrepreneurs who use online businesses to offer services they wouldn't otherwise legally be allowed to offer. As we'll discuss, there's a right way and a wrong way to run your business. There are also easy ways to spot who's acting outside of their scope of practice, which we'll learn how to identify.

As you build your business, it's important to understand the concept of scope of practice. This defines what you're legally allowed to do and teach in your business based on the licensure and regulation of your area of practice in your state and in other states. For example, if you're starting a health coaching business, it's crucial that you don't overstep the bounds of medical, therapeutic, or nutritional advice. If you're teaching about money or finances, all the legal protection in the world won't help you if you offer services, sell products, or give advice that only an accountant or a certified financial planner is allowed to give. Starting an online business is not a way to skirt the laws in your state or that apply to a certain practice area. The rumors suggesting that the online world is the "wild wild west" where anything goes? They aren't true.

connection, you can work with the best coaches and practitioners in the world.

As you'll read throughout this book, running an online business—or becoming the customer of one—isn't a perfect panacea to solve all of life's problems. Just like starting one didn't solve all of mine. But it does offer entrepreneurs an incredible opportunity not only to change others' lives, but their own, too. Starting your own business usually starts with an exit. Maybe it's an exit from something that's no longer working for you. Or an exit from an old way of doing things. My own exit was nothing pretty or smooth, but I discovered that there are many valuable lessons to be learned in the bumpiest parts of life.

GOING ONLINE

Starting now, and throughout the book, we'll get down to business. First, let's talk about why you might want to start or keep a business online, as opposed to opening a brick-and-mortar operation. If you already run an online business, some of these may be familiar to you:

- The start-up costs associated with an online business pale in comparison to the costs of opening a brick-and-mortar store or product-based business. You don't need to rent a space, create or obtain inventory, purchase expensive equipment, or hire employees right away. Technically speaking, you don't even need to start with a website (not my recommendation, but we'll talk about that later).

- A virtual business may offer you time freedom or the flexibility of being able to do what you want, when you want to (or are able to). Maybe it's the ability to earn a living while you care for a loved one, or take care of your family at home. Or maybe you're more of a night owl than a morning person. As your own boss, you set the time that your work gets done.

- The potential customer base for an online business is limitless and has no geographic boundaries, whereas a brick-and-mortar business has to rely on local or foot traffic for its customer base.

- Virtual businesses rely primarily on social media and digital marketing (all of which we'll discuss throughout this book). These tools are much more cost-effective than having to buy ad space in print, billboard, or other advertising media.

Whatever your reason is for having an online business, you probably sought it out because of the perceived ease of starting one (whether or not it's actually that easy is something we'll talk a lot about together throughout this book). The way most people teach it, you can start an online business by simply announcing you're open for business over a social media post. While it may be how you can start one, we'll talk about why growing it is not quite *that* simple and what you should do instead.

What's Really Real?

As an online business owner, you might face two problems right away: a lack of awareness and judgment. Before I started my food blog and later stumbled into an online program to become a health coach, I had no clue what an "online business" was. Most people are still unaware this (giant) industry even exists. Heck, my brilliant husband still asks me, "There's someone who does *what*?! And charges *how much*?!" Most of the world can wrap their minds around bakeries, clothing boutiques, and even e-commerce shops, but when you tell them you're a coach who works with clients all over the world, that you've created an online course that sells millions in revenue, or that you're a content creator who gets paid by brands and algorithms, they'll stare at you like you're a cowboy who just walked into a Brooklyn coffee shop.

In the grand scheme of business things, our industry is still new. But it's important to keep your eye on the prize: building your business and finding your actual customers. We don't need to convince Uncle Jerry that your new business venture is legitimate. If you've done your research and follow the steps we'll talk about in chapter 3 to validate your business idea, then you should feel confident to explore on your own. The earlier you can let go of everyone else's opinions about what you're doing with your own life, the better. They might not ever validate or approve of your path, but you don't need them to.

Beyond the familiarity issue, our industry faces a lot of internal and external criticism about not being as legitimate as a "real" business, like a gym or a coffeehouse. I see it in bro business circles all the time. *"If your business isn't raising capital or isn't 'sellable'—is it really a business?"* they ask. There's the sentiment that people in the online business industry want badly to be accepted and thought of as legitimate, yet some won't take the steps necessary to legitimize (legally protect) their venture. I'm not sure who decided that a "legitimate" business makes a certain amount of revenue or must raise capital, but at least in this corner of the business world, I consider you to have a "real" business if you've registered it and you're trying to sell something. From the outside, you'll have a few snooty high school classmates stalking your social media pages, or a few lurkers on your email list forwarding your email to a friend because they think what you're doing is "so self-promotional." However, you never know when you will inspire other people in your life to make a radical change in their own. Early on in your business journey, it's important to keep your head down and not give too much of your attention to either the naysayers or the bandwagoners. You'll have to protect your time from people who aren't in the arena with you, and also from those who are following closely in your footsteps. Of course, it's nice to help others, and you should do as you'd like. But try to avoid getting caught up in helping others learn what you're doing in real time, when you're just trying to figure it out yourself. The early days of entrepreneurship are filled with distraction and lures—from people wanting to ride your coattails to people wasting your time on opportunities that don't pan out. You don't have to teach everything you learn to others—not now or ever. Should you want to, I'd recommend waiting until you have your business feet under you first. You also have to keep an eye out for people clinging to your progress. Like the time one of my law school classmates pretended to befriend me, only to join my then-private Facebook group so she could privately message each and every one of my thousands of group members to pitch her fat loss pills to them. As time goes on, you'll lean into the confidence and comfort of what you're doing on your own, without seeking the approval or understanding of anyone who's not in the arena with you, as Brené Brown says.

While you may see lots of slimy marketing tactics and baseless advice online, I'm happy to tell you that you'll meet many more good people along the way than bad. It's all about whom and what you give your attention to, which is why I want you to protect yourself and your energy at the start. This is when we tend to be most vulnerable, when we're the most desperate to make things work, but the least sure of how to do so.

Despite being sometimes misunderstood and judged, online business owners all over the world are building incredible businesses that provide them and their families opportunities, prosperity, and happiness. Are they building an Amazon-sized corporation? Likely not. But that's not everyone's goal. And that's not what makes a business legitimate or worthwhile. There are so many ways to build your own unique business, on your own terms. And it's not any less legitimate just because you run it virtually or don't have a brick-and-mortar location. To me, that just makes it full of endless possibilities and low overhead.

Endless Options

Even within the online business industry, there are plenty of broad types of coaching or service-based businesses (health, career, life, mindset, business, money, fitness, travel, etc.) that offer personalized services, online courses, digital products, or have some sort of membership or group program option. You've also got creator businesses who rely on creating content for other brands as their main source of income, as well as product makers who run e-commerce shops off their websites or other e-commerce platforms, like Etsy. Whether you have a service- or product-based business, you can also make money from affiliate sales and sponsorships with your online business. There are also several what I call "sleeper" online businesses that are more specific and unique who are absolutely killing it. Take Richelle Fredson's book coaching business. She had over fifteen years' worth of experience as the director of Publicity and Book Marketing for a major publishing company before she left to start her own online business helping business owners become authors. Richelle uses her decades of professional experience to help aspiring authors write book proposals, navigate the agent/publisher process, and market their eventual books to the masses. Richelle is one of the most in-demand book coaches in the online business industry and she's regularly helping to pull in six-figure book deals for her more established private clients. And like Chris, Richelle runs her business while also taking advantage of her schedule flexibility to spend time with her son and have impromptu date nights with her husband.

Don't get me wrong, building an online business requires a lot of hard work. This is especially true in the first several years, when everything feels new, overwhelming, and hard. Your business might not take off as quickly as you want it too, either. After eight years, my business still requires an immense amount of work—I've just gotten more efficient at handling it, hired a great team to support me, and set up marketing systems that generate sales even when I'm far away from my desk. So when I talk about freedom and flexibility, it often comes after hard work and at a cost. When I take time off or take advantage of being able to do things in the middle of the workday, I'm usually doing so knowing I'll have work to get to later on. There have been times, especially at the start, when I've found myself working more than I did as a lawyer. The difference now is that I reap what I sow, I can feel and see the impact I'm having, and I love what I do. So if attending the US Open on a Tuesday means writing on the weekends—I'll take it.

Nearly every time I log on to social media or open my inbox, I see another online entrepreneur with a brilliant business idea. Don't treat what you see online as a rubric of what's possible for you, though. What you see are only examples. Great businesses are built in the spaces between other businesses or products. Spaces other people don't even know about or haven't seen yet. You might create a product or service that fills the gap people have been looking for. Those spaces are ripe for opportunity, and you can make that a possibility.

No, online businesses aren't the businesses our parents built. They don't require briefcases (sorry, Dad!). Or loads of capital or start-up funds. And that might not make them all sellable, IPO-worthy, or the size of Amazon (do we really need another Amazon, anyway?)—but they offer us opportunities and possibilities that no briefcase job could have ever offered us before. Now that we know we have changed, the world has changed, and the way we do business has changed, it's time to roll up our sleeves and press "play" on the next chapter of our lives.

WHAT WE LEARNED

- The online business industry is booming and continues to grow. There are many opportunities to start your own business online, including those no one has thought of yet.
- If you're unhappy with your current circumstances or career, it's important to identify which parts of it are yours to own and change.
- If you're worried about making a big career or life change, don't put so much pressure on this being your "one big pivot." Life is full of change. It keeps things interesting.
- You don't need anyone's approval to leave your career or start your own business. They might not understand what you're setting off to do, but you'll show them.
- Failures and disappointments are part of entrepreneurship. They will also be the greatest gifts when it comes to lessons learned and future content ideas.

WHAT'S TO COME

- We'll discuss reasonable expectations of what a business will and won't do for your life, including the mistaken belief that starting a business will bring you happiness.
- We'll discuss reasonable expectations of how difficult your business journey may be.

CHAPTER 2

Your Business Won't Fix Your Life

It was a sticky, humid Tuesday morning in July when I trekked over to the Hospital of the University of Pennsylvania to meet with a neurosurgeon, Dr. O'Rourke. Honestly, I thought this was a mistake; some paperwork must have been misinterpreted and I was supposed to see a neurologist instead—but within a few minutes of meeting Dr. O'Rourke and undergoing his physical examination, I realized that, unfortunately, I was in exactly the right place. As my mind raced with thoughts of all the possibilities and outcomes of what he'd laid out for me, he said in what sounded like a language I don't speak, "You have to have brain surgery. How's this Thursday?" I saw his lips moving. And I was pretty sure I understood what he said. But I still couldn't imagine that he was talking about me.

"Brain surgery?! *This* Thursday? But I have so many blog posts to write!" I said with a straight face. I wish I could tell you that my first thought was about my family or how I hadn't visited India yet, but my mind was on one thing and one thing only: blog posts. It's funny what we focus on as business owners and content creators. The things we build as being so "necessary" to our business starting or growing usually aren't.

So how did I end up in a neurosurgeon's office needing brain surgery in two days? The pain started at the back of my head and looped its way up and over the top of my skull, deep behind my eyes. It was only four weeks after I'd started my legal templates business in 2017, so I chalked it up to the hours I'd spent staring at my laptop, embracing my new #girlboss life (hey, it was cool back then), trying to get my business off the ground. But I'd never had headaches like these before. While I tried to ignore the piercing pain of what I now know are called ram's horn headaches, I started to have other symptoms that were harder to ignore: hand tremors, unsteadiness while walking, queasiness, and difficulty speaking and swallowing. Apparently, having nonstop headaches and not being able to walk in a straight line qualifies you for an emergency MRI. The results showed I had a severe Chiari malformation, a structural problem involving the cerebellum, in my brain. Basically, my cerebellum was dropping into my spinal column and blocking the flow of cerebral spinal fluid to my brain. Although it can be serious and debilitating, it's not deadly, which I was grateful to hear. However, according to Dr. O'Rourke, my condition was starting to cause some serious complications that could worsen if left untreated.

In the exam room, Dr. O'Rourke's entire team swirled about and told me of all sorts of scary-sounding things: *You'll be getting a heart scan tomorrow, another MRI right before the surgery, and blood tests to make sure everything's all good. Oh, and then we'll get you set up for admission to the hospital, and you'll have a care team at home following the surgery for a couple of months. You know you're going to be in the hospital and bedbound for a while, right?*

You'll need 24-7 care when you go home, too. You won't be able to drive or use stairs. Did he tell you we will have to shave the back of your head? Don't worry, your hair will grow back.

Welp, there went my blog posts. I asked to have surgery the following week instead of that Thursday so I could get my life in order. I spent the next few days trying to make sense of the fact that I was going to have a very talented, but still very scary, neurosurgeon cut open the back of my head, drill a hole into and remove a portion of my skull, surgically enter my brain, and then close the incision back up leaving me with a giant zipper-like scar. (The thought of it still makes me sick to my stomach, and I've already had the surgery.) The day of the surgery, I begged the medical team to sedate me early. I was used to handling tough things throughout my life, but even I couldn't push my way through this one. I had such a baby business at that point that I can't believe, looking back, that all of this didn't make it fall apart before it ever took off. But I was so determined to make it work that I wouldn't let it.

Even though my business didn't fail, or really falter much at all, having that surgery was my first big lesson in how stressful stuff can still happen after you leave your job or change your life to start a business. I also realized how important it was to build a business that could still generate revenue even when you don't have the time or ability to focus on it. Little did I know, that whole brain surgery thing was just the beginning of a series of unfortunate events that would take over my personal life for the next few years. And I would have been even more shocked to know then that right alongside, I would build a business bigger than I ever could have imagined.

YOUR "WHY" MIGHT BE LYING TO YOU

You'll hear a lot of people talk about the importance of the "why" behind the business you're building. The idea is that you have to know *why* you're starting or running your business in order to successfully grow it. Experts like Simon Sinek have told us that "it starts with why";[1] and Instagram business coaches tell us to keep coming "back to our why" when we feel lost. But hardly anyone tells us that no matter what our why is, it might not be enough to overcome the disappointment that our business won't, in fact, fix our life. And even with the best "why" behind why we are starting our own business, we might not actually be able to build a business that is as successful, flexible, or profitable as we'd hoped (for a variety of reasons that we'll talk about).

It's really easy to make your "why" something outside your control as a business owner. For example, you might say your "why" is to spend more time with your kids. But the reality of running your own business is that it may not give you that time, at least not right away or all of the time. Eventually, when your business is more mature, stable, and self-sufficient, you may have more flexibility and free time. But until then, the truth is what I mentioned in the previous chapter—running a business can take over your life more than any nine-to-five ever did. Sometimes that is by our choice, when we let our business become our life, don't set boundaries with social media or our clients, or we become too focused on growth over everything else. Other times, it's the reality of being a new business owner and trying to get things off the ground. In the beginning, you'll have to make sacrifices and have more of a "hungry" attitude. When I started, I took calls on the weekends and late at night, hours that were normally off-limits for me and against my boundaries, because, frankly, I couldn't really afford to have those boundaries yet. Once my business was more established, I was able to limit my time—for example, by taking calls only between the hours of ten to five on weekdays, but

---

1. Simon Sinek, "Start with Why: How Great Leaders Inspire Action," TED talk, September 28, 2009, https://www.youtube.com/watch?v=u4ZoJKF_VuA.

that wasn't until I could afford it if the customer walked away. If you can, set boundaries as early as you can afford to and stick to them. But if you can't yet, either because you're new, your identity is intertwined with your status as a business owner (like I was), or because you can't afford to yet—know that you're not alone.

Who's Your Why About?

When it comes to defining your why behind starting and running a business, go deeper than what having a business will afford *you*. How will your business impact others? Who are the people you're here to help? What do they need help with? What impact will it have on them, the people around them, and the universe as a whole? What would happen if you didn't start this business? Of course you privately have whys that are more personal and self-serving, but having a why outside of yourself will help you to create something deeper and more connected.

THE WHEN-THEN VIRUS

It's easy to catch a nasty case of the "when-then" virus. "When I start my business, then I'll be happy!" or "When my business is successful, then I'll feel safe and will relax." It's so much easier to blame everything and everyone else for your unhappiness, frustration, and wandering soul than it is to either own your own stuff or realize that life just keeps life'ing, even if you change jobs or sign your own paycheck.

When we're unhappy in our job, it makes sense to think, "If I leave, then everything will be perfect!" If you remove the issue "causing" the problem, then there's no more problem, right? For me, I saw being a corporate lawyer like some sort of infection that I needed to remove and rid my life of. Naturally, I assumed once I got rid of the infection, the sadness, boredom, and feeling of being lost would be gone. In actuality, without the distraction of being able to blame all of my unhappiness on being a lawyer or working for a law firm, I realized that it wasn't, in fact, my job making me feel that way. Sure, working long hours on tasks I didn't love didn't help the situation. But I could have been much happier as an attorney than I was. I didn't make much of an effort to improve my mental health or develop myself during that time because I was too focused on my job and how miserable it made me. Instead of doing anything to try to swim out of the whirlpool I felt forced into, I just lazily swirled in it instead. The problem, in part, was that I tied my identity to being a lawyer, even though I hated it. I didn't develop myself, my hobbies, or much of my personal life outside of a world of briefs, motions, and hearsay. Another problem was that I looked to my job to make me happy, when in reality happiness was available to me all along. If we blame our jobs, our boss, the office, or even being employed by a "Big Brother" company as the reason we're not truly happy without ever exploring our unhappiness on a deeper level, we'll never get to the root of the issue. Without deeper exploration, the unhappiness can linger even if you change your situation.

I've met many people who are so excited to enter the legal profession with a rosy-eyed optimism about helping the world (maybe, like me, they watched too much *Law & Order*). Every one of them says they're going to be one of the good ones, "the kind that actually helps people," they'll say. And while there are many great lawyers out there doing meaningful legal work, the reality is that a large portion of the jobs available to lawyers are not ones that positively impact people's lives. It's actually a joke some professors tell you in law school: "Everyone comes in thinking they're going to argue civil rights cases before the Supreme Court, and they leave doing doc review at a firm."

Lawyers aren't alone in being shocked to find out that their job is, in practice, not at all what they thought it would be when they were in school. People in countless fields, including medicine, education, finance, publishing, you name it, often realize that their actual jobs are nothing even close to what they expected. Once you get in a job, there's a chance you'll find that the idealized version of it you had is covered in heaps of red tape, paperwork, and office politics, making it nearly impossible to accomplish anything of any meaning or importance.

While I can't fix all of these industries myself, I can encourage you to realize the importance of self-development outside of your job. As we'll discuss later in the book, the same goes even when you have your own business. Whether you're a business owner, a lawyer in a firm, or a dietitian working in a hospital—you need a healthy sense of self outside of what you do for a living. Particularly if you don't like what you do, it's important not to make the job, or how miserable it makes you, your identity.

If you're not trying to improve yourself or your life right now, or working to see the glimmers that exist even amidst the difficult times, who's to say you will do those things when you have your own business? Running your own business will bring its own set of stressors, too. It's too much pressure on a new business to expect it to fix your life. I want you to be excited about your business because you're excited to carve your own path, help others, be challenged in new and exciting ways, and make an impact. Will doing so also change your life? Absolutely! In ways you might and might not expect. Although starting a business won't necessarily make everything better, it may change you into someone who can navigate life's challenges in a better way.

As a kid, I carried a sketchbook with me to jot down ideas I had for inventions. When I was out and about, I'd see things and think, "There's a better way to do this!" as I sketched a drawing of a tube-shaped ice cube mold (so ice actually fits in narrow-mouthed water bottles!) or a washer-dryer set with a conveyor belt between the units (so your clothes could automatically transfer themselves from wash to dry). Thirty-something years later, I can't turn this part of my brain off. If you have an entrepreneurial mind, you get it. Sometimes we, as entrepreneurs, get labeled as dreamers or visionaries—people with lots of great ideas, but maybe also people who "flit around" from thing to thing. If you've felt like you haven't quite found your place in the world, and this entrepreneurial spark is becoming a fire, we've got to talk about hummingbirds.

HUMMINGBIRDS AND JACKHAMMERS

I've always felt that life is built a bit backward. You sign up to do something "for the rest of your life" before you've ever lived enough of life to know what you want. Maybe the path you chose at eighteen or twenty-three doesn't work for you now. Maybe the thing you set out to do wasn't what you want to do forever. Or maybe you never thought much about the path you went down; instead, you just sort of wandered into it. *How are we supposed to make such important decisions about our career paths with so little information? Can we really ever pick a career and know it's for us without ever having tried it first? Or are we not meant to be in monogamous relationships with our jobs?* Or maybe you're just a hummingbird.

Author Elizabeth Gilbert asks us to examine whether we're a hummingbird or a jackhammer because each of us, she says, falls into one of those two categories. Laser-focused jackhammers pick one thing and go all in without ever stopping to look up.

Hummingbirds, on the other hand, like to float around and try lots of different things. They can't be tied down by any one thing. By trying so many different things, they cross-pollinate all their experiences with the knowledge they've gained from trying other things. By nature, a lot of entrepreneurs are hummingbird-like because of how multipassionate we are. Even if you are passionate about one thing, you probably get really excited to try new things and enjoy the challenges your work provides. The key to a successful hummingbird life is to stop fighting the fact that you're not a jackhammer. There's no objectively better or right way to be, so set yourself free and fly.

Whether you also carried around an inventions notebook as a child, or you just can't stop analyzing every business's marketing strategies, I hope you embrace both your hummingbird and jackhammer parts. Most "traditional" jobs don't really lend themselves well to hummingbird life. Entrepreneurship doesn't always lend itself well to jackhammer status either. We all have parts of ourselves that are likely a mix of both—but the point is to embrace more of who we are instead of fighting it. Lean into the positives of being a hummingbird, but also keep it in check when it comes to flitting around without finishing what you've started. In the later chapters on content, we'll discuss sticking with something long enough to see if it works.

You might have entered your current path with little to no expectations and found yourself accidentally at a dead end, like I did, resulting in the life lesson that you should go into your own business with a bit more of an intentional plan, considering that your own financial well-being is at stake. It's hard to plan, however, when you don't know what to expect. It's hard to know what to expect in online entrepreneurship when most online entrepreneurs aren't sharing with you the reality (or the truth) of what it's like to build a business. I'm here to share the good, the bad, and the in-between. There's a lot of each, but it can feel awfully lonely and confusing when you're going through it on your own. We'll talk about this more in chapter 3 when we discuss the different stages of building your own business so you know where you are in the process, what to expect moving forward, and that all good things take time.

AMPLIFICATION

Entrepreneurship requires tenacity and resourcefulness. If you've ever wondered if you "have what it takes," entrepreneurship will show you pretty quickly how far you're willing to go to find out. But even early on in your business-building journey, you'll realize that any issues, fears, or insecurities that existed pre-business are only amplified once you hang a shingle, so to speak. There's something about having your name on the (digital) door, your face in every piece of content, and your voice behind every written word that makes everything feel, well, more than a little personal in your business.

No matter what kind of business you build today, it will have to be somewhat personal and offer a behind-the-scenes glimpse of what you do in order for it to be successful. The social media feed of my favorite nail care brand primarily features the day-to-day of their CEO. Would I watch videos of someone doing their nails? No. But I will watch her videos all day long because she's engaging, delightful, and motivating. And that's what makes me want to purchase their nail products.

Today, most consumers look for, or even demand, some sort of personal connection with the companies they buy from. And when your business is primarily or exclusively online, you will have to work even harder to create that type of connection through a screen with people who may be thousands of miles away and totally unfamiliar with who you are and what you stand for. You're also competing for consumers' attention on social media apps filled with millions of other companies or creators screaming in your potential customers' ears about everything from dupe-filled clothing hauls to how to deep-clean their refrigerator. That doesn't mean you have to expose every personal detail of your life. I've found that it's perfectly okay, and healthy, to have boundaries around which parts of your life you share and which you don't. For example, maybe you don't share much about your relationships, but you share your daily workouts or favorite places to go eat. What you share should depend less on what you think you should do and more on the intersection between your personal boundaries and what appeals to your audience. The type of content that appeals to your audience the most is something they can personally relate to. So, if you're a nutritionist and you choose to share about your children, you would talk about your life as a parent in the context of how you help your clients, for example: how you prepare healthy meals for your children in advance when you know you have a busy week at work. The mistake most creators make is to share personal content without looping it back to being helpful to customers. Instead, show us how you "walk the walk" and implement what you teach others.

Unfortunately, as you begin to share and open up to your audience—whether it's through social media, your email list, blogging, podcasting, or even on YouTube, a few pesky friends may show up to the party: comparison, impostor syndrome, and scarcity, just to name a few. When I first started my online business, I felt exposed, raw, and vulnerable, like I was standing in the middle of an open field, with a mic in my hand, and someone had stolen all of my clothes. Maybe our egos kick in when we start sharing about our lives in a more public way. We think that all eyes are on us, even when they're probably squarely focused on themselves. But the truth is, there were more eyes on me once I started sharing about my business and life more publicly than when I sat in my windowless office mowing down entire bags of popcorn. Even if there were only a few eyes on my content, especially in the beginning, it still felt terrifying. Just knowing that my ex-colleagues and high school besties (and frenemies) were watching was enough to make me doubt whether I should show up at all. I would sheepishly take out my phone to document my day in public and record face-to-camera videos hiding behind trees in the park. With enough time, and lots of repetition, I felt like my mission outweighed the embarrassment. People in the park, at the restaurant, or in the coffee shop didn't need to understand or approve of what I was doing. The point was that *I did*. And the more I posted on social media and built my email list over time, the more I saw how much putting myself out there helped other people. So I let people look at me funny and silently judge me while talking to my phone on a walk or in a coffee shop and went on quietly building a seven-figure business behind the scenes. It was my little secret, and the Scorpio in me liked it that way.

There's honestly no magic pill you can take to prevent the feelings of comparison, fear, abandonment, impostor syndrome, or the like from showing up at one point or another. And if you don't let them in, embrace their existence, and work toward recognizing how they used to or still serve you in some way, they will knock down your damn door. Entrepreneurship has been a great blessing in that way. It has pushed me to be a better person, to see my shadow side and flaws, and to finally decide what is and isn't serving me anymore. It's really hard to play victim in your life when you're the one holding the baton. The greatest thing you can do for both yourself and your current and future business is to take ownership over this process, see it as an opportunity to grow, and step into that role the best you can. If you're disappointed because you thought your business was going to fix your life, I'm sorry to be a downer, but it won't. What it can do is give you the opportunity to make many facets of your life richer and fuller. It will gift you the opportunity to be a better person, one who faces their fears and shadows. You can heal parts of your self while also giving back to others.

WHAT WE LEARNED

- Your business may not fix your life, but it can bring you a lot of happiness and fulfillment.
- How to embrace your inner hummingbird or jackhammer.
- Your business, or any career really, won't give you the happiness you're likely seeking. True fulfillment in life is typically found outside of our jobs.

WHAT'S TO COME

- The four stages you'll go through in building your business, what to focus on in each, and how to know what to do next.

CHAPTER 3

From Seed to Pruning: The Four Stages Necessary to Grow an Online Business

Gardening may be a cliché metaphor, but it's apt for many things in life. The stages of gardening, and the patience and care growing plants requires, are similar to the stages you go through as you grow your business. Like a newly planted seed, your business will need a lot of tending to while it develops its roots. If your gardening skills are anything like mine, you usually plant a lot of seeds, knowing only a few will sprout. You wait patiently, tending to them each day, hoping some of your hard work will pay off. The seeds that do survive will blossom into a sprout and grow into a young plant with different needs and tendencies. You nervously monitor the plants' conditions and needs, like light exposure, moisture level, and soil quality, learning as you go what your plant requires more or less of to thrive. A good gardener, like a good entrepreneur, knows it's more important to pay attention to what this particular plant needs versus doing what worked for another plant in someone else's house. While you generally follow plant experts' advice on what steps to take, you also have to learn how to be the expert of your own plants and what's best for them. For example, if you water all your plants indiscriminately once per week without checking the moisture level of the soil, you may be over- or underwatering each plant, guaranteeing its inevitable death. Instead, you need to learn the signs and symptoms of each plant and become the master of *that* plant's needs. In other words, as my mom would say, you have to understand the mechanism of what works for your plants.

As you build your business, you will read a lot of advice about how you are "supposed to" do things. While much of that advice may be helpful, it's still important you "understand the mechanism" of what works, what doesn't, and why in your business. While I'm teaching you many strategies and tips throughout this book, I'm also encouraging you to see what I share here more like a map with many potential routes than a specific set of directions. There are a lot of ways to get to the same destination. Your path doesn't have to look like mine or anyone else's. At the end of the day, we're all tending to different plants in different conditions.

Just as a plant goes through several stages from seed to sprout to cultivation to propagation and pruning, your business will evolve and change between phases, too. Your business might not move linearly through the stages I mention here, or your business might be going through several of them at once. Just like our trusty houseplants, all of our journeys through these stages can look and feel differently. As is true in life, most of business is not so black and white.

Even if your business is more established, I encourage you to read this chapter. I find myself revisiting these stages often, whether it's to create a new offer, revamp an area of my business, or just reevaluate whether things are working. Sometimes you need to zoom out to see the 30,000-foot view.

YOUR MINDSET

Before we dive in to the four stages of business growth, I think it's important to check in on your mindset. Whether you're here because your business is growing the way you had hoped, or you're not sure what to do next, it will help you to recognize and accept where you are on the business stairs. Let me explain.

Think of a long vertical staircase with several landings. Building a business—any business, but particularly online for our purposes—is kind of like walking up these stairs. At some points in our journey, we're stepping up, moving on to the next phase and feeling the fruits of our labor. At other times, we have our heads down putting in the work— while feeling like nothing's happening. At others, we're resting comfortably on one of the landings, or taking a rest before we step up again. All of these stair phases are necessary and natural—but for some reason we tend to fight them.

Now think of the parts of a step. There's the vertical rise, and the horizontal flat part, or tread. Each stage of your business is a step, and ascending the staircase requires a lot of unsexy, hard work behind the scenes, putting your head down and just getting to work. Sometimes I feel like a snail, slowly scooting my way along the flat part of the stair. During this time, the outside world might not see how hard I'm working. "Is this thing on?" I might think to myself. *Why is no one responding to my posts or emails?* These are often the times when you won't be able to see or feel much of your progress (yet): when you're setting your business's foundations (legally and financially), creating a new product to sell, creating high-quality creative content, or upleveling your back-end systems. But these "head down" times lead to growth. After you've put in the hard work during these times, and right before you're about to throw your laptop out the window, you'll suddenly realize your business has taken another step up.

The vertical rise of a step is often the time in our business when we're reaping the rewards of all the hard work we put in previously. That's when we might see or feel the outside world noticing our hard work. Your audience may be growing in size, email list numbers are rising, and you're gaining more clients. I like to think of the flat part of the stair as the time when I set up all of my business experiments—like designing a new freebie opt-in to grow my email list—and the vertical rise as the time when I get to see if my experiment actually worked. *Are people opting in to my email list? Do they stay on my email list after they subscribe? Are they engaging or buying?* But then comes that dang flat part of the step again, and the process starts all over.

In my experience, this is the way business ebbs and flows. It's not only normal, but necessary. By the time I started Sam Vander Wielen LLC, I had learned from the mistakes I'd made with the health coaching business before. With my first business, I had the highest expectations for myself and for it. I figured, as many of us do, that as soon as my website went live, clients and purchases would start pouring in. I had no idea then how much work it would truly take to gain any traction. When I didn't reach these high and unrealistic expectations I'd arbitrarily set for myself, I thought I'd failed. I figured I wasn't cut out to be a business owner or that people must not want to work with me because of *me*. Looking back, I can see just how little I knew about the hard work, methodical steps, time, intentional strategies, testing, and adjusting that are required to build a long-term sustainable business. My business model and marketing strategy were completely wrong. No wonder it never "took off." So, when I started my legal business, I approached it with a different set of expectations, and a wildly different strategy, model, and plan, too.

Whether you're about to hit "publish" on your website, or you're starting your third business after not having had much success with the first two attempts, it's important to know what stages to expect and how to move through them. While everyone's situation is unique and may be different from others', building a business happens in stages.

After eight years of running my own company and teaching others how to build their own, I've identified four common stages of business development and growth. It's important to know what the stages are and to be able to self-identify which one you're in and when it's time to move on to the next stage. Otherwise, you may skip crucial steps that are vital to your business's growth and longevity. You might also find yourself wandering around, wondering if you're doing the right thing in your business, and whether you're making any progress at all. Knowing which stage you're in, or that there are stages at all, is also key to managing expectations as a business owner.

Let's walk through the four stages of business development and growth, from seed to sprout, propagate, and prune.

1. SEED

A business seed starts with an idea: improving something that already exists, offering something that already exists in a different way, or creating something entirely new. Like many entrepreneurs, you might come up with a lot of idea seeds. In my business, I continue to find and plant new seeds every day. So although this is the stage that marks the beginning of an entire business, it can also occur at the start of a new project, creation of a new offer, or building a new branch of a current business. The point of this phase is to cultivate your idea seeds and see which are viable. Knowing that not all seeds will take, there are three ways to determine your idea seed's viability.

Demand

Whether you're creating a business or a product, be careful that you're not the only one demanding its existence. Many people start online businesses or create products in response to their own needs—something they struggled with or wished they had—instead of focusing on the needs of their potential customers. Your own experience can be a catalyst for a great business idea, but only if it's backed up with additional research to make sure that other people need and want it, too. To determine if outside demand exists ask yourself these questions:

> *Is my product or service needed? How can I tell? Are people looking for it but can't currently find it? Why not? What problems are they experiencing and how is it impacting their lives? What have they tried that hasn't worked for them? Why hasn't it worked? What's the missing piece that could solve their problems and offer them the solution they're looking for?*

Start by doing some research. Talk to people and listen to what they struggle with, what they want, and what's standing in their way. If you know people in real life who struggle with the problem you want to solve, meet with them and listen carefully to what they have to say. Don't enter these conversations with an agenda. Keep an open mind and stay curious—they might say something that unlocks an idea for you. If you don't know anyone personally, look online. There are likely Facebook groups, Reddit threads, or a corner of a social media platform where your ideal clients hang out. If you meet with anyone on Zoom, ask for their permission to record your conversation. What they say will be copywriting gold down the line.

Your products need to be demand-tested, too. One of the best ways to find clarity on this is to beta test your product by creating an initial version of it and selling it to a handful of buyers (usually at some sort of discount or introductory rate). Not only do you get to see if your pitch converts to a sale, but you'll also get live feedback on your product and learn what you can do to make it better. We'll talk about how to properly beta test a product in chapter 7.

Supply

When I decided to be a health coach, I wanted to know how many other people out there were doing what I wanted to do, so I checked Instagram to do a little "supply" research. Moments later, I was crushed to find out someone had already taken the exact social media handle I wanted, and offered exactly what I'd thought about offering. To make matters worse, she even lived in my very own city. I can pretty much guarantee you would find people doing something similar to you if you looked on social media right now. But that's not the kind of supply research I'm talking about. And that's not where your journey ends, even if your search turns up a list of competition longer than a Sunday morning Trader Joe's checkout line. I want you to go deeper than that: Look at who's offering what, how saturated the market seems to be overall, and cross-check what you find with the size of the pool of potential customers. Consider:

Who's offering the kinds of products or services you want to offer? What makes you, your business, or even your product

*unique and different from what's out there? Even if your prod-
uct or service is being offered already, is there enough demand
to accommodate your offer? What's missing from what's being
offered that you can provide? What "hole in the market" will
you or your product fill? What's your unique or competitive
advantage?*

For example, when I started my current business, there were
other lawyers already selling legal templates. But my research
revealed two things: First, there was a huge demand (and more on
the way) for what I was going to sell, so having a few people already
in business didn't scare me off. And second, when I dug deeper
into the "supply," I noticed something was missing. Considering
how many people were reaching out to me unsolicited, I wanted
to know why, since they already had options. I listened and asked
questions without an agenda. I wanted to know if those reaching
out to me knew they had options and just didn't like the options
available to them, or if there was a discovery problem and they
weren't finding what they were looking for. In the end, it was a
bit of both. People couldn't find what they were looking for, and
those who did didn't always like what they found. My proposed
products and business's vibe were completely different from what
was being offered (not in a good or bad way— there are different
flavors for everyone). There was room for experimentation in what
was available when it came to customer service, user experience,
and even the marketing tone. Since my research told me that my
potential customers felt like this was all missing, too, I knew I was
on to something.

So if you find others out there doing what you do or want to
do, don't let that alone dash your dreams. Approach this process
like a scientist doing research and go in with an open mind. Maybe
it means your business or offerings need to be tweaked a bit, but

it doesn't mean you can't be prosperous, too. Depending on your industry and how early of an adopter you are, the possibilities may be endless due to a steady stream of new customers.

Your Business Model

Just because there's supply and demand for your proposed business, product, or service doesn't mean it's viable. Ultimately, in order for your business to be profitable, your gross revenue—the amount you generate in sales—must outweigh your costs. You have to charge enough money for your products, and sell enough of those products, to outpace what it costs you to create and sell them. For example, maybe you've created something that would cost around $25, but would be marketed only to college students. Between the low price point, lack of scalability, and the target market likely being short on expendable income, your business model might need a little tweaking before it goes to market.

During the seed phase of building your business, look at what your first one to three offers will be. Consider:

How much will your offers cost? After operating and business expenses, how much additional revenue will you need to bring in each month to build your capital reserves, pay taxes, and pay yourself? How many products will you need to sell of each offer to make enough revenue to cover your expenses, pay yourself, and re-invest in your business? Once someone purchases from you (and they become a customer), do you have anything else to sell them? Or is this product the only product they can buy from you? What will be all the sources of revenue for your business (e.g., products, services, speaking fees, sponsorships, affiliate income, etc.)?

The following are some examples of potentially profitable online business models:

- **Coaching or consulting services** might be offered privately (what we call one-on-one) or through group programs and masterminds. A coach's income can be somewhat restricted since these services are so time- and person-dependent; in other words, it's not a very scalable model. However, many coaches love working with clients privately and scalability is not the be-all and end-all.
- **E-commerce** operates in the form of shops selling goods and products through their digital storefront or online platforms such as Etsy or Amazon.
- Businesses offering **online courses, memberships, or digital products** are typically able to work with more people than personalized one-on-one service providers can.
- **Content creators and influencers** get paid to promote other companies' products and services. They generate revenue from sponsorships, advertisements, and affiliate links (kickbacks for providing a product recommendation or review).
- The online business world is full of thriving **service providers** such as copywriters, graphic designers, website designers, and many other creatives who offer services for both online and brick-and-mortar businesses.
- There are endless possibilities to create **SaaS (software as a service), apps, and other online tools**. Often these are involved, large-scale projects on which you would want to consult with tech experts, software engineers, and a good legal team.

What's a Freelancer?

Freelancers are often thought of as being somehow different from a business owner. In reality, "freelancer" is just an old-fashioned term for a solo entrepreneur, or as the cool kids say: a solopreneur. (Cool kids do not actually say that. In fact, I have no idea what cool kids say. If you're a cool kid, let me know.) Freelancers typically offer services or complete projects for other people or their businesses. Essentially, for legal purposes, you're acting as an independent contractor in other people's businesses when you perform freelance work. But performing that type of work *is* your business. So whether you're starting a side hustle or a "freelancer" business, you're still required to follow all the legal and financial rules that apply to any other type of business.

Avoid the Time-for-Money Trade

You'll also want to consider the long-term viability of what you're building if your business heavily relies on your being the face of it. If you have a service-based business model, as a coach, consultant, or copywriter, for example, it's important to remember that there is only one you, and only twenty-four hours in a day. As you build your offers, try to diversify your revenue streams to include other sources that don't all rely on a time-for-money trade. Of course, your one-on-one time can and should be part of your business model if you love working with clients that way, but your pricing should be structured accordingly to make it the most premium thing you offer. If people are going to get that much of your time, the pricing should reflect that level of access accordingly.

Many service-based businesses often make the mistake of not offering any one-to-many or digital products until they're so burned out on one-on-one clients that they're forced to do so. Some service-based business owners have created those products, but struggle to find the time to market them since so much of their time is taken up with client work. Take Jamie, for example, an intuitive eating counselor, movement expert, and health coach who was a highly sought after one-on-one coach. She charged over $6,000 for a six-month coaching package, and she regularly was at capacity with the number of clients she had. These private client sessions took up every moment of every day. She was so exhausted at the end of each day that she wanted to create a passive product or online course to sell so she wouldn't have to spend each workday in client sessions. But because her private client sessions were so time-consuming, she wasn't able to carve out the time she needed to create the product she thought would free up her time. Jamie also spent a lot of time on social media and writing to her email list marketing her services, but since her private client roster was full, there was really nowhere else to send potential clients. And not all of her followers could afford her $6,000 coaching package. Since she had no other offer available, Jamie inadvertently turned away a lot of business. To finally create and launch an online course that could bring in income even while Jamie was sleeping or vacationing with her family, she had to temporarily stop seeing clients and take a significant hit financially. In the end, she's found a balance between high-ticket private clients and selling her more passive digital product (an online course). But diversifying her revenue streams to include sources other than her one-on-one time is something she wishes she had focused on earlier.

The time you spend in your seed phase can be difficult. Just like a little seed you push beneath the soil to (hopefully) sprout, much of your business growth happens behind the scenes where no one can see it (you included). Be as open and curious as you can during this time. Your purpose here is to test and be a researcher. You can't be emotionally invested in the answers or outcomes, only the possibilities. There may be times where you feel like there's no progress and nothing is working, and just when you're wondering if you should pack your digital bags and go home, you will see that first little green sprout peek its head through the soil's surface.

2. SPROUT

Once you have a proof of concept through beta testing and selling your product or service, and you've gone through the important demand, supply, and business plan viability concepts, it's time to set your marketing and sales foundations. In this phase, you'll focus on building an audience online, learn how to market to that audience, and get them to purchase from you. To build your audience, you can utilize a variety of tools and strategies from email marketing to social media to digital advertising (all topics that we'll talk about in detail later on), but you'll spend a significant part of your time as an entrepreneur trying to figure out which strategies are best for your business, your potential customers, and your wallet. Regardless of which you choose, these strategies take repeated testing and a level of consistency that most entrepreneurs struggle to maintain. If you want to build an email list, for example, you can expect to start with a handful of email list subscribers whom you know (friends and family are most of our first subscribers!), and then you'll see a trickle of initial "random" email list subscribers start to flow in over time. A significant portion of this book talks about how to build an email list full of engaged, ready-to-buy customers—so stick with me.

A lead magnet (otherwise known as a "freebie") is a free resource or download you offer subscribers in exchange for signing up for your email list. This is a great way to start to build your email list subscribers, since it's easier to convince people to receive your emails if they're first going to get something valuable, yet free. It's also a great way to attract potential customers, since the person attracted to your freebie should, in theory, be someone who would also be interested in your services/products.

You'll hear online marketing gurus tell you, "Just create a freebie! Share about it on social media. Post it on your website. Problem solved. That's how you build an email list." But what no one tells you is that you have to actively and consistently market your freebie to people, especially in the beginning. Yes, you might have a website. But how many people are coming to it? Not many at first. And how many views or opens are you getting on social media or your email list? It sounds like crickets over there. You also need practice and time to learn how to pitch your freebie to prospective subscribers, and how to craft no-brainer opt-in copy on your lead magnet page to get people to actually opt in. We'll dive headfirst into how to create irresistible freebies and attract lots of qualified leads to your email list in chapter 6.

For me, it took about five months of sharing about my lead magnet every day on social media to reach five hundred subscribers on my email list. Six months later, I'd doubled my subscriber count to more than a thousand using the same strategy. With time, I learned how to get more email leads each month. But that came only after lots of trial and error, consistently emailing my list each week, and treating my email list as my top priority. Nearly eight years and over forty-six thousand subscribers later, email list growth is still a top priority for me every day. And once you get subscribers on your list, it's a demanding job to keep them on it, let alone engaged. After you've finished this book, you'll have all the info you need to start and grow an engaged list.

As you navigate the sprout phase of building your business, most of your attention will go toward lead generation (building an audience of potential customers) and conversion (getting those leads to buy). It's a continuous cycle that takes time, patience, and persistence to pay off. And it's a cycle you have to consistently nurture, no matter how long you've been in business. But as your audience grows and many convert to customers, it's time to cultivate what you've built so far to achieve even greater growth.

Target <u>Your</u> Audience

If you create a lead magnet resource to build your email list, you'll want it to be something that leads to what you teach or help people with; it should be something that is helpful to your intended customers and encourages them to want to take the next step with you. For example, if you offer a free webinar and want to sell viewers your online course, your webinar should cover the main topics covered by your course. That way, you'll attract people who are actually interested buyers and not random people looking for a freebie. Once on your email list, people should hear from you, ideally once a week, with some valuable content or updates about what's going on in your business and how you can help them.

---

3. CULTIVATE

Once the seeds you've sown have sprouted in your garden, you can cultivate additional growth by tending to those plants' needs and doubling down on what's worked for those plants so far. Similarly in business, all of the sprout work you've done will lead to a more automated business, one with marketing ecosystems that consistently pull in leads on their own and that garners word-of-mouth referrals. In the cultivation phase, you'll start to feel the snowball effects of what you've done so far. You can go all in on what you know works already, finally start to reap the rewards of your business, and experiment in new directions.

By this stage, many online entrepreneurs feel burned out on social media, or by the perceived pressure to appear in all places online at all times. You might get caught in a trap I've been in several times myself, producing too much content in an unintentional attempt to keep up with the online Joneses. By necessity, in this phase you should focus your marketing efforts on one or two main channels, like a podcast or YouTube, so you can grow a deeper connection with an audience in those places, instead of a small audience across many. You'll have a better idea of what is working and what isn't, and, if you've managed your business finances correctly (which we'll discuss in chapter 4), you'll have some capital to invest in the areas that are.

Now that you've been using social media to market your business for a bit, you might be sick of the dopamine crashes, constant algorithm changes, and overstimulating noise there. Or maybe you're sick of shoving your content in to a seven-second dancing Reel, when it really deserves deeper exploration and nuanced discussion. You might be thinking, "How do I build my business, grow my audience, and keep getting new leads without having to be on social media so much?" When you reach that point in the cultivate stage, there are three things to focus on.

Evergreen Content

Often, when you feel burned out on creating social media content, you've been creating too much of it or focusing too much of your marketing efforts on social media instead of a long-form discovery platform. (We'll discuss the difference between discovery platforms and nurture platforms, and how to pick the right ones for you, in a later chapter.) In the cultivate phase, it's time to focus on quality over quantity when it comes to content, and post that content in a discoverable, searchable place that has longevity.

Audience Borrowing

This is where the power of networking (even all-digital networking), collaborating, and audience borrowing comes into play. When you go on social media, or post something online, you're speaking only to your audience—the one you've already built, who likely already know you or like something about what you have to say or offer. But what about all of the people yet to find you who would also like what you have to say and offer, if only they knew you existed? Sure, you could keep posting on social media multiple times per day hoping that the algorithm swings your way and shows your content to the right people. Or you could go where they are already hanging out: your **shoulder colleagues**. These are people who sell to or work with the same people, or the same type of people, as you do, but who do not offer the same exact service you do. You complement each other like peanut butter and jelly. Recently, I spoke with Lori,[1] a registered dietitian who specializes in intuitive eating. After leaving Instagram nine months ago for the exact reasons we discussed earlier, Lori had hit a wall in finding new clients now. I asked her where she was marketing herself and her services. "The usual," she replied. "Other intuitive eating podcasts, intuitive eating websites, and through intuitive eating networks I'm a part of." Bingo, that was Lori's problem. She was advertising her intuitive eating services too far within her own group, to members of her own community (other dietitians, not customers looking for dietitians' services).

1. Name changed.

Cultivating relationships with your colleagues, whether in-person or online, is crucial during this period. Typically, you can offer a training to a colleague's audience, go live on social media together, do a newsletter swap, appear on their podcast, or ask to write for their blog or email list. Of course, they can do the same for you. The key to building successful audience borrowing relationships is to find partnerships in which you both mutually benefit. You offer value to their audience, and you get exposure and potential clients. By cross-promoting in this way, it's a win-win for you both. The key is to put yourself out there and ask. In my experience, the more you ask, the more opportunities become available. And the more opportunities you are able to take advantage of, the bigger the doors are that may open for you.

Paid Advertising and Sponsorships
From Facebook, Instagram, and Google ads, to sponsoring a newsletter or an in-person event, there are plenty of ways to advertise your online business to your target audience. If you want to invest in paid advertising through a platform like Facebook or Instagram (which are both owned by the parent company, Meta), I'd recommend investing in ads only once you have a well-functioning and converting sales funnel set up in your business. We'll talk later on in the book about what those look like and how to start and grow a highly converting sales funnel.

My "cultivate" season came about two years after I started my company. I felt confident in my products and knew that I could sell them; I knew my ideal customer like the back of my hand, and I was starting to see some marketing efforts pay off. That was when I decided to invest in advertising as a more "hands-off" (versus being on social media) lead generation and sales strategy. Since I had saved much of my business's revenue up to that point, I was able to calmly and confidently invest in

Facebook and Instagram ads with a curiosity mindset. I started with a relatively small investment in advertising, and scaled up as the ads had a higher return on investment. But I did not want my business's success or future to rest on an ad platform that could change on a dime, much less one that wouldn't tell me anything about how its algorithm worked. To diversify my advertising and lead generation channels, I dove deeper into cross-promotion and networking by offering trainings to my shoulder colleagues' audiences. I regularly applied to be on people's podcasts, and I even reached out personally through social media to make connections with podcasters whose audiences I could help. Eventually, I started my own podcast so I could ask some of the best creators in my industry to be guests on it. When their episodes aired, they shared it with their audiences, which exposed me to an entirely new group of people who had likely interest in what I had to offer. I started asking each podcast guest if they would do an Instagram live with me on the day their episode aired, which is a great way to cross-promote yourself to others' audiences. (*Note: When you go live with someone on Instagram, it lets both your and their audiences know. Win-win!*)

What If No One's Biting?

As my social media mentor, Natasha Samuel, says: If you aren't getting invited onto stages or shows (yet), build your own. In other words, if you can't quite crack the code on how to get on someone else's podcast, create your own and ask guests to be on it. It's a great way to associate yourself with bigger names in your industry. In the meantime, work on your craft and build your audience. Before you know it, you'll be asked to be on theirs.

During this time, you'll also want to make sure your process and operations are improved and buttoned up. Before it's time to scale, it's important to have most of the kinks worked out of your sales funnels. If there's a tiny hole in the system, it will rupture once you start to run Facebook ads or scale your sales funnel in another way. Do you have clear processes, in the form of standard operating procedures (SOPs)? If not, now's the time to create an SOP for each and every necessary task in your business, exactly how it's performed, and all the places on the back end of your business where someone else could find the resources or links they need to perform that task. That will allow you to hire additional personnel and start to hand off certain tasks in your business that you don't need to (or shouldn't) be doing anymore.

Before scaling even further, take a walk through your customer journey to ensure that the onboarding process is smooth. What is the purchase process like? Is it simple and intuitive? Do the products get delivered—digital or otherwise—properly? Are your current customers finding it easy to navigate and implement? Do you have email sequences to follow up with customers (we'll talk about these later on) or that offer an upsell opportunity?

On the noncustomer side, do you have all nurture sequences linked to all of your opt-ins? We'll talk about those in chapter 6 in depth, but for now it's good to remember that this is the time to get all of your back-end systems in order.

4. PROPAGATE + PRUNE

Just as we prune and cut back parts of the plant that have died in order to encourage new growth, your business will require a similar approach. At some point, your plant might also reach its growth potential. Maybe the point of tending to your plant now is only to keep it alive and healthy—not for it to grow.

I'm the first one to tell you that it's okay if you don't want your business to grow endlessly. Having the biggest plant isn't objectively better than having a small but mightily healthy one. Not everyone wants or needs to create an Amazon-sized business. It's entirely possible for you to make a massive impact even at a "small" business level. This phase will include a lot of time spent on determining how big of a business you really want to build and maintain. Many entrepreneurs I know who cultivated a really big business came to realize they wanted to go back to a smaller, simpler one. Knowing there's no objectively right answer or right size of business to grow into, it's important to think about what you truly want. You might want to save this for a later time if you're not quite there yet. That way, you'll be able to confidently grow and maintain a business on your terms, without accidentally running the one you thought you should. Those unwanted and unintended, yet luring, growth opportunities are often what sink small businesses.

Even if there's no ultimate or objective business size you're trying to reach, you will reach certain peaks based on the structure and viability of your business. Maybe you hit a ceiling because your business is so heavily reliant on your one-on-one work with clients, or because you've capped out the market. If you are an early-ish adopter like me, you might not know ahead of time exactly what those limits are, because you're setting them as you go. I never dreamed that my business could grow to the size that it has. I didn't intend or plan for it to become this big. My time in this phase has largely been spent asking myself the hard questions: *How big do I want this to get? At what cost? Why do I want it to grow so much? What does success look like to me these days?* I check in with myself often about growth and especially around why I'm seeking out that growth.

When I first started working with my mindset coach, Jennifer Diaz, she asked me what my ultimate business goal was. Instead of giving her a revenue amount or a stage I wanted to speak on, I told her about the two goals I had: (1) Get a book deal with a Big 5 publisher (you're holding that dream right now!); and (2) build the biggest business ever. "Okay, build the biggest business ever…," she lovingly repeated as she jotted down my ridiculous goals in her notes. "What does that even mean?" she rightfully asked.

"Well, I want this business to become as big as it possibly can," I replied.

"Why? Why is it important that it become so 'big'?" Jennifer asked.

This, my friends, is why working with talented professionals who can hold your feet to the flame as a CEO is so important. At the time Jennifer asked me that self-reflective question, I had more of a "because!" attitude. But over the course of the next year, as my world collapsed around me, my answer not only changed but became painfully and distinctly clear to me.

When Life Hands You Crapola

Before my dad's leukemia diagnosis, and his devastating death in 2022, I was totally committed to those "build the biggest business ever" goals I shared with Jennifer. But especially after he got sick and I became his caregiver, I was forced to revisit my priorities, goals, and desires. You, too, might be in a situation where life has handed you a bag of crapola, as my grandfather would say. And to you I say, first and foremost, I'm sorry. You are not alone. But I'll also tell you that you have an opportunity to make your business work *for* you and the situation you've been dealt. Hopefully, sharing my experience will help you to imagine how you could reorient your own.

Seemingly overnight, I started attending his chemo appointments, picking up meds, calling doctors to advocate on his behalf, getting him the supplies he needed, and, during COVID, administering his treatments myself through his chest port. If you've ever been a caregiver or faced a loved one's terminal illness, you know it's sort of like encountering a burning building. You run in and do what you can without stopping to think or consider what all of your options are. It's an experience that changes you permanently as a person. But what I didn't expect was how much better an entrepreneur it would make me, and in turn how much more efficient it made my business.

I'd sit with my dad on the fourth floor of the University of Pennsylvania's blood cancer unit and type away on my laptop to distract myself while a nurse dressed like a beekeeper (they wore these hazmat-looking suits to keep themselves and my dad safe) administered his chemotherapy. Over time, my attempts at distraction felt useless and inconsequential. *Do I really need to post a legal tip on Instagram today? I'm watching my dad fight for his life.*

When he got sick, I realized my business relied too much on me to constantly create new content. If I didn't show up on Instagram every day, my sales dipped. It felt like I'd built a really powerful sports car, but it ran only when I had my foot on the gas. The moment I let up, the whole thing came to a screeching halt. Since taking care of Dad was my priority, I would have to figure out a way to still make sales with the car in neutral (or more like self-driving mode, these days).

Out of Bad Comes Good

Sometimes things happen in your life that don't just objectively change how much time or attention you have to dedicate to something. Sometimes life slaps you straight across the face and teaches you a valuable lesson. Most of the stuff we fret about in our businesses—how many likes our Instagram post has, how many email subscribers we have, how much money we make—is just flat out not that important in the grand scheme of life. But we all have to make a living, right? How do we balance those two things? Prioritizing our health, time with loved ones—and putting food on the table. I had to figure that out because I wanted to be there for my dad, and I also needed to make a living. I couldn't shut down my business, and I couldn't afford to let it slow down. There was no other option but to figure out a way to make my business run even more smoothly.

Whether you've got a lot going on in your life or you need to reorganize your priorities in some way, the first thing to do is to prune. *What tasks do you not have to do? Could they be axed completely, or could you hire someone to complete them for you? What projects are you working on that can wait until later?* Especially in moments of crisis, you might find that some of what you do can wait or be scratched entirely.

When you go through something in life that leaves you with very little time to accomplish what you need to do, you quickly learn how to prioritize. Besides cutting unnecessary tasks out of your business, you can also audit your time. *How much time, for example, are you spending on creating content? And how well is that content performing for your business?* As we'll discuss throughout the book, this is where it's important to focus more on evergreen, long-form content, and less on churning out lots of what I call "toilet" content, short-form, non-searchable content (usually posted on social media) that has a very short shelf life. Instead, as we'll discuss, you could spend less time creating fewer pieces of content that have a bigger impact on your bottom line. You also want to focus most of your time on revenue-generating activities, like sending out emails, creating new freebies to attract leads, and cultivating relationships with your shoulder colleagues. As you audit your time, keep track of which tasks can be scrapped completely, which can wait, and which can be assigned to someone else. If you're in a position to, now is a great time to hire your first virtual assistant or independent contractor to delegate those tasks to.

Sometimes, the hardest moments in life offer the greatest lessons. While you may have hoped that life would be smooth sailing once you started your business, the challenges you've had to overcome might actually help you in the long run. My mom always said, "Out of bad comes good." And out of a very bad experience, I figured out how to optimize and scale my business to work smarter, not harder. When my business reached a certain point and my dad's leukemia raged on, I also learned to define what my "enough" level was.

In May 2022, my dad spent what would turn out to be his last weekend at my house in New York. We had the best time doing what we do best: going to the farmers market, putzing around grocery stores, and taste-testing in every bagel store within a ten-minute drive of my house. The season was shifting and the sun was shining brightly as we sat together and talked in my greenery-filled backyard. At that point, we had navigated his cancer diagnosis together for nearly four years and he was doing relatively well. But just days after this incredible long weekend together, my dad passed away. When the doctor came to say what I dreaded to hear for so long, I was alone. It was the worst moment of my life. All I could whisper into his ear repeatedly was, "You did so good. I am so proud of you. I love you so much," as I watched the light dim from his hazel eyes as he drifted away from this earth. As much as I naively thought I had prepared myself for that moment and what would come afterward, I was sorely mistaken. *How can you be prepared for something so bad that even your mind can't imagine it until it happens?* But it wasn't long after my dad passed away that life handed me another gut punch. My mom, the eccentric, vibrant, energetic physician who wore sparkly high heels to the grocery store, took ballroom dancing lessons, and loved ocean kayaking, died suddenly under tragic, traumatic circumstances. To say that my life was shattered would be an understatement.

After losing both of my parents back-to-back in a year's time, I questioned nearly everything I had thought I wanted in my business and my life. Fortunately, I had built evergreen funnels and marketing ecosystems (the same ones I'll teach you how to build later in the book) that continued to bring in sales at a normal pace, even while I took time to reevaluate things. I also had an incredible team that supported me and my customers behind the scenes. All of this wouldn't have been possible if I hadn't followed my own money-saving advice that we'll discuss in chapter 4. So while I was in a privileged position to stand back and ask how "big" I really wanted my business to be, I also see how the strategies I'm going to share with you led me to being able to do so. Why did I want it to be *that* big, and did it need to be? Could I still go on after such devastating loss and suffocating grief? I wasn't, and still am not, sure that I could now physically do what I used to. Even though my business continued to do well, would that always be true? I needed the income from it, so letting go wasn't an option. But grief humbled me. I wasn't the same "build the biggest business ever" entrepreneur I was before. I'm still not.

For years leading up to Dad's cancer journey, my business was my priority. But after he got sick, and especially since losing my parents, my priorities have shifted. Maybe that's a forever thing. Or maybe that's only temporary after being completely knocked down (and then kicked again in the gut) by life. We all have income goals and needs, but my point is that having a business and having a life are not mutually exclusive. What I want you to take away from this book is that you can build a scalable online business that makes money whether you're working nonstop, going through a rough patch in life and needing to work a little less, or anywhere in between. There are very few entrepreneurs I know who have been able to prioritize their businesses at all times, regardless of what else was going on in their lives. One of my entrepreneur friends had a baby with significant health issues, while another recently lost her mom to a sudden heart attack. They both stepped back and revisited their relationship with their businesses. Your business, and your relationship to it, can ebb and flow as you want or need it to. Yes, there's a practical level of what you need to make to earn a living. But there's usually an opportunity to reevaluate your relationship to your business, too.

Remember, building your business is going to involve times that are nothing but grunt work and other times that finally feel like progress. These winding paths are so much more common than the handful of overnight sensations you might hear about online. Knowing that these four macrolevel, and many microlevel, stages exist will help you quiet the noise that inevitably bubbles up from time to time as you run your business. You can come back to any of the phases I've described here and determine what next steps are right for you. Your journey may not be linear or look like anyone else's. Grade school rules apply: Keep your eyes on your own paper. It's only natural to wonder whether all your effort is going to pay off or whether what you're doing is actually working. But as you're making your way through and between these stages, know that you're becoming a member of the very cool and unique club of entrepreneurship.

WHAT WE LEARNED

- The business-building journey is similar to that of growing plants from seeds: It might require you to tend to a lot of ideas first before one of them sprouts and becomes "your thing."
- To make sure your business or product idea is viable, you need to evaluate the supply, demand, and your business model.
- When it comes to attracting and building an audience, you want to focus on building your email list as a top priority.
- If you're looking for additional ways to grow your audience, consider paid advertising and collaborations (audience borrowing) to get in front of your ideal customers.
- As you build your business, you might run into life roadblocks. These are opportunities to reevaluate how you spend your time in your business and also work toward focusing your time on things that actually generate revenue and move the business forward.

WHAT'S TO COME

- How to financially plan and budget to start your own business.
- What you need to know about putting financial pressure on a young business.

CHAPTER 4

What It Really Costs to Start and Grow an Online Business

When I took my first ever cold plunge in Sayulita, Mexico, it felt as if all the blood in my body froze—but, had I stopped to test the water temperature first, I would never have jumped in. When it comes to cold plunging, jumping in without thinking is key to success. However, the same is not true when it comes to starting your own business. In this case, it's crucial to be as prepared as possible and do things right, even if that means going slower than you want to.

Once you tell people you want to start a business, you might hear advice to "start before you're ready!" or to "dive right in!" (Of course, that's in addition to all the people who will tell you how many businesses fail in their first year. Thanks for that helpful info, Uncle Larry!) This type of irresponsible advice leads to many entrepreneurs with failed businesses and dashed hopes. Don't get me wrong. There is a certain element of "diving in" involved in starting a business. But there's a difference between diving in without a plan or realistic expectations and some careful planning.

We've talked a little about how online businesses are smart businesses to start because of how much more affordable they are to run than a "traditional" brick-and-mortar store—the price of entry is a bit lower. Of course, as with any business, though, there are still start-up costs involved. And as with any business, brick-and-mortar or purely digital, getting to a profitable stage where you can comfortably pay yourself as much as you want or need can take time (or at least more time than you want!). Sure, with an online business you might not have up-front commercial rent to pay or a store build-out to fund as you perhaps would if you started a bakery, but you are still starting a full-fledged business. Businesses require a proper legal setup (which costs money), an online presence (which costs money), and some initial investment to get going (you guessed it: money).

For all these reasons, a solid foundation and plan are crucial to building a successful business, which I define as a business that:

- lasts for the long run, or at least as long as you want it to;
- offers quality services or products that actually help people, make the world a better place, or fulfill a need; and
- gives you some peace, joy, pride, and fulfillment (not all of your fulfillment, as we'll talk about later, but at a minimum I'd love for you to be proud of your business and the impact it has).

LET'S PLAN

Let's talk through what your own plan would need to look like so you can safely and successfully leave your job or plan to launch a new business.

I crafted a plan to leave the law and start my business once I knew in my gut that it was time to go. There were lots of steps to accomplish on the "start my own business" checklist, such as getting a domain name, designing my website, and starting social media accounts. However, there were also several things I wanted to do to be *financially prepared* to be out on my own before leaving my nine-to-five.

I saw it as a three-step process: save, sell, and make. I first looked at my spending habits and noticed patterns that weren't helpful for my financial wellness. Once I made some cuts, I saved money and began adding to a small-yet-mighty slush fund for my future business. Next, I looked around my house, especially in the basement and garage, and boxed up items I wasn't using anymore but that could easily be sold for quick cash. Finally, I looked for additional work opportunities through side jobs, extracurricular work activities, and the first beta clients for my coaching business.

With some careful planning and consideration, you can enter the early stages of entrepreneurship with a more realistic idea of what is actually required moneywise to start and grow a business, and what will be required in terms of time, resources, and attention to become successful. Most people don't spend enough time thinking about these things before they start a business, which often leads to a frantic, pressured start to an early stage company that they expect to make them money right away. Finally, it's also really important to learn how to pay yourself and responsibly manage your business and personal funds so that you don't accidentally violate any laws or tax regulations.

1. Save

You may find this part of the plan sort of ironic considering that your primary reason for starting a business might be so you can make more money to spend. But this is where part of my Philly-style tough love comes in—unless you've got a pile of cash lying around somewhere, you've got to build up some capital. The first step is to take a good hard look at your personal budget. You need to have a clear picture of your personal expenses and exactly how much it costs you to live every month, with or without a business. Your personal expenses could include

- housing, including rent/mortgage, HOA fees, maintenance, and emergencies;
- food;
- utilities;
- clothing and entertainment;
- insurance (health, car, house, pet, rental, etc.);
- medical and health-care costs not covered by insurance; and
- transportation (personal car, public transportation, rideshare, etc.).

Some of your personal expenses will increase when you start your own business, and others will decrease. For example, if you're commuting to work each day right now, you will have fewer transportation expenses (assuming you will work from home). Until I worked on my budget, I never realized how much I spent going out to lunch or for coffee nearly every day. When I started working from home, those expenses virtually disappeared.

On the other hand, your job might pay for some of the above-listed expenses as benefits right now, whereas you will be financially responsible for them when you're out on your own. A good starting point to investigate health-care options as a solo entrepreneur is at healthcare.gov, the US government's health-care marketplace, where you can price out what it would cost you to get health insurance as a self-employed individual.

As long as we're taking a good hard look at your personal expenses to determine how much you need to live, now is a good time to identify any unnecessary expenses in your personal budget. You might catch recurring subscriptions you didn't even know you were still paying or pick up on a regular expense that costs a surprising amount each month. When I looked at my own credit card statements in anticipation of quitting my job, I noticed how much I spent trying to cure the unhappiness I felt in my career. My lunchtime online shopping habits, long lunches out to get away from the office, and overpriced car payment stacked up. Considering how badly I wanted to leave, those were all expenses I was happy to cut back or completely cut out of my budget if it meant not having to work there anymore.

For any necessary, yet high, expenses, try to negotiate them down. You would be surprised what one email or phone call can do if you call a company and express your intent to leave or cancel. For big companies, Google "[company name] cancellation retention" to see if you find anything online about deals offered on their website if you try to cancel your subscription. Recently, I found one for 60 percent off my subscription for one year.

While it's always possible, it's unlikely your business will generate enough profit for you to be able to pay 100 percent of your personal expenses off the bat (or even for a good while). Your personal living expenses budget will give you a good idea of how much you'll need to save or continue to earn elsewhere to cover your expenses until that happens. (*Quick note: You don't pay your personal expenses from your business account. We'll talk later in this chapter about how to properly pay yourself so you can pay your personal expenses.*)

Once you know how much money you need to live, I recommend starting to build yourself a "runway fund." This should consist of the following:

1. Money to pay your personal expenses for at least six months *without* relying on business income. If your business generates profit within those first six months, save it in your business account for reinvesting in your business or build back up personal savings you used to start the business. If your financial situation allows for it, you can also let the profit build up in your business bank account to ensure you can reliably pay yourself a consistent amount over a long period of time.

2. Start-up capital that you will use to pay one-time expenses to start your business, including website costs, business registration fees, legal documents and policies, business insurance premiums, and equipment (e.g., a computer, camera, mic, etc.).

3. Additional start-up money to pay recurring business expenses for at least six months, including any website maintenance fees, email marketing software, or professional fees, online software and tools costs, and anything else your business requires to function online.

Thinking of Renting an Office?
Not So Fast.

Although it's tempting, one of the earliest expense mistakes entrepreneurs make is renting an office space. Unless you're starting a business that requires customers to see you in person or a brick-and-mortar store they need to visit, save yourself the expense of an office for now. If you can, work from home, your local library or university, your favorite coffee shop, or even the lobby of a local hotel or gym. If you need to meet

> with clients in person, consider a co-working space that allows those types of meetings. With good coffee and a strong Wi-Fi signal, you really can work from anywhere.

I know you might also be reading this thinking, "I don't have time for all that number crunching!" I know you want to get started now. You might feel like your already tight budget can't afford to be cut any further or that it doesn't allow for much saving at this point. I recognize that many of my tips come from a privileged position and access to many resources due to that privilege. If saving in this way isn't an immediate option for you, there are several others you can explore.

Free money is always the best option, so first look into whether there are any grants or other free or low-cost support options available to help you start your business. Here are a few resources to check out:

- Grants.gov, a federal government website with a plethora of information on grants and how to get one.
- Sba.gov, the US Small Business Administration website, which gives information on how to start a business, get funding, and connect with someone locally.
- Mbda.gov, the Minority Business Development Agency website, has business and financial resources to foster growth for minority-owned businesses.
- Your state's Small Business Association, which may have additional resources available for you as a state resident.
- Alumni associations, professional organizations, or even larger companies like Verizon and Amazon that have programs for start-ups.

If grants are not available, talk to your financial adviser or CPA about whether a line of credit or a small business loan makes sense for you. You may have to pay interest and fees with loans and lines of credit. When you speak with your financial adviser, ask them:

- Are you a Small Business Association (SBA) preferred lender?
- Based on the type of business I'm starting, what type of loan or line of credit is best?
- What types of documents do I need to sign for a loan? Do I have to personally guarantee the loan? (This means you're personally financially responsible for the loan. If this is required, speak to your CPA and attorney first.)
- Can I apply online or in-person? How long does it take to get approved or hear back?
- What are the interest rates and fees associated with this type of loan? Are the rates fixed or variable? Are the fees one-time or recurring?
- Are your interest rates negotiable?
- How long do I have to pay it back?
- Is there an early payoff penalty?
- How and when can I access the funds? Will I be able to use the funds for anything I'd like?
- How long do I have to keep the account open? Even if I don't use the funds?

As always, I highly recommend (or, if I were your business bubbe, I'd require!), that you seek professional advice before ever taking out an interest-bearing loan or opening a line of credit. As we discussed above, you must be aware of how much you actually need to operate your business, and you want to be sure you're able to pay it back as required.

2. Sell

The stack of old baseball cards in your attic isn't doing much good collecting dust. If there was ever a time to do a spring-clean, this is it. When I started, I sorted through my basement, garage, the trunk of my car, and even what I had at my parents' homes and got to work selling what I could. Some of that money went toward the cost of registering my first LLC ($125); purchasing my website domain ($50); and getting my website hosting set up ($50). Whether you've got collectibles or items you're not using or could simply let go of, you may be sitting on some start-up cash. Unless you have high-value vinyl records or a few rare coins lying around, the amount of money you will make from selling used items isn't going to make you rich, but something is better than nothing.

Now that you're starting a business, you want to get scrappy. Although it may be relatively easy, fast, and cheap to start an online business, the reality is that you're going to have to be creative to get started. Selling personal items is just one of the ways you can cover some start-up expenses (and avoid dipping into your personal savings).

As you're looking through items to sell, this is also a great time to declutter and clean your space. As you start your business, you want to have a clear and organized area to work and live in. You're about to take on a massive new project and phase in life, and it's very helpful to have a space that reflects the mindset you're going in with.

You'll have additional moneymaking opportunities if and when you leave your old job behind and go full-time into your business. You might be able to sell your old work clothes, supplies, or other items you no longer need now that you're not working your nine-to-five. The day I sold all of my lawyer suits was one of the best days of my life. It was still early days, so the few hundred dollars I made selling those clothes helped to cover some of my business expenses for months. Even after you start your business, don't stop looking for opportunities to cover your expenses. To this day, I still sell things I'm no longer using. I call it my "coffee money," but I definitely use it to cover much more. If you need a little motivation, try this quick activity: Set a kitchen timer for thirty minutes and see how much you can get organized in any one room or area of your house before it goes off. Organize what you find into three piles: toss, donate, and put away. I like to put "like with like"—so I place all of my notebooks in one place, all of my candles together, and all of my papers to be filed in another, for example.

A clean-out also presents you with the opportunity to decide where to dedicate some space, whether it's an entire room, a nook, or a part of your kitchen counter or table, to your business. If you run your business from home, it's important to have a space you do your work in and other spaces where you don't. You might not be able to stop your mind from thinking about your business all the time—still, there should be spaces where work is *not* being done. Plus, having a dedicated workspace in your home will be important for tax purposes come filing time. You'll be able to claim the space you use in your home exclusively for your business as a business expense. Talk to your CPA to find out whether your space qualifies for the home office deduction and how to maximize the amount you can legally claim.

3. Make

If you already have a job or another source of income, now is a great time to see if there are any additional earning opportunities within your same job or industry. If you're able, you could take additional shifts or hours, assume an additional role or set of responsibilities, or seek outside work opportunities should they become available. It won't be forever, or long-term, but try to take advantage of those kinds of opportunities as you're saving for or building your business.

If possible, you could try to negotiate a raise or, if your business's launch is imminent, try to negotiate a different schedule. After I set my business up, but before I was ready to be a full-time entrepreneur, I negotiated a half-time job with a firm for the same pay I made as a full-time attorney. See what works for your circumstances—any way you can get or create more flexibility will allow you to slowly but surely start to build up your business on the side.

Depending on what type of job you have and what's going on in your life, it might not be possible for you to work additional hours. Or, strategically, it might make sense for you to take the time you would have spent at work making more cash and instead use that time to start your new business. There's a balance between investing time in your new business for a payoff later and generating more money so you have enough for your new business to run smoothly. After you've evaluated your own budget, you will know which option is best for you.

For you, starting your business and taking on clients might be the best way for you to generate cash. If possible, complete the legal and financial start-up steps and open your business's doors *before* you leave your nine-to-five. Not only can you start generating revenue without financially depending on your new business quite yet, but you can also move through the crucial proof-of-concept phase. Use the time when you still receive a paycheck from someone else to work out the kinks in your own business after hours. As we'll discuss later on, you can use this time to find the best marketing channel to reach your customers, develop a great product or service, and find your optimal pricing structure and scaling strategy. Depending on how your early business days go, you can always adjust your exit schedule up or down to allow yourself more time to get things off the ground. As soon as things take off, I will be the first one to help you pack your bags.

A Foot in Both Worlds

I'll be real with you, as always. The time when I worked as an attorney on weekdays *and* started working on my own business on nights and weekends was one of the most stressful times. I want to honor and recognize it is a lot—especially when you undoubtedly have other responsibilities in your life. You might feel like you want to give up at this phase, but I want you to know how normal this challenging time is. When you're planning your exit or transition to entrepreneurship, I want you to factor in this time period and how difficult it is to juggle so many areas of your life at once. It took me longer than I wanted or anticipated to exit, but because of utilizing the planning, saving, and budgeting tips I gave you here, I was prepared for it. I also learned during this time that many of my business ideas weren't viable, and by the time I was ready to go all in, I was able to hit the ground running much faster and smoother than if I had dived in headfirst.

THE EARLY DAYS

You'd think after all these years I'd finally stop having nightmares about middle school. But if you've ever walked into a lunchroom and felt like you didn't have anywhere to sit (or anyone to sit with), you know that terrible sinking feeling well enough to have recurring dreams about it. Honestly, entrepreneurship can feel a bit like that early on. You come in with all this enthusiasm and your cute new work-from-home outfit, only to find out there are all of these already established friend groups set up. It's hard not to feel late to the party, even though you just found out the party exists.

So it comes as no surprise to me that most people don't know what to expect when it comes to the money side of entrepreneurship. You're not only entering into a bit of a clique, but one partially built up around a facade of making hoards of money. Some of the people in online business aren't formally educated or trained in money or finance topics. (It's a dead giveaway when coaches refer to themselves as "millionaires" because their business allegedly generated $1 million in gross revenue. If you're looking for someone to show you the ropes in business, look for a coach who understands the difference between gross and net revenue, income, and net worth.) Yet you'll have lots of earnings claims and "money mindset" tips thrown at you, all in the name of getting you to spend money on their products or services.

When I started my legal business in 2017, I wrote, "GOAL: $2,000" on a bright pink Post-it note. My goal for the month was simply that: to generate $2,000 worth of gross revenue. Given that most of my legal templates cost $347, it meant I had to sell nearly six legal templates to hit my goal. Achieving my goal would mean I turned a profit my first month in business, given that my fixed (recurring monthly) expenses were only a few hundred dollars at the time. I crossed off the tally of what I still needed to make to hit my goal that month as each sale came in. At the end, I wrote +$2,447 on the sticky note to reflect the amount I had exceeded my goal in my very first month. In just four weeks, I'd sold $4,447 worth of legal templates with a teeny-tiny email list, hardly any social presence, and an accidentally smart SEO strategy. I easily could have paid myself most of that profit, especially given how unexpected it was and how low my expenses were at the time. It would have been easy to assume that because I exceeded my expectations the first month, surely more success was to come. In the end, I paid myself only $500 (what we call an owner's draw, which is taxable and does not count as a business expense, by the way) and kept the rest ($3,947) in my business bank account. Let's talk about why.

Business Keepsakes

I still have that pink sticky note in my desk drawer. I'd encourage you to document and save some of your early entrepreneurship treasures like these. Sharing your journey on social media is actually a great way to build an audience and create a connection with future or potential customers online. If you're not actively teaching something on social media, like a tip about your area of expertise, then I think it's a great idea to document what you're actually doing. Show your audience how you're building your business, and tie it back to the transformation you help others achieve (e.g., to follow their dreams, be uniquely themselves, get healthier, own their power, etc.).

As your business begins to generate revenue, you'll want to divide it into four categories:

1. Taxes

As a general rule, most tax experts will encourage you to set aside 25 to 30 percent of your gross revenue to pay your taxes. You may or may not have some left over at the end of the year, but setting aside this safe percentage ensures you won't be left with a big tax bill and nothing to pay it with come tax time. As a self-employed business owner, you will have to pay federal taxes to the IRS, as well as any state taxes owed where you live and work. Once you set up your business, meet with a tax professional/CPA to determine how much and when you should make quarterly tax payments to both the IRS and your state tax department. Your estimated payments are based on your estimated tax liability, which is based upon your gross revenue minus your (legitimate) business expenses and deductions.

I hear lots of rumors floating around about how you shouldn't register your business until you have made a certain amount of money (or even just turned a profit). This inaccurate myth is based upon the false assumption that registered businesses, like limited liability companies (LLCs) or sole proprietorships, have some sort of special tax tacked on to them. Here's how taxes work, on the most basic level, for us business owners:

When you have a sole proprietorship or an LLC, the money you make in the business "passes through" to you and gets reported on your personal income tax return. Unless you elect to be taxed differently, LLCs are considered "disregarded entities" in the eyes of the IRS. That's just fancy tax-talk for "The money you make in your business becomes your personal income," essentially. So if your business makes $50,000 in gross revenue, but has $30,000 in legitimate business expenses and deductions, you are taxed on and report the $20,000 of profit on your personal income tax return as income. Your business's profits, or the amount you report as income, is taxed the same way a salary from a nine-to-five job would be, with one exception. As a business owner, *you* pay the self-employment taxes that your employer, if you had a job as a full-time or part-time employee, would automatically deduct from your paycheck for you. The federal self-employment tax rate is 15.3 percent as of August 2024. Self-employment taxes to the IRS contribute to your future social security and Medicare coverage.[1] Other than taxes you'd already pay in a "real job," there are no additional secret LLC or sole proprietorship taxes tacked on just because you have a business.[2]

Of course, taxes and personal finances are more complicated, individual, and nuanced than I can really break down here (or else you'd end up with a treatise and not a book!). Plus, I really don't want to put you to sleep any more than I might have already. Just remember: You should speak with a tax professional to fully understand what your tax liability may be and how much to pay in quarterly state and federal taxes.

2. Operating Expenses

You want to save and maintain at least six months' worth of operating expenses in your business bank account at all times. This way, if you have a slow month or an emergency that takes you away from your business, you will still be able to cover your expenses. As you generate revenue in your business, it should flow into and be kept in only your business bank account. All of your business expenses should be paid directly from that account or from a business credit or debit card that draws from the business bank account's funds. You want to use your business's money to pay for your business expenses so you can reduce the tax liability you will owe. Forming a limited liability company is also an additional way to insulate yourself from personal liability, a limited protection offered but not guaranteed by an LLC.

---

1. IRS, "Self-Employment Tax (Social Security and Medicare Taxes)," https://www.irs .gov/businesses/small-businesses-self-employed/self-employment-tax-social-security-and -medicare-taxes.

2. Some states have certain annual fees that are tacked on, typically for LLCs, that you will want to familiarize yourself with so you have a full financial picture of how much it costs to operate a business in your state. Other states have no income tax, so it all depends on where you live!

3. Business War Chest

When I first got started, I didn't have much money left over after saving for taxes, expenses, and paying for my basic needs. I saved whatever I had left; I told my friend Margo that it felt like I was saving ten cents at a time. It was sort of the money-saving equivalent to running on a hamster wheel—putting in a lot of work, but with very little progress to show for it. But Margo told me, "It feels like that now. But ten cents every day adds up. And gains interest. One day you'll look back and you will have saved a whole lot of ten cents over, and over, and over again."

Fortunately, I was saving more than ten cents at a time, and the amount I was able to stash grew significantly. So, I panicked a bit less when three years after I started my business, a worldwide pandemic left many business owners feeling unsure of the future. I had no idea how or if it would impact my business, but I knew if the impact was significant, I could stay in business because not only had I saved my operating expenses for way more than six months, but I'd also built up my war chest over the past three years. I like to think of a business war chest as:

- insulating you in case of emergency or unforeseen circumstances (situations that would go beyond your six months of operating expenses—like a global pandemic or a serious injury or illness); and
- giving you the ability to make investments and business moves that will catapult your business success, without fear that you're betting all your business's money on something that may not work.

At the time, my business war chest gave me the opportunity to use the money I'd saved to invest in Facebook ads to accelerate my business. During the pandemic, digital ads were cheaper and people were online more. It was a win-win situation. You could use your business war chest to invest in a new project, to comfortably get through a rough business patch, or to invest in more team support.

4. Paying Yourself

After you've paid your operating expenses, topped off your six-month fund (if needed), set aside money for taxes, and put a little money into your war chest (even ten cents!), it's time to pay yourself.

Many entrepreneurs have unrealistic expectations when it comes to paying themselves. They think if their business makes $5,000 per month and has $1,000 in expenses, they can pay themselves the remaining $4,000. By now you understand why that's not a good idea. How will they pay their taxes come tax time? How will they be able to pay their expenses if they have a few slow months or a personal emergency, as I did? Also, the amount you pay yourself as a business owner is not a business expense. It won't reduce your taxable income, and you will be expected to pay taxes on that amount of money.[3]

This is where it's very important to have a clear grasp of the personal budget you calculated earlier in this chapter. You may have to delay your full-time entrepreneur status until your business is a little further along, depending on your personal budget needs. You really don't know how quickly your business will grow, so this plan is always subject to change. But even if your business begins to make revenue quickly, I still encourage you to take the steps outlined here and plan for the long run. I've seen some businesses take off quickly, but not be prepared for slower months ahead.

---

3.   Unless you have elected to be taxed as a corporation and receive a paycheck from your own company, like an S corporation, for example.

Even if you experience quick success, you want to build a strong foundation to last the test of time.

In terms of *how* you actually pay yourself, it's easier than you might think. If your business is registered as a sole proprietorship or an LLC, you can make what are called "owner's draws" at any time. Owner's draws are the money you pay yourself from the business's revenue as the owner of the business. You can simply write a check from your business account to yourself and deposit or transfer it into your personal bank account. Make sure to mark or notate the transfer as "Owner's Pay" or an "Owner's Draw" in your bookkeeping software or spreadsheet. Remember, *owner's draws are not business expenses.* That money is still part of your taxable revenue, and you should be prepared to pay taxes on it. I recommend you set aside 25 to 30 percent of your gross revenue *before* you pay yourself, so you won't have to worry about having enough come tax season.

There's no official correct amount or schedule for paying yourself after budgeting properly so you have enough to cover your expenses and taxes. Personally, I prefer to pay myself a set amount at a consistently scheduled time. Think about how much you could pay yourself consistently for the next three months instead of only looking at the maximum amount you could pay yourself this month. You'll be better able to plan ahead and follow your personal budget if you know you're able to consistently pay yourself over a longer period of time.

So here's what a typical month could look like:

1. You make $8,000 in gross (total) revenue.
2. You set aside 25 to 30 percent of your total revenue in a separate business bank account designated to fund your quarterly tax payments, plus any taxes you may owe at the end of the year.

3. You pay your recurring monthly expenses, plus any one-time or annual expenses that may be due that month, from your business bank account.
4. You set aside some money for your business war chest to invest in future projects.
5. You pay yourself by taking an Owner's Draw.
6. At the end of the year, after you've paid all of your tax liability, you can take what's left over from what you set aside for taxes and put it toward your war chest or use it to pay yourself an end-of-year bonus. Confer with your accountant about what's best for you financially.

Finding a CPA

Find a CPA and a bookkeeper you can trust as soon as possible. I highly recommend working with both of them early on in your business. At the start, there are a lot of moving and confusing parts to running a business. As you grow, you'll settle in and understand more of all that's required, but I find that having someone on your financial team whom you feel comfortable reaching out to can save you lots of nights of lost sleep (not to mention financial missteps, missed deadlines, and fuzzy vision from staring at the IRS website).

GROWTH FACTOR

As you grow, you might be tempted to invest in all sorts of opportunities. In the online business world, we have courses, masterminds, trainings, and retreats being thrown at us constantly, all with the promise that what they're offering is exactly what we need to "get to the next level." It's not that these opportunities are not helpful or that they won't bring you any positive learning or growth opportunities. However, you do not have to invest in them all *in order to become* successful. Rather, invest only in things that support your growth, provide connection and the opportunity to meet and collaborate with your peers, broaden a skill or area of interest, or that feel expansive to you.

Of course, you want to be at the top of your game. It's important to stay current with what's going on in your field, to be aware of new research, and to better your skills. Some entrepreneurs, however, get stuck in a cycle of investing in furthering their education in lieu of getting started at all. It is natural to feel like you have to learn and know everything before you launch your first course or begin coaching clients. And while I certainly do think you should command a certain level of expertise, knowledge, and education around your topic area, it is unnecessary to require yourself to know everything about what you do before you start a business. Sometimes we stall because we're afraid to be seen or get called out for not being an "expert." So while it's important to continue to invest in your education and foster your desire to learn and improve, these two areas need to be balanced with actually moving your business forward. I would add that it's equally important to invest in your copywriting skills. As an online business primarily relying on digital marketing channels, you will need to write copy for your website, social posts, emails, and opt-in pages. Out of all of the products or courses I've purchased over the years, copywriting related courses had the best return on investment.

It's only human to invest in things that turn out to be mistakes. Recently, I asked my social media audience, "What's one thing you invested in early on in your business that turned out to be a waste of money?"

Some responses:

- Business cards and other physical items, like a bulky office printer, which they didn't end up using because they had a virtual business with very few in-person interactions.
- Expensive custom-branded packages and websites, purchased before being clear on what their niche or vibe really was.
- Rent for a physical office space, which was a large expense they could not afford and did not need to start an online business (but thought they needed to be considered legitimate).
- Time-consuming online courses that took them in all directions on topics like webinars, Pinterest, YouTube, and more before they ever knew what platform was right for them or whether they had a proof of concept.
- Coaching programs or coaching support that was purchased before realizing it didn't align with their values or ways of marketing their businesses.

Some of them felt so defeated by their wasted purchases that it took them months to recover. Others experienced significant financial setbacks after spending nearly all they had on a shiny new website or office space, because it was what they thought they were supposed to do. Those early spending mistakes made them apprehensive to invest in things that would have been a good opportunity moving forward. It's important to invest in yourself and your business—yes—but it's equally as important to avoid "wasted" investments when your business is still so vulnerable.

There are lots of worthwhile investments to make in yourself and your business, too. The business areas I see as offering the "best return for your investment" are:

- copywriting, considering you use it every day, in many different ways, in your online business and life;
- professional branding, photography, and a website, once you have proof of concept, a business plan, voice of customer research, and a clear picture of your overall feel and tone;
- financial support, including a bookkeeper and a CPA;
- legal services, support, and contracts through a retainer agreement with your own local small business attorney, contract templates, or a membership;
- mindset coaching and self-development;
- masterminds or other peer-support groups once your business is off the ground; and
- business training from a qualified, experienced coach with clear expectations and goals.

Your being clear about why you're investing in something can be the difference between a wasted investment and a worthwhile one. Investing in a course, coach, or product only because you think that investment will bring you success or change your business's trajectory will typically result in failure. When I polled my audience on this topic, they responded again and again with, "I thought that buying the course/coaching package/ membership would make me money." What they didn't realize then was that no coach or course alone can or will make your business successful. Your business will need to be built by you, over a period of time, with a lot of hard work. Often, we think what we're doing already isn't working, when in reality we just needed to give it more time.

It's important to vet the person or product you're thinking of investing in, as well as to have in mind what you expect to receive from your investment. Realize that not every opportunity you invest in will be 100 percent applicable to you or your business. Some of the best experiences I've had came after I went in to a course or program thinking, "I'll take what I need and leave the rest." Often, others in the program would struggle with the fact that they did not find the entire program helpful to them. They spent all of their time focused on what didn't work, rather than gaining from the things that did.

Beware of Lifestyle Creep

Lifestyle creep is what happens when you allow your standard of living, and the cost to maintain it, to creep up as your income increases. For reasons that will never quite make sense to me, the online business industry is plagued with lifestyle creep. Judging by social media, at times it seems the only reason to even have a business is so you can buy more stuff. Of course, you can choose to buy whatever you would like. If starting a business is a way for you to buy more purses, go for it! But I'm also here to warn you that many of us unconsciously participate in lifestyle creep because of the culture of the industry we're in.

When I first built my business and felt the urge to start buying more and more things, I realized two things. One, I was consuming way too much on social media. So much of what we see on social media is capitalism gone wild. Watching content creators share daily clothing hauls that would cost thousands of dollars a piece is not normal. Keep in mind that many of the creators make a living off of getting you to buy more things. And since you're human, seeing everyone else buy things makes you feel like you should, too. Two, I realized that I wasn't actually getting to the root of my core values or wants. When I was an attorney, I bought stuff to make myself feel better. (*Newsflash: It didn't work.*) But I came to realize it wasn't my business's job to make me happy. And buying more things wouldn't either. In the long run, it only puts more stress on your business because you have less in reserves. And guess where that leaves you? Having to work more, to make more, so you can buy more, which leads you back to working more. It's a vicious cycle.

If you follow my business war chest strategy and save revenue to build capital, you won't feel the urge to buy more stuff because you know that's all about short-term happiness, and you're planning for the long term. As my business has grown, and my business bank account has grown along with it, I have chosen not to significantly increase my standard of living, but rather to increase my salary slowly and steadily, which I knew I could consistently do for a long period of time. Not only did this allow me to better predict and plan my personal budget needs, but it prevented me from wildly spending only to have to pull significantly back. This gave me a lot of breathing room during times of crisis or when I wanted to devote my attention to other projects. I've also chosen to invest in real estate, put away money in my retirement and high interest savings accounts, and give back to charities with personal meaning to me. I could have purchased a lot of G-Wagons by now, but I know better than to think my happiness exists in those buttery leather seats.

WHAT WE LEARNED

- How to properly plan to leave your job or prepare to start your own business.
- Why setting realistic expectations and a clear budget helps avoid disappointment or early business failure.
- The importance of setting aside money for taxes, business expenses, and a business war chest.

- How to pay yourself.
- What investments are worthwhile versus early investment mistakes and how to avoid them.

WHAT'S TO COME

- The common mindset blocks that come up for entrepreneurs and how to overcome them.

CHAPTER 5

Five Mindset Obstacles to Overcome as a Business Owner

I don't know what it is about becoming an entrepreneur, but when you do—you almost immediately catch the "entrepreneur virus." While not an *actual* virus, this nasty little bug seems to affect the mindsets of entrepreneurs everywhere. The worst part is, when you initially catch it, you'll think you're the only one experiencing the resulting feelings or thoughts. In reality, every entrepreneur I know, including myself, has felt the symptoms of the entrepreneur virus at one time or another. Unfortunately, there's no cure—the virus keeps coming back, even as you grow your business. You're not free from it because you build an audience or start to make a good income. Truthfully, if we're putting our growth mindset hats on (which we'll talk about in a bit), these challenges are actually opportunities for growth, expansion, and curiosity. In this chapter, I'll walk you through five of the most symptomatic mindset obstacles, "excuses," and challenges that come up for entrepreneurs and give you a set of prescriptions to help resolve them. Let's jump straight into the symptom that typically appears first.

SYMPTOM #1: PERFECT TIMING

The universe agrees with a made-up mind.

—AIDA RODRIGUEZ

As we discussed in chapter 4, there's a difference between careful, responsible planning and waiting for the perfect timing before taking action. In the first scenario, you're taking some time to fully understand what you're getting yourself into; and in the latter, you're, well, frankly, coming up with excuses to delay taking action because it feels scary. You're right, trying something new *can be* scary. Putting ourselves out there feels really vulnerable and makes us feel like popping back into our shells, wishing we had never stuck our heads out in the first place. If you stall, then maybe you can prevent the scary stuff you're worried about from happening. If you wait long enough, you'll make sure you never get the chance to find out.

I've known I wanted to write a book since I was little. I first thought of writing a book about business a few years ago. I researched how to get started, only to walk away with the conclusion that my audience wasn't nearly big enough and I should wait. Years went by and my audience grew exponentially, but I was still too afraid to take action on my dream. I made so many excuses about it not being the right timing, but I couldn't tell you when the timing would be right either. After my dad got sick in 2018, I took it as another sign that it wasn't the time. But after caring for him for three years, I thought he might outlive his terminal cancer diagnosis. I realized that perfect timing was never going to happen.

I dove in and wrote a book proposal (if you want to write nonfiction, you write a book proposal first and then shop it around to editors at different publishing houses). It took me three times longer than it should have to write my proposal because life didn't stop doing what life does once I finally decided to step forward with my dream. Looking back, it was so hard to balance caring for my dad, running my business, and trying to write a book proposal at the same time. But if I had waited any longer, my dream would have been squashed entirely. I would not have felt up to writing a proposal once he passed, and I probably would have only kicked the can even further down the road once my mom passed away shortly after. Since you're holding my very dream in your hands, you know what ultimately happened once I took the leap. Timing has a way of working things out, as long as you don't stand in the way.

Although there will certainly be better times than others, there may never be a perfect time for you to start your own business or for you to take your existing business to the next level. Only you will be able to tell when you've done your due diligence in responsibly planning for the next step in your business versus when you're hitting snooze (repeatedly) as a means to stave off doing something seemingly scary to you. Here are a few questions to ask yourself if you're not sure whether the time is right to take the next step in your business journey:

- Have I calculated my personal budget/living expenses and start-up expenses?
- Have I taken any steps to save for both my personal budget and start-up expenses?
- Do I have the right qualifications, education, and skills to get started?

- Do I have a viable business plan, an idea of what products and services I'll offer, and an idea of how I will initially market those items?
- Do I have any benchmarks or to-do items that must be taken care of before I start my business? What if I got started and then tackled them alongside my new business?
- Journal prompt: If I knew it would all work out, I wouldn't wait to _____.

Perfect timing excuses come up throughout our business journeys, not just at the start. As your business grows, you might tell yourself the timing isn't right for you to launch a new course, apply to be on a popular podcast, write a book (!), or speak on a big stage. Fear might sneak up on you with each opportunity to try something new or when it's time to level up. Your fear may tell you the timing isn't right and you should wait until things are better/perfect/easier. But that's just your mind's way of keeping you safe. Trying new things, taking risks—these all bring about a bit of uncertainty. And our mind's job is to keep us safe. "If where we are now is safe—or at least known to us—why try something new?" your mind says to itself. After more time, experience, and practice, I like to thank my mind for trying to keep me safe and then go about taking risks anyway. Well, at least when it comes to business. I will still let it talk me out of skydiving and bungee jumping, if I ever get brave enough to try.

The Prescription for Perfect Timing

Action steps:

- Refer to the budget and plan you created in chapter 4 to determine when, financially, you can afford to start your business.

- Journal, using the prompts below, on the natural feelings of fear coming up for you.
- Take the first step forward, no matter how small it may feel.

Journal prompts:

- If not now, when? What will be different later?
- List three reasons it's better to start or grow your business right now versus later. *What are you risking by not taking action now?*
- List all of the things you've done to prepare for this moment. Remember your education, investments, research, business planning steps, and any other steps you've taken so far to be prepared as a businessperson.

SYMPTOM #2: IMPOSTOR SYNDROME

I still have a little impostor syndrome...It doesn't go away, that feeling that you shouldn't take me that seriously. What do I know? I share that with you because we all have doubts in our abilities, about our power and what that power is.

—MICHELLE OBAMA

So now that you've stopped waiting for the perfect moment, you should be all clear of any future mindset hurdles, right? I wish I had better news for you. You're about to get a visit from what is likely our most common, and persistent, friend: impostor syndrome. No matter where you are along the entrepreneurial success spectrum, you might have moments where you yell, "*What have I gotten myself into!?*" In these moments, you'll wonder who the heck you ever thought you were to go and do something so bold and drastic as hanging a digital shingle with your name on it. You may experience impostor syndrome by

- worrying that someone (or everyone!) will discover you're a "fraud" and call you out because you don't know every single thing about your subject area;
- thinking you don't know enough yet about your subject area, so you stay in an information gathering stage and rack up additional certifications so you can build up a fortress of knowledge, trying to avoid the feeling described above;
- thinking it's crazy for you to be so "narcissistic" and self-centered as to chase after your own dream, create content about your life, claim your expertise, or think you could ever achieve success; or
- worrying that your past successes and wins were simply luck; you won't be able to repeat them because you didn't earn them in the first place.

Just like the perfect timing symptom, impostor syndrome has a funny way of showing up throughout your business journey. Every time I've launched a new program, run a promotion, or otherwise stepped outside of my comfort zone in my business, I've had one or more of these thoughts pop up. After my business hit multi-six-figures in its third year, a business mentor of mine prompted me to set a new, bigger revenue goal. I balked at this, saying, "But why? I can't even believe I hit *this* revenue mark—why should I deserve any more? This is good enough." Truthfully, I was afraid I didn't deserve or actually cause the success I'd had so far. "Who am I,"

I thought, "to build a seven-figure business?" On top of that, I worried that my multi-six-figure revenue earnings in year three were a fluke. Instead of planning to hit seven figures the following year, I anticipated a decline in revenue.

But then I learned of the power of future-proofing. Often, we make decisions only from the place we and our businesses are at right now, which will maintain about the same size and success rate. If you keep taking the same steps as you have before, you'll end up in the same place. But what if you took different steps? What if you headed in a new direction before you knew exactly how to get there? That's a future-proofing mindset. Before I adopted a future-proofing mindset, I'd been able to picture only what I'd done so far. But thanks to my impostor thoughts, I couldn't see a bright future ahead. I figured if I ever got there—and that was a big *if*—then I'd take steps to act like the type of person who ran a bigger, more successful business. But after realizing—with a lot of encouragement—that I might have the type of business that could grow, I decided to let myself dream about what the business I truly wanted to build looked like. Instead of waiting to become that business first, I started acting like I was there already (or, at the very least, headed in that direction). When I became clear on what my futuristic, ideal seven-figure business looked like, I could see who I would have to become to lead it. Instead of spending hours each week giving free advice and going on coffee dates in the middle of the day, I would protect my time and know my worth. Would I be posting several times a day on social media, or would my time be so valuable that I would instead be working on bigger, more impactful pieces of content with lasting power? It wasn't an overnight shift. I just decided to adopt the mindset of a seven-figure business owner before my bank account actually reflected it. But even embodying this attitude most of the time had a significant impact on my bottom line. Suddenly, my business started heading in the exact direction of the business I'd imagined. If you can't picture where you're headed—or even buy into a part of it—there's no way you will take action steps to get there. Pushing through and overcoming impostor syndrome is about addressing it head-on and recognizing it for what it is, ultimately flipping the script to take more of a growth-minded approach.

Before we talk about some of the times impostor syndrome might show up for you as a means of keeping you safe and in your comfort zone, we have to talk about a time it may come up that's actually worth paying attention to. Every once in a while, I get a frantic email from someone, worried they are going to be "found out" or called out for something they're doing in their business. For example, a health coach recently wrote to me worried about an online tiff she was having with another online business owner. The other business owner happened to be a licensed dietitian who was calling the health coach out for teaching about a topic the dietitian thought was outside the coach's scope. The coach was furious. She wanted to know what her options were for libel and slander lawsuits. On the surface, this looked like a spat between two creators. But on a deeper level, I knew something else was bothering the coach. I suspected she had always been worried that what she was doing online wasn't "legal" (aka, outside of her scope of practice), and now she felt called out for it. She mentioned needing to "learn the bounds of what she can legally say and do" in her email.

Remember, if you're starting a business on a topic you've been trained, educated, or licensed in, you're most likely not an actual impostor. In my experience, most of my friends who struggle with impostor syndrome, myself included, are highly educated and qualified to do what they do. Impostor syndrome is about feeling like a fraud or a phony, regardless of how qualified you are or how much success you've had in that area. Some of us can experience a lot of success, and receive lots of positive feedback, and still feel like we don't deserve it. With that being said, there are times when impostor syndrome crops up because we do, in fact, feel out of our depth. Some of our uncomfortable feelings, such as, "Should I be saying this?"; "Is it okay for me to teach on that topic?"; "Is this legal for me to sell?" should be paid attention to because they might actually be legitimate concerns.

Scope of Practice

Your scope of practice is what your state's laws and regulations say you're legally allowed to do, say, teach, offer, sell, and so on, based on how you're licensed, educated, or credentialed. Your state may not define exactly what you can or can't do. For example, no state I know of defines what a "money coach," a "career coach," or a "mindset coach" can legally do. But what nearly all states *do* define are those coaches' "umbrella professions": doctors, lawyers, therapists, social workers, physical therapists, accountants, dietitians, and so on. Your "umbrella professions" are the professions that hover around, and maybe even "above," what you're doing. They're the professions in which you don't want to be accused of practicing without a license because they are, in fact, regulated by the state. Just because your state doesn't define your job title doesn't mean you're free to do as you wish. It's important to familiarize yourself with these umbrella professions and make sure you don't offer services, sell products, or create content that goes beyond your scope.

The desire to go outside of your scope of practice doesn't come from an insidious place or because you want to do something wrong. Most people operate outside of their scope of practice for one of three reasons:

1. They're unaware of what their scope of practice is, or that it even exists.

2. They've heard of scope of practice, but they don't understand how it works and think the online space is a free-for-all where anything goes.
3. They're scared that if they don't offer services or speak on content that's outside their scope of practice, they'll lose customers and attention to someone who does.

If you're in group #1, I hope you know what scope of practice is now. Same goes for #2 and your understanding of how it does, in fact, apply to you. But if you find yourself in group #3, feeling like you have to interpret lab results as a health coach (*illegal!*) or give personalized investment advice as a money coach (*illegal!*), I hope you know how much good you can do in a business that follows the rules. We'll talk about this more when we get into the next symptom: scarcity.

I know most entrepreneurs aren't feeling impostor syndrome because of scope of practice scares, but the lawyer in me doesn't feel right not addressing what could be a dangerous elephant in the room! When impostor syndrome bubbles up for me, I take it as a sign that I have to look seriously at how I'm spending my time online. The times I've felt the worst about myself and how I stack up correlate, unsurprisingly, with my highest levels of screen time. When you spend time on social media as a big part of your job, it's impossible not to soak in some (or lots, to be honest) of what you see. It's equally as hard to see everyone's highlight reel on social media, and then mentally compare it to the reality of your situation in full display. Keep that in mind: You're not seeing their full picture, but you do see yours. It's an uneven playing field.

The greatest gift you can give yourself is freedom from knowing what everybody else is doing online, especially in your industry. When you feel cruddy about how you're doing in your business and how it stacks up, it's time to look at what you're consuming every day. Start by unfollowing or muting anyone on social media who creates icky feelings for you. Don't judge yourself for feeling this way. Just honor the feelings and do what's best to protect yourself and your business for now. It doesn't have to be forever.

I also recommend unfollowing anyone who does what you do, regardless of how their content makes you feel. It's not that you don't support your competitors, but you really have to treat yourself like an elite athlete. When elite athletes train for a big game, they block out the noise and focus on their own mission. Building your business is no different. You're on a mission to build something for yourself, and you can't let everyone else's noise ruin your experience. From a creativity, and even a legal, perspective, it's also healthier not to consume your competitors' content because you won't have to question where your ideas came from. If we consume too much content in our industry, it can lead to a lot of doubt as to the validity of our ideas—did we come up with it on our own, or did we accidentally borrow it after looking through another business's window?

Ignore Your Competition

Community over competition is sort of bs, in my opinion. Online, everyone will tell you you're not supporting your fellow entrepreneurs and competitors if you're not cheering them on 24-7. I say that's nonsense. I'm not here to wish any ill will or harm toward other entrepreneurs in my space. But I don't think it's my job to help them grow their business or audience, either (that job belongs to them and their business coach). My growth isn't dependent on their lack of success, and vice versa. We can all prosper in this market. But I don't understand why there's pressure for online businesses to support competitors differently than traditional businesses would.

Do you see Target cheering on Walmart? Do you see them following each other on social media, or commenting on each other's posts? No, you see two major companies doing their own thing, focusing on *their* customers, and building their brands. It's okay to have "competition"—it's healthy to have other businesses in the marketplace doing the same thing as you. It means there's demand (remember chapter 3?). But following them and incessantly consuming all of their content isn't helping you. And it's not helping them, either. Ask yourself if you are really "supporting" your competition by following them, commenting on their content, or reading everything they write (or, more accurately, stalking and judging their IG stories). Kindly unfollow, unsubscribe, and mute. It's the greatest gift you'll give your mental space and your business. In the eight years I've been in business, this is the tip I get thanked for giving the most.

The Comparison Trap

Research shows spending too much time on social media can cause issues like addiction, depression, loneliness, reduced self-esteem, and the inability to create or maintain meaningful personal relationships.[1] Most entrepreneurs don't realize just how much damage social media is doing to their businesses until it's too late. We don't mean to do this consciously, but when we spend lots of time on social media, we take in so much information about and from other creators. Since we're human, we naturally take that content and apply it to ourselves. If you see a very successful business owner you want to be like, you can't help but compare

---

1. Sean Withington and Alexandra Punch, "There Are Costs from Spending Too Much Time on Social Media," October 2019, Lerner Center for Public Health Promotion and Population Health, https://www.maxwell.syr.edu/research/lerner-center/population-health-research-brief-series/article/there-are-costs-from-spending-too-much-time-on-social-media#

yourself to them. If she's wealthy, funny, fit, or has some other attribute you see as being absent in or out of reach for you, it's only natural to wonder if that's why she is successful and you are not (yet). We're not meant to know so much about people, their lives, or their businesses. Does the CEO of Target share what they have for lunch each day, what their workout of the day was, or teach their audience how they "balance it all"? Could you imagine if the CEO of another big-box or department store who performed worse than Target had to sit around and watch Target's CEO gloat? It's unnatural.

When Julie started her online nutrition business, she immediately noticed how different she looked from the "typical" nutritionist on social media.[2] Julie spent hours online learning strategies to help her grow her business. In doing so, she saw loads of content featuring her "competitors." While Julie's content garnered little attention, her peers seemed to be getting lots of it. She couldn't help but wonder if the physical differences she saw in her peers versus herself were the cause of her business's slow growth. She wondered whether she would ever be able to grow a successful online nutrition business if she didn't look the "part" of an Instagram-typical nutritionist. Julie's feelings worsened as she began to question who she ever thought she was to become a nutritionist in the first place, given how she looked.

It wasn't until Julie spent less time consuming others' content on social media and more time creating her own that she began to realize just how qualified and desirable she was as a coach. Without knowing what her peers were up to online every day, she was able to find her own, unique voice and discover what topics her

2.   Note: For the record, I'm sharing Julie's story, not my personal or objective opinion on how someone within a profession "should" look. Your looks, body size, or any other physical attribute does not and should not qualify or disqualify you from any profession. But honestly, these feelings are common and pervasive in our industry, which is why I'm sharing Julie's story here.

customers wanted to learn about from her (and therefore attracted new customers). She more confidently owned her qualifications and nutrition knowledge. She took pride in, and shared, her clients' transformative results. With time, Julie redefined what a good nutritionist was—someone who was highly qualified and knowledgeable about nutrition, not someone who simply looked a certain way. And by her new and empowered definition, she finally felt like she belonged.

You may or may not struggle with feeling that you're qualified to teach about your subject area, but many entrepreneurs face the "Why me?" part of impostor syndrome at some point or another. You might question who you are to even think about starting a business or wonder why someone like you would ever be considered for a top podcast interview, a big stage talk, or another major growth opportunity. As my incredible mindset coach, Jennifer Diaz, reminds me, when these types of intrusive thoughts pop up, we have to ask ourselves: "What's the underlying belief I'm buying into here?" When it comes to our "Why me?" doubts, we typically have negative underlying beliefs around worthiness and being deserving of success.

Given what I've shared about my difficult childhood, you may not be surprised to know how hard it is for me to take up space or feel comfortable with things being about me. For years after I started my business, I struggled to put myself out there, take up space, or really own how successful my business had become. I wanted to stay as quiet and small as possible because then, I figured, people would leave me alone. As a child, making myself invisible was a necessary survival mechanism. But being left alone isn't a great way to build a business. I've had to learn to become more comfortable with being seen, regardless of the type of feedback or response I get.

When I do get a mean or aggressive comment from someone

upset about something I said, I wonder if they've been similarly impacted. When you see someone else doing something you've told yourself for so long you're not allowed to do (e.g., "I'm not allowed to take up space or have things be about me"), it's really triggering to see someone doing just that. It's natural to react by saying, "Who do you think you are to do that?!" because on the inside you're thinking, "I'm not able to do that, so how dare she think she's able to!" or "I wish I could do that, but I can't because of XYZ, so she shouldn't either."

Comparison-itis won't go away overnight. In fact, it might not go away at all. It tends to rear its ugly head at various points throughout the entrepreneurial journey. This is an opportunity to be aware of and own the stories you tell yourself about who you are and what you can do. As you've already read, building your business isn't just about marketing strategies and tactics. Often, the things you do "off the field" have just as much impact as the stuff you do on the field. You have unique strengths, approaches, thoughts, and opinions. Now is the time to proudly share them.

The Prescription for Impostor Syndrome

The key to kicking this symptom to the curb is uncovering your deeper beliefs behind the feelings that come up, working to rewrite and shift those beliefs, and standing in your power and ability to do what you do. Though consuming less content will not cure it, limiting your time on social media will certainly help.

Action steps:

- If you know this is an area of needed development for you, seek out professional help through therapy, coaching, self-development materials, or a support group.

- Every morning, write two or three sentences of your future bio as if it were the present tense. For example, I would write: "Sam Vander Wielen is the author of multiple bestselling books, a TED talk alumnus, and the go-to legal educator for online business owners."
- Learn your scope of practice and stay within it.
- Boost your confidence by setting goals, creating habits, and sticking with them.
- Work on developing a mindset that is open to learning, growing, and changing over time. Lead with curiosity.
- Each time you experience a "win" in your business, no matter how small, recognize and celebrate it.

Journal on:

- What are you truly afraid of? Why does that scare you? Go deeper—what's underneath this fear and what are you afraid it means about you if the "worst" happens?
- Write about a time you thought you couldn't accomplish, finish, or complete something, but you did. What helped you to overcome your doubts? How did you feel afterward?
- What do you and your business stand for? What are your core values? How are you embodying them as a business owner and also as a business?

SYMPTOM #3: SCARCITY

Nobody goes there anymore. It's too crowded.

—Yogi Berra

In ecologist Carl Safina's *Alfie & Me*, the author shares his incredible journey of rescuing and rehabilitating an injured baby owl during the pandemic. For months, Carl tended to, fed, and protected the owl, whom he affectionately named Alfie. Eventually, Alfie's wing healed and she grew to her full size. On the one hand, Carl wasn't ready to let Alfie go. He had developed a bond with her and was afraid of what would happen to her if she went back into the wild. He thought she had the skills and resources necessary to survive on her own, but there was no way to know for sure beforehand. Setting his desire to hold on tight aside, Carl set her free. (In case I haven't yet tugged at your heartstrings enough, even after being set free, Alfie has essentially parked herself in the trees outside Carl's home full-time. Alfie calls and waits for Carl to come outside to say hi. She even responds to Carl's attempts to do an owl call. Animals are amazing.)

I use this story to illustrate that it's only natural to have a fear of trying new things, a desire to keep things safely the same, and feel intimidated by the idea of letting go. Running your own business can be hard. And it feels scary to expose yourself, especially on social media. Simply doing some mindset exercises or trying to shift from a scarcity mindset to an abundance mindset will not cure this for you. It will take work not only to prevent yourself from going down some of the inevitable mindset detours, but to learn how to navigate your way back to your path, too. You might love your business and what you do like I do. It's only natural that we want to protect and hold on tight to the things we love.

A scarcity mindset tends to focus on the lack—what you don't have, and what you will never have—and the underlying belief that because this lack will continue, you must conserve and be stingy. Those with a scarcity mindset typically believe there is only a certain amount of things, whether it be money, time, energy, or resources, to go around. Even if someone with a scarcity mindset experiences success, they never feel like what they do have is enough and that their luck or success will run out. Unfortunately, having a scarcity mindset is a bit of a self-fulfilling prophecy in business. If you hang on too tightly to what you've got, or focus only on what you don't have now, you won't be able to make the strategic and sometimes stretch-worthy decisions necessary to grow your business. (*Note: Scarcity and lack are very real, unfortunate realities for many people. This, of course, is not their fault and is not something that will be adjusted by a simple mindset shift.*) The scarcity mindset we're talking about here is one that someone adopts even if they have all of their basic needs (and then some) met. If that sounds like you, the goal is to recognize this pattern in yourself and slowly but surely shift into an abundance mindset.

An abundance mindset adopts the view that there's more than enough resources in the world to go around. Instead of making impulsive decisions out of a place of lack or fear, those with an abundance mindset make decisions from an excited, optimistic, open, and curious place. The possibilities are limitless considering there's enough resources for everyone.

I'm not into the spiritual bypassing thing in our industry (that's when some creators will encourage you to look past, or completely ignore, very real fears and blame your perceived failures on you and your lack of manifestation). *But for $499 you can get their manifestation course—just as soon as you unlock your mindset block around spending the money on it!* The fear and hesitation you feel are real and are just trying to help you stay safe. Every time I'm afraid, I thank my body and mind for doing its job. All of these feelings should be paid attention to or they will only grow louder. That said, not all of them need to be honored and followed. If you did, you wouldn't be able to grow your business. Assuming it's your goal to grow and develop, then it's time we address and shift some of the scarcity mindset moments you might have so you can build your business.

We have to acknowledge how many online creators, coaches, and service providers there are these days. Therefore, it makes sense that you might be easily discouraged by the sheer volume of competition. If you opened a coffee shop in your town, there may be a few others already in operation in your area, but you wouldn't be competing with coffee shops around the world. When you remove the physical location barrier of being able to reach only customers within a reasonable distance of your shop, the entire world becomes your oyster...I mean, potential customer. If you're a career coach or a copywriter, you're technically "competing" against coaches and copywriters around the globe. At first, you may panic. A cascade of scarcity-driven emotions comes on: *There's no room for me. Everyone is already doing what I want to do. My business isn't unique and won't stand out. Nothing I have to say is original. There's no way I can thrive here.*

This is where much of the work we've done together already and that we will do in the next chapter is key. Yes, it's true there may be lots of creators already doing something similar to what you've set out to do. Researching the market to determine if it's fully saturated or already has the supply to meet a limited demand is generally a good idea. But there's a difference between doing your due diligence and haphazardly deciding there isn't room for you to belong without research or statistics to back it up. Our scarcity tendencies might tell us there's no room (which assumes there's a cap on participation), but a new abundance mindset would encourage us to see the possibilities in our industry as endless. That might mean switching up your niche or tweaking your messaging to stand out more, but it doesn't mean you can't start your business or be successful in it.

One of the ways to conquer a scarcity mindset is to focus on facts over stories. Simply seeing other creators do what you want to do is not reason enough to back out. It doesn't mean there isn't enough room for you in the industry. Online businesses are rapidly expanding both on the supply and the demand sides. For as many creators as there are starting businesses, there seem to be just as many customers seeking new ways of learning, being coached, or working together online. When I started my health coaching business, I naively thought I was the only person in the world to have thought of the business I started. After I opened my Instagram account, it took about three minutes to discover that not only were there hundreds—if not thousands—of other people already doing exactly what I wanted to do, but there was a woman in my town with the exact business model I intended to use. I wanted to quit before I even started. But as naive as I was to think no one else could ever think of my business idea, I was equally if not more naive to not realize there was more than enough room for us—and many others—to thrive.

Since I didn't know about the scarcity and abundance mindsets then, I got completely derailed by the existence of my local competition. I tried so hard to not be like her that I forgot to be myself. I shape-shifted left and right to create a business that was rebelliously different. In reality, even though we had a similar business idea, our approaches, personalities, writing styles, and methodologies were completely different. But I was so afraid of being edged out by one small fish in a giant ocean that I completely exited the water.

Seeing others who are already successful in what we want to do can make us feel like we've already missed out. If we're this late to the party, is there anything left for us to add? It can feel like everyone has already said everything that needs to be said on your given topic, and they've gobbled up all of the customers along the way. Plus, when you see how successful they are already, the distance between where you are now and where you perceive them to be can feel gargantuan. It might even make you feel jealous or envious of their success.

To shift through this, I'd encourage you to start by practicing gratitude and admiration. Build a one-minute habit into your daily routine where you write down things you're grateful for. Sometimes my list can be as simple as "a warm mug of tea," and it nearly always includes my dog, Hudson. But occasionally you might also be able to list things you're grateful for about your work, business, colleagues, or clients. No matter how small it is or may seem to be, add it to your list. It's really incredible how much this daily practice starts to show up in your day-to-day. I find myself noticing beautiful flowers, or a kind gesture from one stranger to another, and thinking, "I can't wait to add that to my gratitude list later!"

When it comes to envious or jealous feelings toward another, I like to practice some admiration. I challenge myself to name three things I really admire about that person or their work. Recently, I saw someone given an opportunity I would have loved to receive myself. When I felt envious pangs bubble up, I countered with the thought, "Wow! She's worked so hard for this. She shows up week in and week out. And she's gotten really good at editing her videos. They're professional-level quality, and I know that takes a lot of work, dedication, and practice." In reality, her receiving the opportunity had no impact on whether I will receive a similar one. There are loads of opportunities to go around. And the truth is, I know I also have received opportunities that others may look at and wish they had. It's just how the world works. At times, I also have to be honest with myself and reflect on how I'm not doing the very thing I admire about the person I'm envious of. If I'm envious of a big speaking engagement they got, I will ask myself, "Have you been applying to speaking gigs you want? Are you networking and letting people know that you want to speak?" Oftentimes, the answer is no. It helps me to reset my priorities, and set aside more time in my weekly schedule to go after those things I want more of. Bonus points if you reach out to that person directly to let them know what you admire about them. I bet it would make their day.

When you start to think about how there's not enough to go around, you have to focus on what you can control, which is yourself, your business, and your content. You might feel intimidated by how much success someone else has (or you perceive them to have, or they advertise that they have), but only you can control how dedicated you are to learning, growing, and showing up. And when you do, show up and share fully. Don't hold back on the type of content you share because you're worried it's "too valuable." In the online world, there's no such thing. Plus, this type of giving attitude will begin to feed an abundant mindset. One that trusts that good people, with good intentions, are rewarded.

Creator's Block

If you ever feel like you don't have anything to share content-wise, now is a great time to try something new outside of work. Sign up for an art class, go on an owl prowl, see a movie, or even try taking a walk in a new-to-you park! When I've felt like I didn't have anything interesting to say, it was usually because I wasn't doing anything very interesting. I don't want you to try something you're not actually interested in just to share it on Instagram, but I do want to encourage you to use this experience as an entrepreneur as a time and a way to get to know yourself better, create your own identity outside of your work, and to become more comfortable when vulnerably sharing (some) of those parts with others.

Challenging limiting beliefs is a great way to shift through a scarcity mindset. If your space feels crowded or like you're late to the party, I invite you to see this as an opportunity rather than a roadblock. There's a reason entrepreneurship isn't for everyone. No one (other than a few spammy business coaches) said it was going to be easy. You should take pride in the fact that entrepreneurs are creative, forward-thinking people. So if you want to actually build your business, you might have to tap into the core of what it means to be an entrepreneur. To me, that's being innovative. Entrepreneurship involves a lot of thinking on your feet, being resourceful, and learning how to pivot. These skills are crucial not only to beating out the competition, but also to staying in business long enough to thrive. If you see someone out there doing what you want to do, don't let that deter you. Yes, you should be smart and do your research to make sure the market demand is there. But you can also get crafty and innovate past your competition. How can you do things differently? Better? In a way no one has thought of before? Dig deep and get creative with your answers, without judging them or saying why they won't work first.

My dear friend and incredible intuitive eating and movement coach, Simi Botic, once told me, "What if it all works out better than you could have planned?" *What if, right?* What if you could create something even better than what you see being offered right now? What if your innovation ends up being a key breakthrough, helping more people? Now isn't the time to limit your own dreams. The world has a funny way of trying to do that for you. Simi's sage advice reminds us to dream without limits and to open our hearts and minds to the possibility that our futures might be greater than we can predict.

The Prescription for Scarcity Syndrome

Action steps:

- Do your research on how crowded the market really is, and whether there's viable demand for your product, without basing a pre-conclusion on what you see on social media.

- To foster more creativity and feel confident your ideas are your own, unfollow people on social media whom you're following to see how successful they are or to whom you compare yourself.
- Consume less content than you create, and always create before you consume.

Journal prompts:

- If you could create anything without judgment, fear, or thinking about what others might be doing already, what would it be? Why would you create it?
- What are three limiting beliefs you hold about abundance, success, or achievement? How do they come up for you? What shifts can you make to take a more abundantly minded approach?

SYMPTOM #4: BEING A BEGINNER SUCKS

Maybe the yes comes before the readiness. Maybe you say yes and then you become equipped to handle whatever is about to happen.

—GLENNON DOYLE

A few years ago, I started playing tennis. For my entire life, I'd played volleyball and easily picked up any other sport I tried. But as I laced up my tennis shoes and put on my white tennis skirt, I felt like this time was totally different. Tennis was a sport I grew up admiring, but never playing. I wanted to be Serena on Day 1. But I wasn't even hitting like Serena did when she was seven. As I slipped and slid across the clay court, I felt like such a newbie. I didn't know where to stand when the coach said, "Go to the baseline," or what he meant when he said, "Be on the deuce court." I had one of two options: quit and give up, because the distance between me and Serena was bigger than the Grand Canyon; or stay and embrace the discomfort of being new at something.

The worst part about being a beginner is when you can feel the distance between where you are and where you want to be. In a world where you can have coffee delivered to your doorstep through the tap of an app, or hire people for minimum wage to show up at your house to assemble your Ikea bookshelf, we've come to expect immediate results. If you're coming from another job or career you were comfortable in, it can be really hard to jump into a world you're relatively unfamiliar with.

Even if you know your subject area, you're about to dive into a whole bunch of really confusing-at-first stuff. When I started, I distinctly remember having to google every new-to-me phrase I came across—"funnels," "email list," "landing page," "opt-in," and "trip wire" were just a few that had me stumped. I was exhausted after a full day of googling and trying to set up my new business. I felt like each day I would discover more and more things I didn't know or understand. Realizing what I didn't know was scary. *What else is out there I don't know? Am I way out of my depth? Maybe I got in over my head.* Seeing everyone else running their businesses seemingly so confidently on social media, I thought I was the only one who didn't know what was going on. This intense discovery phase went on for months, but eventually it got better as I became more comfortable with the lingo and all the moving parts of an online business. But even as I have learned more and my business has grown, there are still times when I feel like a beginner.

If you have an online business, the one thing I can absolutely guarantee is change. Things are always changing in this industry between AI, social media regulations, algorithms, platform popularity, content preferences, consumer behavior, and so much more. So although you might get over the major beginner hurdle at the start, you can expect to be humbled by this industry at times down the line. I like how it keeps me on my toes and invites me to learn new things. Part of being an entrepreneur, in my opinion, is adapting and innovating. See, there's that abundance mindset kicking in!

It's one thing to feel out of your comfort zone, but it's another to be so afraid to fail that you don't even try in the first place. If you don't even try, you can't fail, right? But that puts you at a crossroads. If you want your life to take a different path, you've got to take different steps than you've taken before. Forging a new path inherently means you're signing yourself up to be a beginner. Having started and closed down one business within a year of starting it (I think we can all agree that equates to "failure," at least on paper), I knew starting another business would be yet another humbling experience. But this time, I had "failure" on my side.

With my first business, I learned how to set up a website, create social media content, navigate sales conversations, and email my list each week. I didn't necessarily do any of those things correctly or well. But it was the act of doing it that allowed me to do it better the second time around. When I started my legal business, I was still a beginner. I learned a new way of speaking to my customer, had to learn how to build an audience online talking about preconceived "boring" legal content (if I can do it, you can build an audience on anything!), and navigated an entirely new and complex scope of practice. Eight years later, I'm still learning because things keep evolving. Part of your job is to stop expecting a "mountain peak" moment. There will never be a time when you have it all figured out, because that doesn't exist. When the game keeps changing, you just keep changing with it.

Remember the children's book *Everyone Poops* by Taro Gomi? Gomi taught children not to be afraid or embarrassed of something everyone does. As entrepreneurs, we sort of need the *Everyone Starts* equivalent to that book. Maybe we would all feel better if we saw the first time Oprah was ever on camera, or the first time Serena tossed a ball high above her head for a serve. When I see a brilliant athlete like Serena Williams play tennis, yes, I'm absolutely impressed by how incredible she is. But I'm more impressed with her journey than her performance. I think of all the early mornings and late nights Serena spent practicing. All the trials and tribulations she endured. I think of all her sacrifice and the times it didn't work out. Sure, we see the end result and the incredible number of times it *did* work out for someone like Serena. But what about all the times she fell and all we saw was her triumphant rise back to the top? When she stepped onto the court the day after a devastating loss. Or when she got back in the gym to make herself stronger, faster, and more flexible after an injury. Even Serena was a beginner at some point. Even she has faced defeat and setbacks. Maybe she became who she is *because of* those setbacks and speed bumps and how she navigated them, not despite them. The same goes for Muhammad Ali, Alex Morgan, LeBron James, Kobe Bryant, Abby Wambach, and many other athletes.

Why would we be any different from Serena? We must be beginners too. We must be awkwardly bad at something before we can become great at it. Would it help take some of the pressure off if I told you, "At some point you *will* fail"? I'm not saying you're going to be a *failure* and not ultimately be successful. But I can absolutely guarantee that you will experience failure, or disappointing results, at some point or another—likely more than once. I've gotten a lot better at tennis in the three years since I took it up. I've lost a lot of games, won a few here and there, and had more tennis lessons muttering expletives at myself under my breath than I can count. But I'm a heck of a lot better than when I started. It's actually really cool to look in the rearview and see just how far you've come, no matter how far the drive you have up ahead is. If you don't appreciate the journey, what makes you think you'll enjoy the destination?

But this beginner's symptom isn't just about grinning and bearing it. It's about shifting your beginner mindset in the first place. You can view being a beginner as a bad thing or as an exciting opportunity to carve out your own path. Beginning something new is fun—or at least it can be! Sometimes I think back to the time when I started my business and I miss it. There were a lot of flubs that I wouldn't repeat, but there was something to be said about that time because I didn't yet know what I didn't know. I didn't know enough to care about how good my video quality was, or even know what an open rate was to worry about how many people read my email. And thankfully I didn't know just how important email marketing was; otherwise, I would have spent too much time obsessing over how good it was instead of just getting my email reps in.

Embrace and feel grateful for the messy but quiet beginning rather than being frustrated that no one is watching. This is a time to dig deep and find the perseverance that probably led you to wanting to become a business owner in the first place.

The Prescription for Being a Beginner Sucks

Action steps:

- Make a list, no matter how small or minute-feeling, of things you've already accomplished in your business.
- Measure the distance between where you are now and where you started, instead of where you are now and where you're headed.
- Give yourself compassion. You're learning so many new things and being a beginner can feel overwhelming.

Journal prompts:

- Think of something in your life that you're really good at. Do you remember being a beginner? What was it like? How did you move past the beginner stage?
- What would it feel like to surrender to the beginner stage and release the expectation to have it all figured out right now? What would that allow you to do more of? Less of?

SYMPTOM #5: LONELINESS

Being famous on Instagram is basically the same thing as being rich on Monopoly.

—ANONYMOUS

When I first moved to a quiet, beachy area on Long Island, New York, I wouldn't leave the house for the entire workweek. I'd putz around the house Monday through Friday in my pj's and slippers and couldn't for the life of me figure out why I felt so blue. My old house in Philadelphia backed up to a fire station and a bustling colonial town, so "quiet" wasn't a word I'd ever used to describe my old living situation. As much as I valued peace and quiet, I worried I might have taken "quiet" to another level. As I ventured out into my new-to-me Long Island community each weekend, I realized there was a whole world out there beyond my MacBook and my Instagram feed. I knew I was desperate when I found myself attending a three-hour talk at our local historical society on the history of the area's lighthouses (honestly, it was fascinating!). Eventually, I joined a local, community-oriented gym so I would have to change out of my sleepwear, slip on my leggings, and actually interact with other humans every day. I met my dear friend and brilliant podcaster, Michelle Rubinstein, who also understood the sometimes isolating-feeling online world. Almost immediately, I felt my mood and spirits lift.

If you're not careful, running your own business can lead to a bad case of loneliness. As a work-from-home business owner, you have to intentionally cultivate social connection, community, and play. During the pandemic, I heard one expert comment, "We don't work from home; now we live at work." With your laptop on your dining room table, and your phone, which you can essentially run an online business from, always in your hand anyway—it's easy to slide into bad habits. And while some of those habits might be helpful for your bottom line, they won't be good for your sanity. (Yes, working all of the time will probably grow your business; you just won't have the stamina to do it for very long.)

If you're feeling lonely in your business, there are two ways you can introduce more variety and socialization into your routine.

First, you could intentionally add things to your calendar that put you around other people and get you out of the house. This is especially helpful if you, like me, don't mind running your business day-to-day relatively by yourself, but you don't want to be by yourself for the entire day either. Your companionship doesn't necessarily have to come from your business. It could show up in the form of an after-work yoga class, a book club meetup, or a community event. For me, I got lucky by finding an incredible gym. Between my trainers, the staff, and the incredible members, I feel like I've got a group of people around me to connect with nearly every day.

Intentionally creating space for socialization and connection outside of your business is also a great way to further separate your identity from your business. As we've discussed, starting your own business can easily send you down a rabbit hole where you start dreaming in email sequences and landing pages. But I've found being around other people who aren't online business owners (or online business owner friends who like to talk about non-business things), and further developing hobbies outside of my business, has been a very rewarding and grounding experience. My mom always said, "It's important to be interested and interesting." Not only do your weekly classes or group experiences get you out of your house and around others, but they have the added benefit of giving you all sorts of creative inspiration and fodder for content, too.

The second way to boost socialization is to incorporate collaboration as a part of your business model or as part of your educational development. Once you know this is something you want more of in your business, you can intentionally seek out opportunities—big or small—that put you with other business owners more often. You could even seek out educational opportunities—like masterminds, online courses, or memberships—that put you around your peers more often. If you wish you had an actual partner in your business, consult your attorney independently before doing this. There are a lot of legal implications and steps that should be taken before adding a partner to your business.

But loneliness doesn't creep in only when we work from home or when we don't see other people that often. I've experienced a different kind of loneliness—one I never felt before I started a business that relies on social media. In 2016, I hosted my first live webinar in my health coaching business. I'd spent weeks advertising it, begging people to sign up, and shouting from the rooftops about all the reasons why it would be helpful. When I finally hit "LIVE!" and no one came, my heart sank. "How embarrassing," I thought. "No one even cared enough to show!" I started to spiral, listing all the reasons why no one bothered coming to my class: I wasn't good enough, pretty enough, smart enough, interesting enough. Or that it was already too late; they probably got this information from someone else. How stupid was I that I thought anyone would even want to come to this. *Sound familiar?*

Is This Thing On?

Those experiences (*yes, there were many*) were so difficult to go through that it kept me from wanting to put myself out there. I felt so alone in those moments. I wanted to retreat back to where I came from. Not back to a law firm, per se. I wasn't *that* desperate. But I'd convince myself that I didn't really need social media, or to be on video, or to do anything else that I'd decided was the hindrance to my success. And for some reason when you experience a flop, or you don't get much engagement on social media, you have this tendency to think you're the only one. Everyone else is doing well but you. And it's because of you that you're not doing as well as you perceive everyone else to be. Now *that's* loneliness.

First things first, we have to work on separating ourselves from our work and the outcome of that work. If you approach your launches, content creation process, sales, et cetera from a place of curiosity, you won't feel like a failure when they don't go according to plan. If a piece of content doesn't perform well on social media, it likely has nothing to do with you personally, and more to do with factors very much outside of your control like algorithms, time of day, trends, and sheer volume of output. Sure, maybe your content was bad—but it's not because you looked bad while presenting it. But when viewed through the lens of experimentation versus judgment, we can take a "flop" as additional data instead. The same piece of content posted today might perform completely differently than if you posted the same exact piece of content next week or presented the same information in a new way. That's why you need to enlist a more scientific approach and not make generalizations or take drastic moves based on one flop or underperforming content or promotion. The more you practice approaching content and your sales this way, the more your negative self-talk will ease when something doesn't go as planned.

Second, as much as I love a good mindset shift, I wouldn't be doing my job if I said it was the only thing that might help you overcome low turnout or poor engagement. Sure, sometimes content flops for reasons completely outside of our control, but the way we create or post the content can also affect its performance. Later on, we'll talk about changes you can make to your content to attract more engagement and ensure more people see it. Often, it's a mix of topic, visuals, and messaging.

Quiet Sales

It's not just your content that can leave you feeling a little lonely sometimes. When your sales are quiet, you may similarly feel like you're the only one onstage in a very empty theater. If and when your sales are slow, take a look at your approach. Ask yourself the following questions:

- Have I been dedicated to growing my audience and nurturing that audience? Have I shown up consistently?
- Even outside of a specific sale or promotion, how often do I talk about my product, what it is, who it's for, and how it helps them?
- If a recent sale flopped, did I warm up my audience by teasing that something was coming for at least seven days prior to the sale?
- Have I properly educated and made my audience aware of what my product is before the sale, so that during the sale they're simply deciding if they are ready to buy (not trying to figure out what I'm talking about)?
- Did I use acronyms or nicknames to describe my offer, instead of realizing it may be someone's first time hearing about my offer (for example, referring to your program on social media as "the BP" instead of "the Business Program")?
- During the sales period, did my content address people's time, money, and right-fit objections?
- Did I show up consistently, regardless of how my sale went? Or did I start to withdraw from my content and my audience once I felt sales were slower than I'd hoped?

Regardless of whether you implement every tip here, I hope you now feel less alone. It takes time to find your way in your business and the content you create for it. Allow yourself the time to be a beginner and work out the kinks when fewer people are watching. By the time you have more eyeballs on you, you'll not only feel less personally impacted by each post's performance, but you'll have a better idea of what actually works.

The Prescription for Loneliness

Create community for yourself, both inside and outside of your business, to maintain social connections and relationships. Seek out new-to-you hobbies and activities as a way to stay committed to openness (and get the added benefit of boosted creativity).

Action steps:

- Book a class, activity, or block some time out on your calendar to do something else you've wanted to try.
- Carve out time this week to spend with someone who makes you feel more connected.

Journal prompts:

- Check in with yourself. How are you feeling about your social connections and relationships since starting your business? What are some ways you can get out and into your community this week?
- What are ways you can create a deeper connection even among your online community this week?

WHAT WE LEARNED

- There may never be a perfect time to launch your business or your next product.
- It's natural to feel like you're out of place, don't know enough, or won't be as successful as other people you see online, but don't let that stop you.

- Being a beginner is hard. No one said this would be easy. Let yourself be open and curious about all of the new things you're venturing into.

WHAT'S TO COME

- If you're worried that the online business space is crowded, let's learn how to stand out from the crowd in a way that's uniquely yours.

CHAPTER 6

Be a (Content) Leader, Not a Follower

Thanks to an early love of reading as a child, I was able to start school a year early. Although that might sound like a good thing, it was really tough to be the youngest in the class by nearly a year. There were many times in elementary and middle school that I would try my hardest to just fit in. I was so sick of being different—the youngest, left-handed, and a child of divorce. But my dad was always quick to remind me, "It's always better to be a leader, not a follower." I've come to appreciate how much he instilled in me a desire to be a unique, different, and strong individual. His wise words apply to how we build our businesses, too.

As we've chatted about already, the relative ease it takes to start an online business, paired with marketing coaches encouraging you to use formulaic, plug-and-play strategies, leads to a whole lot of sameness online. Whether you're starting your own business or you're revamping your existing marketing strategy, it's hard not to get sucked in by all of their promises. It's easy to gravitate toward strategies that appear, at least on the surface, to work, especially when you're confronted with any of the symptoms we discussed in the previous chapter.

But sameness doesn't build empires. Coaches selling you outdated, carbon-copy marketing strategies aren't telling you how many of their customers don't see any success with them (*no, all you'll hear about is how much money they are making off of their products as an incentive for you to purchase them*). Sameness is also destroying creativity. There are days when, as I scroll through social media, all I see are creators sharing the same regurgitated content in the same way. It's not only boring to watch, but I imagine it's boring for your ideal customer, too. So, while you might feel like your space is too crowded or like there's too much competition for your product already, I say this:

> There are too many of the same people, saying the same thing, already selling what you sell, in the same way. A whole lot of sameness.

> But there is no other *you*.

How do you show up in a way that grows your audience and business? You've got to

- show up in your uniqueness, consistently, for a long period of time;
- keep showing up even when you don't immediately see results, especially if you have been inconsistent;
- commit to the long game because you know these things take time; and

- actually *be* unique (if you're not doing anything interesting, you won't have much to share).

When I was a kid, I was the most uniquely me I've ever been. From my printed leggings paired with striped T-shirts, to being the first in my school to sport Nike Shox (my classmates called them bowling shoes!), to reading things no one else my age cared to crack open (hello, Albert Einstein's biography in fourth grade)—I was unapologetically me. Or, at the very least, I didn't try to fit myself into anyone else's mold of what they thought I *should* be, because I didn't even realize there was a mold to shape myself into. Thanks to a lack of social media at the time, I had no idea what everyone was eating, reading, and watching. You could develop a pure sense of what your actual likes and dislikes were without knowing about everyone else's. What a time to be alive.

It's no surprise to me that when we start our own businesses, social media sort of forces us to shrink and morph ourselves into the mold created by the industry. I was open earlier about how I tried to package my first business in the way I thought all coaching businesses needed to look, but there was a personal molding going on behind the scenes, too. Starting an online business felt like the school cafeteria all over again. Suddenly I felt like I didn't belong in nearly every way possible. With time, and showing up consistently despite the engagement (or the lack thereof) I got, I learned to own who I was a bit more. And then this wild thing happened: The more myself I was, the more other people felt like they had permission to be themselves, too. People wrote thanking me for being so vulnerable and open about something going on in my life or my business, not because we necessarily had the same exact things in common, but because they felt it gave them the permission and safety to do the same. Your being uniquely yourself will help inspire those around you—creating a ripple-like effect of people embracing more of who they are. What more could we ask for?

Sometimes an accidental or subconscious attempt to blend in or do what's popular can actually lead to legal trouble. For instance, just because you see someone doing something online doesn't make it legal. When people comment on my content with "I know you're saying this isn't okay, but I saw so-and-so doing it...," I remind them of what our parents told us: "Just because so-and-so's doing it, doesn't mean you should." Not only will this argument not fly from a legal perspective, but you also want to embody the mindset of a leader, not a follower. We're not here to do things the way other people do them.

On a related note, in an attempt to build a successful business, be careful that you don't accidentally mimic or even partially copy someone else's intellectual property. For example, Andrea was a successful in-person personal trainer who wanted to start an online fitness coaching business. She didn't have to look far to find other successful trainers online whose businesses she admired. She didn't even realize it, but as she consumed more of her competitors' content, hers started to look exactly like theirs. Soon, her copy and visual designs were nearly identical, too. It wasn't long before a pointed message landed in Andrea's inbox from one of the coaches she admired asking her to take down her content. Whether Andrea's content actually infringed on the other creator's content is a legal analysis for a different day—but I can tell you this story is far from rare. Nearly every day, I receive a message from someone like Andrea, panicking about whether they've done something wrong (or from the creator who felt infringed upon *by* Andrea, asking me if it is, in fact, infringement and what they can do about it). Those kinds of messages and, in many cases, threats can derail a young business. And they most certainly throw off your mindset. Once you get a message accusing you of copying, you will inevitably struggle to create content out of fear of being accused again or not knowing whether what you're putting out is uniquely yours.

Cloudy Competitors

I've said it before, but it bears repeating: I strongly discourage you from following or consuming the content of your competitors. Not only do I not find it useful from a mindset perspective, but it seriously clouds your creativity. You will forever question whether something you've created is purely yours or the result of having seen it somewhere else. Many of the ideas and tips we see out there aren't uniquely "owned by" the creator talking about them. But they do own *how* they talk about them. So go on and talk about the same topics or concepts—just do it without knowing what they're saying about it.

PERSONAL UNIQUENESS

Legal issues aside, there's another reason I don't recommend trying to look like everyone else online (or, better put, why I recommend trying to be uniquely yourself instead). Honestly, it's just flat-out boring to see the same person, voice, personality, and viewpoint expressed on the same issues online. Whenever my mom strutted into a room, everyone noticed her. Yes, she was absolutely stunning. But it was also because she confidently carried her vintage doctor's bag (as a purse, no less) with her go-to favorite outfit: Adidas track pants, a see-through top with a lacy red bra, and her Bottega Veneta high heels. She owned who she was and took pride in being different from everyone else. Trust me, most people don't want to dress exactly like my mom. But people were envious of how confidently she carried herself. *That's* what got people's attention (the lacy bra didn't hurt).

When you feel like your niche is overcrowded, maybe what you're actually feeling is the effects of homogeneity. I rarely ever go to the mall, but the other day I waited in line at a popular workout and athleisure clothing store to buy a new shirt. I looked at the long line in front of me only to notice that every person in line had on the same shoes (short UGGs); pants (leggings); white crew socks (Alo); and jewelry (gold huggie hoops). Middle school wasn't *that* long ago, so I hadn't forgotten what it was like: Just blend and hope no one calls you out. Sticking out was a bad thing. But with a little bit of age, traumatizing life experiences, and lower back pain, I thought to myself, "I'm grateful I can be myself now." Remember how badly you wanted to blend in when you were young? How funny is it now that so many of us would pay to be seen?

If you're wondering whether you require some newfound confidence *before* you can successfully grow your business, I want you to know that my business is the catalyst that actually allowed me to embrace myself for who I am. Not because the more I shared about myself, the more people liked me. But the more confident I became in my business, the more I stopped caring what everyone else thought. With that quiet confidence, I felt freer and more relaxed to be myself. The more relaxed I felt about myself, the more other people felt they could do the same. That cycle of permission and acceptance was the final piece of the puzzle that enabled me to start to learn, own, and accept who I am.

Like many things we've discussed here, my own self-acceptance and confidence journey is ongoing. While you might not be ready to confidently strut into a crowded room in Adidas swishy pants and five-inch heels (but if you are, you go!) like my mom could, you can start by taking one step at a time. Let your audience know about one hobby you have or a quirky fact about you. Start sharing about that hobby or thing consistently with your audience until you become known as "the woman who travels for ghost tours" or "the person who can't stop reading romantasy." Whatever your thing is, own it. To help your niche and the online business space to become a more diverse, inclusive, and, frankly, more interesting place, let's commit to being more uniquely ourselves and owning what sets us apart.

BUSINESS UNIQUENESS

We've talked about how sharing your uniqueness helps you to stand out from the crowd. But uniqueness in business is about so much more than whether you wear high heels with sweatpants or how off-the-beaten-path your hobbies are. Maybe you're thinking, "I'm just not *that* unique" (you are, but I hear you) and feeling like there's nothing particularly interesting about you that might make you stand out. But perhaps even more important than your personal quirks is how unique your approach, product, vibe, message, or methodology is. If everyone else is talking about the same thing in the same way, tell me how you approach things differently from most people in your industry. Why is your unique approach better than the more familiar and traditional approach? For example, I'm obsessed with pottery. If you go to an art festival or something similar, you will normally see lots of the same styles of pottery being offered. I happened to discover my favorite ceramist at a crafts fair while she was demonstrating the ancient Japanese technique of raku. Her products' uniqueness, and the story she had to tell along with it, stood out. Guess whose pottery I purchased that day, and have continued to purchase ever since? Here are some prompts to help you pinpoint your unique business approach:

- Do you have a unique skill set or educational experience to talk about (that most others don't)?
- Have you created a unique methodology (a step-by-step approach, set of procedures, or strategies) that works? How often do you share that methodology? Have you named it and shared about it so much and for so long that you've become (or are on your way to being) synonymous with it?
- Do you have a unique way of approaching your given topic in terms of your vibe or overall feel? For example, are you an unstuffy lawyer who tries to make legal easy instead of scary, boring, and overly expensive? (Just a random example ;))
- Have you created a product, service, or offer that's different from anything else currently available? If so, how and why is different better in this case?

One of the *worst* ways to stand out is to do illegal things outside of your scope of practice. That's not the kind of uniqueness you want to be known for. On the other end of the spectrum, it's equally important to differentiate yourself when you are licensed or qualified to talk about a topic. For example, if you're a physician (MD or DO), or a registered dietitian (RD) who teaches people about food and nutrition, yet you consistently get asked by future customers whether they should work with you versus an unlicensed or unqualified person in your field, you may want to spend time educating your audience on what an MD, DO, or RD is, how they're trained versus other types of coaches, and why it is important to seek guidance from a qualified professional.

The fact that you are licensed, experienced, or highly educated in your field can be a great way to set yourself apart. As we've discussed, the ease of starting an online business has made it possible for a lot of people to sell products or offer services for things they have no actual experience with. For example, when I hear an inaccurate myth coming from some marketing or business "experts" in my field regarding legal matters, I use it as an example to teach my audience what the reality or facts are and emphasize how important it is to get your information from a reliable source. Not only do you further establish yourself as a trustworthy source your future customers can rely on, but you further educate and empower them to learn how to navigate the murky waters online. My friend Keila Hill-Trawick is a CPA who often educates her audience about the differences between a bookkeeper, an accountant, a CPA, and a financial adviser. They each have important, but different, roles. By educating her future customers on the benefits of choosing a highly qualified professional, Keila positions her tax-preparation services to be the solution to one of their needs.

You can use your differences to overcome some of your ideal clients' fears or stereotypes that are keeping them from getting your help. For example, maybe you're an accountant who has great people skills, focuses on how knowing your numbers helps grow your business, and isn't yelling at people to ditch their daily latte. (*Not that this is what traditional accountants do!* It just might be what your ideal customer imagines when they picture an accountant.) Maybe your ideal client has a fear of going to the doctor or discussing medical issues, or they think all mindset coaches will tell them to meditate for sixty minutes each day. Whatever stereotype doesn't feel right to you—emphasize that, because there are surely people out there not getting help because of it.

You can and should put everything we've discussed so far into the way you approach ideating, making, and designing your content. With social media, sometimes it's not about what you say, but how you say or present it. Don't be afraid to be unique in your creative process, too. You certainly don't need to follow all of the trends. You can pick and choose which trends work for you and which don't and still do really well in business. Honestly, the main focus should be your audience and the needs of your future customers, not what everyone else is doing.

We'll discuss a more detailed content strategy later on, but for now I advise this: Create the content that best teaches your information or makes the point for your customer. If that's visual with props and drawings, or audio—do it! The most stand-out unique content is created by people being themselves while having fun doing it. The more relaxed you are, the better teacher you'll be. The more people learn from you, the more they will keep coming back to watch your content. If and when something you create works for you and turns out to be a hit with your audience, try to repeat that formula as often as you can. Many creators burn themselves out trying to be different every time they post new content. In reality, it's better to find what works, understand why it works for your audience, and create spiderweb-like content related to what works.

Jenn Lueke (Jenn Eats Goood) is a content creator who shares meal-prepping tips, recipes, and weekly menu ideas through her blog, Instagram, YouTube, and Substack newsletter. While she cooks each Sunday, she films her meal prep and then shares an Instagram Reel dissecting one of the tips, strategies, or recipes she used to prep that week. The content approach is nearly identical week-to-week, but what she teaches is always slightly different. Her style works for me (and millions of her followers). She turned her weekly meal-prep videos into a series, which keeps us coming back for more and checking in to see when a new "episode" drops. Sort of like the old days when we used to tune in to Must See TV on

NBC to catch the latest episode of *Friends*. How can you re-create that kind of bingeability for your audience with your content?

Your business, and what you offer, also has to be unique enough to overcome the common question all creators who sell products or services online get: Why should I pay you for this when I can just get it online for free? Whenever people ask why they should buy my legal templates when they can download a freebie off some website, or when they ask a personal trainer why they should work with them when there are thousands of free YouTube workout videos, the righteous knee-jerk response may be, "Because! I went to school for this! I worked for this! I deserve to get paid for it." While you're right to feel that way, I can promise you people won't stop asking.

The truth is that most free resources aren't going to be enough for your ideal client to see results, solve their problems, or save them time. Access to the overwhelming amount of free information out there can actually have an adverse effect and set our clients back. They waste more time spinning their wheels, searching for answers or bouncing around from resource to resource, without making any progress or achieving results. As you hear from your audience members or clients about how much your work or paid resources helped them, be sure to save those responses to use in future marketing. It will help to overcome the objection someone might have to pay for, or even opt in for, your services or products. Make it clear to your future customers why it's beneficial to pay you for what you do instead of continuing to seek out free information. Show them

- how much time you'll help them save, not only because they can quit researching and bouncing around, but because you'll give them the exact information they need (and nothing more) so they can progress;

- the amount of money you will end up saving your client, whether it's because "time is money" or because of the actual money they might have wasted on low-cost alternatives instead of buying what they really need;
- that the results they aren't seeing may be due to insufficient advice, feedback, or guidance, and they may need a professional's eye on their issues to help create a customized game plan to move forward;
- why their situation or problem is so unique that it needs a professional's touch; and
- the quality differences between your product or service and those that can be found online for free.

Being unique isn't something that can be manufactured or planned. My hope here is to empower you to confidently step into more of who you are, not who everyone else is expecting you to be. You might get frustrated and feel like you're not making any progress, so you reach for a bad habit: mimicking a competitor, following trends, searching for the magic bullet. If that happens, I hope you will come back to this section, remember how important it is to be yourself, and reset.

Now that we all know how important it is to lean into our uniqueness and stand out from the crowd, let's talk about actually *building* that crowd.

EMAILS ARE EVERYTHING

I know what you might be thinking: "I already get too many emails. Aren't emails dead? Don't you just want to text someone?" Part of the bs I told myself early on was that emails were for two things: (1) nine-to-five jobs; and (2) sales emails (preferably with coupon codes) from my favorite stores. That may have been more true at the time. But in the online business world today, email marketing remains supreme. Of course, social media, SEO, and text messaging are important and can be additional options in your marketing toolbox, but emails have remained consistently popular over time; as of this writing, newsletters, Substack, and email lists are growing in popularity. So while it's true many of us get too many bad emails that aren't worth the energy it takes to click to open them, the truth is that really good, valuable emails are performing well in the online business world.

In this section, and everywhere else throughout the book, when we talk about "emails," we're not talking about one-off emails you would send to a friend or family member. We're talking about *email marketing*—the act of collecting email addresses of people who want to hear from you (what we'll call your "email list") and sending out emails related to your topic, services, or products to those people regularly (what used to be called an "email blast," but what we would now refer to as an "email newsletter"). Whether you have five people (whom you're related to) or five thousand people on your email list already, this list is one of the most important parts of building and growing your online business. It's going to be your tried-and-true way to establish credibility, provide value, and build the know-like-trust connection that's required for people to want to work with or purchase from you. When carefully built, consistently nurtured, and strategically handled, your email list will likely be where the bulk of your sales come from.

To get started, begin collecting a list of email addresses (we'll talk about how to do this in the next section) of people who have elected to hear from you or your business using an email marketing platform like Kit (formerly ConvertKit) or Mailchimp. Then, send out a newsletter to your email list at some consistent interval, perhaps once a week or every other week. The content of your email can be anything from sales/promotional material to an offer or coupon, to value-driven emails, which offer educational tips, stories, strategies, or information to your ideal audience as a means to build rapport, trust, and awareness. I focus 98 percent of my efforts on value-driven emails (while still strategically talking about my offers, which we'll discuss in a bit), and I run sales to my email list a handful of times per year.

Audience Preferences

When we talk about email, we have to acknowledge that there are some people who don't like to read emails. Just as there are many people who aren't on social media. And even for your social audience, some of them might hate one platform while the rest love it. Ask ten people, and you'll probably get ten different responses regarding where they prefer to consume their content. As always, I'll encourage you to focus on what you like to create. (For example: *Do you prefer writing, video production, or audio? Which are you best at? Which is the best medium for presenting your information?*) Another area to focus on is where your ideal audience generally likes to hang out or how they like to consume their content.

For example, my ideal customers are the type who enjoy sitting down and reading a longish, more detailed email from me versus watching a seven-second TikTok clip, so the engagement for my email list is very high. There's no right or wrong; you have to know your people!

Emails with Benefits

Utilizing email marketing for your business isn't just a safe choice, it's one that can seriously help you grow your business when used correctly. There are a lot of reasons to give email marketing a huge portion of your marketing attention over other methods like social media. Unlike social media, with email you have the opportunity to capture someone's undivided attention without all of the noise and distraction of ads, pop-ups, and content from other people for them to click away to. These days, the primary purpose of social media platforms is entertainment. With email, you can still provide entertaining content—but given the long-form nature of emails, you can also dig deeper into various topics in a way you can't in a dancing TikTok video or a lip-synching Instagram Reel.

On social media, even when people choose to "follow" or "like" you, the algorithm gods make an unknown-to-us decision about how, why, when, and who gets to actually see your content. It's possible the people who follow you will never see the content you create or post. If you're ever looking for a reason to feel discouraged, open up the stats on your latest Instagram post and see how many people actually saw it, including the people who have chosen to follow you (so, presumably, they could see your content). With email, on the other hand, we know someone receives your email when they sign up for your email list. You can't control whether or not the person actually *opens* or *reads* the email, but there are lots of crafty things you can do to try (we'll chat about those later). Given the fact that social media doesn't even guarantee delivery of your content to those who sign up for it, email is a safer bet from a reliability standpoint.

An important aspect of email marketing is how much access you get to user engagement and behavioral data. You can see which emails they open, what links they click on, and typically where they're located. I check our open-rate data (that's the percentage of people who actually opened the email I sent); click-through rate (the percentage of people who clicked on a link in the email I sent); and the unsubscribe rate (the number of people who opted out of my emails moving forward because they no longer wanted to hear from me). That data informs what topics I write about in the future, what kind of subject lines I use, and how often I email my list. Through some fancy link technology that's beyond me, we can also tag people who have clicked on a link before and then send a future email only to those people on my email list with the tag "Customer interested in 'X.'" I can send emails based on their location, how long they've been on my list, or any of their other clicking or engagement behavior. Having access to that level of detailed information allows me to send targeted emails to smaller groups of people on my email list (what we call "segments"), which helps to avoid tiring out disinterested people.

Kit (formerly ConvertKit), the incredible email service my business uses, allows me to A/B test our emails. For example, I can send out the same email to a percentage of my email list but send half of them the email using one subject line and the other half using a different subject line. That way, I know which subject line performs best with the same exact content in the email. I pick whichever subject line wins and send out the email to the rest of my subscribers. I especially like to use this feature for my sales sequences, which we'll discuss later, so I can improve my open rates and sales over time. See? Data is cool!

Last but certainly not least, email marketing also gives you the benefit of being able to "set it and forget it." Although there are social tools out there to help you schedule and auto-post content, they are far from perfect. You are also limited a bit when prescheduling and auto-posting to social media, with many features unavailable to those not posting in real time natively on the app. With social media, most experts believe your content performs well only if you engage a certain amount on the app. If you "post and run," even fewer people may see your content than the finicky algorithm may have shown it to had you stayed and engaged. With email, on the other hand, you can prewrite, schedule, and send emails to whomever, whenever you would like. Whoever has signed up for your email list will receive that email. No algorithm intervenes and says, "Not today, sucka!" But email isn't a panacea. We still have to work to get people's attention these days. It's best if you create a connection with subscribers when they first join your list. So let's chat about how to do just that.

Most, if not all, of the main email marketing services allow you to create "welcome sequences"—a series of emails that a new subscriber receives after they've opted in to your email list (e.g., when someone downloads my freebie, I send them Welcome Email #1 immediately and Welcome Email #2 in 24 hours). Let's get into the different types of emails you can send on behalf of your business, including those crucial welcome sequences.

Welcome Sequences

Whether someone joins your email list as just a plain ol' opt-in (like on a sign-up sheet at a live event or via an opt-in form on your website) or they download one of the freebies we're going to discuss later in this chapter, you can use a welcome sequence as a way to welcome them not only to your list and familiarize them with you and your brand, but to your community, too. A welcome sequence is an automated series of emails you send to someone who's signed up for your email list. Since these are prewritten and triggered by some series of events, once you set them up, you won't have to do a thing to welcome people to your list. Welcome sequences are your way to set the lay of the land for your new audience members. For example, the four to six emails in your welcome sequence might perform the following functions:

- **Deliver the freebie.** If they opted in to receive a freebie, the very first email should quickly and clearly give them access to it. It's a great way to start off the relationship.

- **Introduce yourself.** Who are you and why should they trust or listen to you? This isn't the place to share your entire life story, but rather why your experience or credentials establish you as an authority. This is also a great time to share some of those unique skills, quirks, and parts of yourself that we talked about in the previous chapter.
- **Set expectations.** What types of emails do you typically send? What kind of things will they learn here? It's not just about having lots of people on your email list; you want the right people who actually want to hear from you.
- **Give value.** Why should they stay on your list? Literally give them something valuable, like a free resource or a hot tip, even if they didn't sign up for that. Let them know that's just a little taste of the kind of value they can expect if they stick around.
- **Your stories.** Share a core story or a time when you faced adversity, overcame it, and how (what we call a "hero story"). For example, that near-death experience you had that got your tush in gear, or the struggles your family faced in your childhood that spurred you on to become a financial expert.
- **Get a reply.** Your welcome sequence is a great time to open up the floor and ask them one targeted question, like "What's the number one challenge you're facing in your workouts?" One welcome sequence reply prompt that works really well for me is asking the reader to reply with something simple like "Got it!" or "I'm here!" to prove they're listening. It's a great engagement hack, plus, it gets them to read the entire email. Getting them to reply isn't just good for email health (email services

see replies as a good sign you're not a spammer!), but also for their overall engagement and the chance they'll read your future emails.

- **Pitch your products.** This is the time to strike while the energy is high. Your ideal customer joined your email list for a reason: They're interested in what you're doing! You've got to start talking about your offers and products and can even consider a sales pitch toward the end of your sequence. Typically, I like to start to familiarize my new subscriber with my products, the product names, what they are, and how they can help the subscriber. That makes the sales hurdle a little easier to jump over later on.

Remember that you may have to create different welcome sequences for different parts of your business. I tailor each welcome sequence to each freebie I offer. I also have specific welcome sequences for new customers, too. Instead of pitching a sale (since they just purchased from me) or trying to set the stage of what to expect, I focus those emails more on getting to know the product, where they can find certain things, and what to do if they need additional help. As we'll discuss later on, I know the key to creating a product that sells well for a long time is getting people to use it, like it, and tell other people about it. Welcome sequences come in many shapes and sizes, and what works for me may not work for you! It's important to test out what works on your audience.

Hire a Copywriter

When you can, I highly encourage you to hire a copywriter familiar with your area of expertise who can write email sequences for you. A great copywriter will gather the voice of customer research, review your freebie, and have a clear strategy and pathway to build out your welcome sequence. A copywriter was one of the earliest investments I made in my business and it was well worth it. Not all copywriters do the same type of work, though. So make sure you look for a copywriter who focuses on what you need (e.g., website copy, conversion/sales copy, ad copy, etc.).

Weekly-ish Emails

Imagine stopping by for a tour of a brand-new gym near you. The manager takes you around, shows you all the features and benefits of being a member, and even lets you talk to a few happy members who have already joined. But instead of inviting you to sign up or following up with you after your visit, you never hear from the manager again. Will you actually end up purchasing a membership? Or will you forget about that gym when life gets busy and you see ads from other gyms? That's what it would be like if you set up a welcome sequence to your email list, but never sent them weekly emails. Your weekly emails are the follow-up. They continue to provide value, even if someone didn't purchase from you right away.

Each week, I send out my *Sam's Sidebar* newsletter to my subscribers. In contrast to an automated sequence like a welcome sequence, these are emails I'm writing from scratch each week that go out to nearly everyone on my list. I can segment and exclude certain groups of subscribers from receiving these emails when it makes sense, but usually, all subscribers receive an email from me that includes a personal narrative with a lesson (connection and value); a legal Q&A (high-value); a behind-the-scenes look at what's going on in the Ultimate Bundle® (familiarity with my product); and a blurb about that week's *On Your Terms®* podcast episode (additional value).

Your weekly-ish email strategy can certainly vary from mine, but you should keep a couple of goals in mind. First, your weekly email is a great way to stay top-of-mind with your subscribers. They live busy lives and might not see your social media content, so this is your chance to cut through the noise and get some one-on-one time with them. Even when I'm not trying to sell my product directly, I make sure to mention it several times throughout the email. I don't mention my products in a "You should buy this," type of way, but by sharing a lesson or tip and then saying, "That's actually something I teach in my program, the Ultimate Bundle®!" or sharing a behind-the-scenes look at what's going on in my customer community. That way, not only are my subscribers more familiar with the products I sell and even what they are called, but I sort of slyly create a little FOMO. The next time a product is on sale, that subscriber won't be able to wait to hit "purchase."

Second, your emails should continue to build on the know-like-trust connection you have set the foundation for in your welcome email sequence. People need time to make purchase decisions. They also often need to be presented with certain information—which varies depending on the psychological makeup of the person you're dealing with—in order to feel ready to purchase from you. Personally, I welcome subscribers regardless of whether they can buy right away, one month from now, two years down the line (I've had some people purchase my product and email me afterward to say they've been on my email list for five-plus years!), or never. I see my weekly email as a way to stay top of mind and continue earning their trust, respect, and time. Some of the people on your list might never purchase from you—either because they're not the right fit or they cannot afford it. That doesn't mean they don't deserve to be there. Providing free content to people who don't become customers is just the cost of doing business. Plus, a core business value of mine is accessibility. It's a privilege to make legal information, which is typically out of reach and costly, available to those who wouldn't have access otherwise. Never underestimate the power of word of mouth and referrals, too. Therefore, make sure your weekly emails continue to provide free highly valuable content, center your products as the solution your ideal customers are looking for, and seek their engagement and replies.

Last but certainly not least, if you brand your weekly emails/newsletters or give them a theme by naming them (like one of my favorite YouTubers, Jules Acree, whose *Slow Brew Sunday* newsletter is the first one I open each Sunday) and make sure they're full of value, you can use the emails/newsletters themselves as a reason to join your email list (versus luring them in with a freebie). Instead of asking your audience to "sign up for your newsletter," pitch your newsletter as a themed weekly (or however often you send it) piece of valuable content. Position the value of your newsletter with an explanation of "what's in it for them" to give them a reason to join. For example, to get people to join your recipe and cooking newsletter, you could say, "Sign up to get free 30-minute, one-pot recipes with custom shopping lists and my go-to kitchen tools each Sunday!" I'd sign up for that one in a heartbeat.

Sales Sequences and Sales Promotions

The great thing about having a solid welcome sequence and a weekly-ish email strategy is that your audience will be primed to purchase by the time you run a sale or promotion for your products. Imagine if you never talked about how you work with people or the types of products you sell, and then you just ran a sale. You would have to spend an even larger portion of your sale period educating your customers and creating awareness around your products before they knew why or whether they wanted them. Knowing your audience's awareness level is a crucial step that we'll discuss later.

Instead, if you follow the nurture and weekly email tips we've discussed so far, you will have properly educated, and brought awareness to, most of your email list subscribers by the time you run a sale. You will still have to do some educational work around promoting your product, but you're going to make your life a lot easier by consistently mentioning it.

Like a welcome sequence, a sales sequence guides your customer along a journey—only this time, the destination is to purchase your product. Although you can send a series of emails to your email list at any time to promote your products or put them on sale, right now I'm referring to an intentional series of sales emails that are triggered by a subscriber taking some action (like signing up for your webinar or challenge) or attending a virtual event. For example, if you sell an online course and offer a webinar as a way to introduce your topic and pitch your product to your customer, your sales sequence would be the series of emails the subscriber automatically receives after signing up for, and ideally attending, your webinar. As another example, if you sell products and run a Black Friday sale, your sales sequence would be the series of emails subscribers receive leading up to and during the holiday to notify them of the sale, offer them a discount, and remind them it is expiring.

Sales sequences typically consist of six to eight emails, depending on your topic, sale structure, and your product's price point. The higher the cost and the bigger the investment required for your product (either in time, money, energy, or some combination of the three), the more emails are likely required to fully nurture and convert a subscriber to become a customer. A sales sequence usually addresses a number of topics, including the following:

- **Objection busting.** People typically have one or more objections to purchasing products, so you need to make it clear why your product is worth their time, money, or energy, and how it meets a unique need (we call these "snowflake" objections). It's crucial to address these objections in one or several emails throughout your sales sequence. You can even sprinkle objection busting throughout your email sequence in small but mighty ways, like including a customer testimonial from someone who had one of these objections ("I thought it was going to take so much time!") but who realized after getting your product it wasn't true ("it ended up being so fast and easy!").

- **Social proof/customer-generated content.** Showcase real customer stories, real-world application examples, and wins as a way to show potential buyers what is possible for them. Your potential customers need to see *themselves* in the stories you share. My customers love hearing from my once confused and overwhelmed customers about how they quickly legally protected their businesses with my product.

- **Features and what's included.** Everyone makes purchasing decisions differently and considers different information before eventually pulling the purchase trigger. Some people (me!) need to see exactly what's included to justify and understand the cost. Although some entrepreneurs tend to spend too much time focusing *only* on the features of what's included (e.g., your package includes 10 personal training sessions, 1 customized 6-week workout plan, and 15 breakfast recipes), there are people who want and need this information in order to make a decision. It's really about *how* you present the features as benefits to your customers. If your feature description is simply "includes a 6-week workout plan," ask yourself:

Why is it beneficial to get a customized six-week workout plan? Why is it helpful to have a workout plan from a personal trainer in general?

Then, you might change the feature description to something more like this:

Includes a six-week workout plan, so you know exactly what to do in the gym each day. You don't have to wander around the gym for two hours, wondering what types of exercises you're supposed to do anymore. With all that extra time, snap a few extra mirror selfies—your progress is too good not to share!

- **Emotional triggers.** A good sales sequence will speak to what a customer is feeling, dealing with, frustrated about, and how they wish things were different. People want to feel seen and understood. If it's true your product is the solution to help them go from sad/mad/frustrated to feeling better, you should spend a few emails positioning your product to do so. For example, I know that the fear and anxiety of being legally unprotected in their businesses is often what keeps my future customers up at night. My emotionally driven emails connect with them on this pain point, make them feel less alone in it, and show them how my product leads to the solution of not feeling so vulnerable anymore. Instead, they'll feel confident to promote their business and can finally start growing it.

- **Frequently asked questions.** Use at least one email to address customers' most commonly asked questions about your product, process, or whether it's the right fit for them.
- **Urgency.** It's important to sprinkle urgency, or to give people a compelling reason to buy now versus waiting until later, throughout your entire sales sequence. Without a reason to purchase by a certain time, there's no incentive for someone to purchase now versus six months from now. Big companies do this all the time. How many sale emails do you get over Memorial Day weekend or for Black Friday from your favorite companies reminding you about an upcoming or expiring sale? This is just your version of that. There are three main components of urgency to consider:

1. **Time:** You can limit the amount of time someone has to purchase your product by creating an open/closed cart product. That means it's not on sale all the time. If your product is evergreen, like mine, in that it's something people need access to purchase at any time, you can offer a discount for a specific period of time and give people a reason (e.g., an expiring bonus) to purchase before the sale ends.
2. **Money:** There are many ways to play with financial discounts on your product. You can offer a discount for a specific period of time. You could also use a ladder system to offer the best discount for the first three days of a sale and then decrease the discount over the course of the rest of the sale. You could even introduce a new payment-plan option that's not available outside of this specific promotion. That gives people an incentive to take advantage of your sale early and get the best deal.

3. **Limited-time value:** When I run sales, I include certain trainings or items I've created as an additional bonus. Using the same scale-down system for financial discounts, you can offer other products, additional resources, or other items you've created as part of your bonus suite, too.

If these sequences or email ideas feel overwhelming, I hear you! Here's what I'd recommend to get started:

1. Begin writing your weekly-ish emails, even if you have five people on your email list. Create the habit now. Through time and experience, your list and writing skills will flourish.
2. Create your first freebie (I'll teach you how in the next section) and write a welcome sequence for it.

Keep emailing weekly, because those who opt in for your freebie and go through your welcome sequence will need future nurturing to become customers.

Voilà! You've got a simple email strategy in place.

Integrity

I try not to use a lot of high-pressure tactics in my emails, nor do I try to change someone's mind about not being able to afford my products. Trying to shift someone's mindset or perspective on the value of something, or the value of taking action, is different from saying, "Just buy it! You'll definitely get your money's worth! Even if you have to open up a new credit card account... just do it!" I see that type of (less on-the-nose) language in our industry often, and it's not how I choose to do business. On the flip side, some business owners become too cautious in their copy and won't address their subscribers' objections head-on. The truth is, some of your subscribers do have objections; it's just a matter of whether you address them or not. I draw the line at encouraging people to take truly uncomfortable or unsafe risks and encourage you to do the same. At the end of the day, we have to empower our customers to make the decision that's best for them. But we can also sleep tight at night knowing we didn't encourage anything we don't feel proud of.

CREATING THE BEST FREEBIES

One of the best ways to build your email list is to offer something free and valuable—what's called a *freebie*—in exchange for someone signing up. Typically, freebies come in the form of a handout, like a guide, checklist, webinar, video series, challenge, trial, email series, or something similar. It's best to offer variety to your audience by having more than one freebie and to test which freebies convert most highly. You can swap out low-performing freebies with new options from time to time in order to test what your audience likes and needs. There are two purposes to freebies:

- To build your email list by giving subscribers something valuable in exchange for signing up.
- To educate your audience on your area of expertise with just enough information to be helpful, but also to further familiarize them with you and what you do—so you're their logical choice when they're ready to hire someone to help them.

The key is to create freebies people actually want and that actually support your business goals. So how do you do that?

No-Brainer Freebies

Years ago, my brilliant copywriter, Katelyn Collins, and I were brainstorming ideas for bonuses for a big sale I was running. Katelyn said when it came to bonuses, and even our order bumps (low-ticket products included as an option to add on at checkout, sort of like the online version of sticking those Trader Joe's dark chocolate peanut butter cups in your cart at checkout), it's crucial to make them a "no-brainer" for people. In other words, you need a bonus so enticing that customers won't even have to blink before clicking "BUY!" After seeing how well that strategy worked for bonuses, I tried out the same logic when it came to my freebies. People often create freebies they think they *should* create, or that they see offered by other people. Instead, create something for your audience that would be such a no-brainer decision (because it's *that* good) for them, they would click "SIGN UP!" and be on your email list in an instant.

Once I adopted this no-brainer approach, my email list sign-ups skyrocketed (thanks, Katelyn!). I stopped creating freebies I thought sounded good and approached them from the perspective of a potential customer instead. I also thought about how they wanted the information presented to them. Would they want this information via a checklist, webinar, or Google doc? Ask yourself: What would be so valuable, so helpful, and so enticing *to them* that they wouldn't hesitate to sign up for it? If you're worried that your freebie is "too good" or "too valuable" and borders on something you should really charge for—jackpot. That's your new freebie. Giving it away for free should make you sweat a little.

Reverse Engineering

Freebies should be no-brainers, but they still have to be related or adjacent to what you do. Create freebies that lead back to your products. One way I like to do this is by reverse engineering my product into what would make sense for a freebie. If your product is an online course about email marketing and creating great email sequences, maybe your freebie would contain a checklist of the ten things every highly converting email sequence must have. Or it could be a guide that includes your one hundred best email idea prompts. Or a video training on how to write better subject lines, with a PDF of your top-performing subject lines of all time. Since you want to attract ideal potential customers, your freebie should be related to what you do and sell. The idea here is that someone who prioritizes email sequences and wants to get better at writing them will want to get your freebie on email marketing. That person will then see that you have a course on email marketing and email sequences. Your product then becomes the no-brainer next step in their email-sequence writing journey.

Adjacent Freebies

Although the majority of my freebies are heavily related to what I sell, I do have several high performers that are more adjacent to what I do. Here's how I think of it: There are only so many legal freebies I can create. But what else do my ideal customers struggle with? Well, basically everything you're reading about in this book: email marketing, social media, overcoming mindset struggles, and making more sales, among other worries. Over the years I've experimented with freebies that, although they aren't directly related to what I sell, are highly valuable to my customer base.

For example, each year I promote an Annual Planning Guide freebie—a template of the annual business planner I created to plan and execute my business's marketing strategy for the following year. We get many new sign-ups using this freebie. I don't sell anything related to planning, but I know people who want to plan their business year also need to get their legal ducks in a row. These types of freebies are certainly fewer than my reverse-engineering approach, but they work extremely well. If you can get people on your email list and use the weekly-ish email strategy to further nurture and educate them, there's still a chance that they'll become a customer in the future. These types of freebies can also be used to provide additional value to subscribers already on your email list. I never make current subscribers sign up again to receive a new freebie. Instead, I email it to them as an additional gift. Providing too much value doesn't scare me. What scares me is not providing any, and their finding it elsewhere.

WHERE TO PROMOTE YOUR FREEBIES

In order for people to opt in to your freebies, you have to post and share about them nearly everywhere in your online universe, not in just one place. We're going to take a holistic approach to sharing our freebies in numerous places to try to catch our potential leads' attention. Let's start with your website.

Your Website

You should have several places on your website where customers can opt in to your freebies. Ideally, pick one or two strong freebies to emphasize on your website; this is more effective than including a dozen different options in many different places. When I choose which freebies to emphasize on my website, or even social media, I like to consider variety. If I pick a guide or PDF, I might select a video or an audio-based freebie for the other option. I wouldn't pick two similar guides, or two webinars, because I know not everyone likes to learn that way.

It's best to include freebies on your website via opt-in boxes or forms, as well as integrating them into your blog posts or content posted on your website. Experts have split opinions on how effective website pop-ups are, but I tend to err more on the side of excluding them—they tend not to work so well on mobile devices, and they can decrease the amount of time spent on a website. When done right, opt-in boxes throughout your website are more user-friendly and have a higher conversion rate. I also like to include my most popular freebie in my hello bar—the thin bar that can appear at the top of your website across all its pages.

If you're utilizing SEO-optimized blog posts as a marketing strategy, your freebies should be top-of-mind when creating them. If you're going to put effort into creating a blog post that people can search for and find, give those new visitors a reason to stick around your community by offering them a "content upgrade" (a fancy term for a freebie!). If your blog post is about the steps needed to legally start a business, give readers the opportunity to opt in for a checklist of the steps. The great part about this strategy is that it's a "set it and forget it" approach. I'm still getting opt-ins on blog posts I wrote in 2017! This is another place in my business where I reverse engineer my approach. I create blog posts that naturally lend themselves to my freebies, instead of creating freebies based off of my blog posts.

Social Media

Another great place to share about your freebies is on social media. You can use your freebies as calls to action (the action you ask viewers to take after watching your content) at the end of your social media posts. For example, if your post is about dating tips, you could encourage viewers to grab your dating guide freebie. That way, you're taking people off of social media—a place we don't "own" or fully control as to who sees our content—and inviting them somewhere you do own (your email list) and can control much better. I like to use my reverse-engineering strategy again and create content that's been backed out of my freebie itself. So if your freebie teaches five things, or includes ten steps, just take one of those and create a piece of content around it. That way, the call to action can be to download your freebie for the full list.

Your Marketing Platforms

Beyond social media, you should also share your freebies on your podcast, YouTube channel, Substack, or anywhere else you're building an online community. Just as you would with a blog post content upgrade, you could include a freebie for a podcast episode or YouTube episode, too. If you ever get asked to be interviewed on someone else's podcast or teach in their community, make sure you include a link to your freebie for viewers to opt in to.

Remember, there's not any single strategy that will be "the thing" to go viral or grow your business. It's a brick-by-brick approach that can accrue a whole lot of compounding interest. All of the things we've talked about might work better for you than others. But no matter how each performs, they add up over time.

As an online entrepreneur, email marketing is one of the things I love to play with the most, and the opportunities are endless. I have given you a lot of ideas and a place to start, but what is most important is to just start doing it. You will learn what your audience likes, clicks on, and buys from only once you start experimenting. This is a great time to embody the experimenter, scientist mindset we talked about earlier. Be open. Stay curious. Send lots of emails. And always look at the data (but don't take it personally).

WHAT WE LEARNED

- In a crowded online space, uniqueness is key. It's not that you're trying too hard to be unique, you're actually emphasizing what is unique about you, your approach, and your methods.
- Email marketing still reigns supreme in the marketing world. It's a great way to build a community off of platforms you don't "own" and where you can, generally speaking, reach people more consistently.
- By creating irresistible freebies, you will consistently attract new leads to build your email list full of engaged, future buyers.

WHAT'S TO COME

- How to research, build out, and beta test your first $1 million product so it sells consistently, for years to come.

CHAPTER 7

How to Build Your First $1 Million Product (Without Losing Your Marbles)

From a small seed a mighty trunk may grow.

—AESCHYLUS

When I first started my business, I only offered a suite of individual à la carte legal templates. Sometimes people would purchase just one of those templates, and other times people would purchase several. It wasn't until I conducted more than twelve hundred free "legal checkup calls" with people (a free opportunity to ask me questions and find out what items they might need from my template shop) that I realized I was actually sitting on a potential million-dollar product.

The more people I spoke with, the more clearly I saw two significant patterns emerging in my business:

1. People wanted several legal templates—more than they had purchased—but it felt cost prohibitive to get all the ones they needed at once.
2. My potential customers had the same exact questions as the twelve hundred people I spoke with on my free checkup calls, and I found myself repeatedly answering with the same information.

That's when I knew something had to change. I joked with my husband, "I could record myself answering their questions, just leave it on speaker, and walk around! Everyone wants to know the exact same things. And I give them all the same answers, again and again." Instead of continuing to be frustrated about what felt, at the time, like a waste of energy, I realized it was actually an opportunity to create something more "passive." Instead of conducting so many calls and giving away so much of the same valuable information for free, I could record videos answering each one of these questions, package them into an online course, and sell it. Knowing from my calls that customers *also* needed a more affordable way to get all of the legal templates they needed at once, I included a pack of ten of my legal templates as well. Packaged together, and utilizing the marketing system I'm about to teach you, the Ultimate Bundle® became my first not just million-dollar, but multimillion-dollar product.

Before we get started, I want to set the record straight on a few things:

- When I say "product" here, I'm generally referring to something scalable like a course, digital product, downloadable item, or membership. Although you can make great money offering high-ticket services through coaching and consulting, you will inevitably hit a ceiling in both revenue and the amount of time and energy you have to sustain it. If you sell physical products, your scalability could depend on how much hands-on work is involved or how unique your product is, and whether you have the resources to scale production at a cost-effective rate. As you will read about, there's something uniquely special and doable about creating an educational digital resource and scaling it.

- You don't have to want to make $1 million in sales, nor is your product deemed successful only if it actually makes $1 million in sales. I want to encourage you to set your own bar for what you want to achieve in your business. I, admittedly, did not set out to make $1 million, and I don't like to focus on "money" as the only or sole object of my business success. Remember: You can set goals on your own terms.

- The plan I'm about to share with you took me *years* not just to learn, but to implement. I learned all of this firsthand by getting my hands dirty, moving forward even when I didn't know what I was doing, and even more so by making (costly) mistakes. I'm passing all of this on to you, but know this: The sole act of getting started will be your best teacher.

- Of course I encourage you to read my strategy and implement what works for you, but I also encourage you to leave what doesn't work for you (or what you don't want to do, for whatever reason). Sometimes entrepreneurs get too hung up on whether or not something fits and works for them perfectly. If it doesn't, we use it as an excuse for why we can't get started. Nothing in this book, or that you'll read elsewhere about business, is one-size-fits-all. Adapt it and make it your own.

Knowing all of that, are you ready to build your version of a million-dollar product? Let's do it. You can build your $1 million product by:

- conducting thorough research and development on your product niche;
- beta testing and adapting;
- taking a customer-first approach;
- having a solid marketing plan; and,
- eventually, creating a sales funnel.

Having built and marketed many different products, I know it's tempting to want to skip to the good part (for me, that's marketing!). But looking back, I know what made my products successful was going through a methodical, step-by-step approach. On your business journey, you might hear stories of people who scaled faster or who went viral and experienced more immediate success. But how many of them could tell you *why*? How many of them could replicate what they've done, and do it again, and again, and again? How many can adapt to the changes in industry, messaging, social media, technology, and consumer behavior? The next time you see an online entrepreneur touting their overnight success with their secret formula, for which they ask you to pay $497, come back to the mantra of this chapter: brick by brick. You're doing it.

PHASE #1: RESEARCH AND DEVELOPMENT

Although we touched on this quickly in chapter 3 with regard to your *business idea*, the idea of researching and developing your *product* before it goes to market is an entirely different conversation. Although in an ideal world, we would have all researched the heck out of our businesses before we ever hung a digital shingle, I also know that's not the reality of how things work. As I shared with you, my million-dollar product was born from an idea I had once my business had been up and running for more than a year. In fact, I'd argue that I needed to run my business for a time in order to even come up with that idea in the first place. So, don't fret if you're already in business or already sell products and now you're like, "Wait, we were supposed to do research *first*?" If you already have a product that isn't selling as well as you'd like it to, make sure you go through this section in its entirety. There's always time to adjust.

Demand

Just like you do when starting a business, you need to make sure there's demand for your product before you actually create it. Remember: Although it's great that *you* want your product and wish it existed (maybe even for yourself if you suffered from the same problem your clients suffer from now), ideally, you want to make sure there are lots of other people out there with the same or similar concerns who need your product.

In order to determine whether there's demand for your product and the solution it offers people, I recommend starting with a casual search online. A few places to start your search include the following:

- **Social media:** Search hashtags, keywords, and trends to see what people are already saying about your topic.
- **Search engines and search engine optimization (SEO):** Find out what people are searching for related to

your topic. I like to use the Google Chrome extension "Keywords Everywhere" to have access to data while I search. I can type in a question or phrase to search on Google, YouTube, et cetera, and Keywords Everywhere tells me what the search volume is, geographic statistics, and what additional words, phrases, and questions people search for related to these terms. I also recommend using the free website Answer the Public, where you can see exactly what questions and phrases people are searching for around your topic.

- **Chat threads:** Reddit, Quora, X (formerly known as Twitter), Threads, LinkedIn groups, or Facebook groups are gold mines to find out what your ideal customers are searching for, what they are struggling with, and where they're coming up short.

- **Beta sell:** A great way to see if there's demand for your product is…to try selling it! Keep it super simple, casual, and without all of the bells and whistles. Those can come later. For now, if people already ask you about what you offer or you're finding yourself in a lot of conversations that would lend themselves well to selling your product, create it! We'll talk in more detail about beta testing later in this chapter and how to best go about it.

- **Competition:** Are there already other people out there doing what you want to do? We talked about this earlier, but, again, don't be scared if there are! That's proof of concept. Now the question is whether the market share is large enough to accommodate more competition. In the online space, the answer is often yes because, as we discussed, there are also more clients looking for help online as these options become available to more people. Depending on the industry you're in, there are some niches that lend themselves to always being relevant, like legal, food, fitness, money, and career. But even if there's room for you and your offer, you should still want to make it unique and different to stand out.

One of the ways a million-dollar product idea might come to you after some experience in business is that you'll begin to notice trends. Jaime Mass, a registered dietitian (RD) who became a business coach for other dietitians (and dietitians-to-be), teaches her students how to create their own online nutrition practices and businesses. After working dietitian jobs herself, she left her nine-to-five and started her own online nutrition practice. Similarly to what happened to me when I started my health coaching business, eventually Jaime's RD colleagues sought her advice on starting their own practices. Jaime loved helping her colleagues avoid some of the same mistakes she made early on in her practice. In late 2018, Jaime shut down her own nutrition practice and officially pivoted to helping other dietitians learn how to start their own practices full-time. Over the years, she has offered different styles of programs and coaching packages to hundreds of her clients. But it was through her own nine-to-five nutrition practice, and working with several other dietitians online, that Jaime noticed so many trends in what was missing for dietitians to become successful online. Combining all of that experience, Jaime created various programs with the different resources, levels of support, and training her current and future clients needed. Now, because her clients actually experience incredible results, get premium customer service (we'll talk about that later!), and consistently refer their peers to her, she's one of the go-to dietitian business coaches in the online space. Jaime is a prime example of a successful online business owner who combined all of the key factors we'll discuss in this chapter. Be careful if you ever run into one of her clients—they won't stop talking about how much they love her.

Last but certainly not least, a survey is one of the best research tools you can use to gauge demand. Surveys are an easy way to get honest feedback from potential (or current) customers to see what they are really struggling with, what they wish they could find, and what they feel is getting in their way of breaking through or having success in this area. Instead of using your own language to talk about a product you've created, it's better to use your respondents' exact language, concerns, and questions. This is especially important if you, like me, haven't experienced the "pain point" or problem that your ideal customer has. For me, I've never started a business and not been an attorney. But all of my customers have. Therefore, it's crucial that I pay close attention to their language, the way they phrase things, and their specific self-identified pain points—not the way I'd put things or what I think they should be worried about.

Besides posting links to your survey on your content platform, like YouTube, Pinterest, or podcast, consider sending it directly to

- current customers, if you have them;
- email list subscribers;
- social media followers;
- friends or family members who fit the ideal client profile (if you feel that they will be honest and are actually a good fit); and
- online communities filled with your ideal customers, like Facebook groups, Quora threads, or Reddit communities.

Through your survey results, you want to get a clear picture of what your ideal client is both struggling with and looking for.

Your goal is to figure out how your product would help them solve whatever problems they are having. Here are some examples of survey questions you could ask:

- What frustrations or challenges are you currently facing when it comes to [your topic]?
- What isn't working for you right now when it comes to [your topic]?
- Why is that? What's getting in your way?
- What do you think would help you move past it?
- Imagine if I solved [the problem you help people solve] for you today. What would your life be like instead? What would having this problem solved do for you? What would it allow you to do, let go of, do more of, or do less of? Be thorough and descriptive.
- What would you like to learn about [your topic]?
- What would keep you from investing in a solution that would help you solve this problem?
- If a solution to this problem existed, what would it have to include?

The answers to these questions will give you an idea of not only what your customers are struggling with, but what they're looking for, too. As I mentioned, sometimes it's a good idea to actually create a product based on these responses (and the other research you've done) so you can ensure the product will be in high demand (versus something you personally want to create or think they should want). If nothing else, your survey responses will offer loads of helpful voice-of-customer data for you to use when writing copy for your website, social media posts, or email marketing. If you're able to, schedule Zoom meetings or phone calls with a handful of the respondents whose responses stick out to you. Go deeper and ask them follow-up questions. They may become your first beta testers down the line! Bonus tip: Ask their permission to record your meeting so you can hand it off to a copywriter.

Supply and Unique Differentiators

As important as it is to find demand for your $1 million product, it's equally important to ensure there's not too much supply of that product already. As we talked about when it comes to "supply" research for your overall niche or business idea, a little supply isn't a bad thing. It could mean there's actually demand for what you want to do. Existing supply can also serve as proof of concept— meaning people have already shown they're willing to purchase what you have to offer.

But if you want to sell a product that other people already sell, what reason will you give consumers to purchase *your* product instead of the ones already available to them? Is your product different or better in some way? Is there something about the current offers available to them that isn't resolving the problem they hoped the product would solve? That's where your product can come in.

For example, when the online graphic design tool company Canva launched in 2012, there were plenty of other graphic design apps and software available for people to use. But Canva entered the already busy graphic design market to resolve users' biggest complaint about those other tools: They were difficult to use and expensive. Although considered the "gold standard" for design, tools like Adobe's Photoshop were thought to be prohibitively difficult for newbies to use. Canva allowed inexperienced entrepreneurs and everyday people to design their own digital assets—for way less (or many times, free) than the competition. Not only did Canva remove the complexity and cost as barriers to entry, but they created such a helpful tool that they gained raving fans who spread the word about Canva like wildfire, too. As of

2023, Canva's total annual revenue has exceeded $2 billion USD. Given Canva's recent entry into AI-generated copy and design, I imagine people's reliance on, and use of, Canva as a design tool will only increase from here.

Using Canva's story as an inspiring example, ask yourself:

If my product already exists in a similar form in the world—how is my product going to be different? What do the existing products not do that mine does? Why is that helpful? What do people find frustrating about the existing product? What about the existing product stands in the way of offering a solution to customers?

Focusing on your unique differentiators—the factors, features, or ideas that make you stand out from the other companies doing what you do—is crucial to overcoming a "supply" issue. Your product might introduce a new feature or benefit that consumers didn't know they wanted. Or it might solve your product niche's biggest problem and customers' biggest pain points. Either way, utilizing the various stages of customer awareness outlined by copywriter Eugene Schwartz in his book *Breakthrough Advertising*, your job is to

- educate the customer who's unaware the problem exists;
- speak directly to the customer who knows the problem exists, but doesn't yet know there is a solution out there to resolve it; and/or
- get the attention of the customer who knows the problem exists, knows there are solutions out there, but is deciding right now which product they would like to buy; and
- convince the customer who knows the problem exists and even knows that you and your product exist that they should actually buy it.

Here's a familiar example: Take a walk down a city block and you will see plenty of people lugging 40-ounce, $60 reusable water bottles around like some sort of cool water club status symbol. So, when the water bottle company LARQ launched their LARQ Bottle PureVis™, they focused on educating consumers about a problem unknown to bottle loving consumers: how dirty and gross your water bottle gets inside. With new information in hand, these consumers were now stuck with a new pain point: *How were they going to clean their giant, hard-to-clean water bottles as often as they needed to, to avoid the bacteria they now knew about?* Easy. Enter: LARQ Bottle PureVis™, a self-cleaning bottle. For the unaware consumer, this entire campaign would be news to them. For the problem-aware consumer, we got their attention with a solution. And for the solution-aware buyer, we've introduced a product. Not only did they solve a problem most weren't even aware of (potentially) and introduced a solution (LARQ Bottle PureVis™), but they also resolved a common problem among nearly all customers in any industry: time. Who has time to clean their water bottle every night? And now we know about all of these disgusting germs?! Gross. LARQ's bottle seems more and more valuable. We'll discuss customer awareness as a marketing strategy further in chapter 8.

Pain Points and Desires

As you conduct your demand, supply, and unique differentiator research and surveying, it's important to take note of all the pain points and desires your customer has along the way. Pain points are the things that aren't working for your ideal customer right now. They might be things that aren't going well or a hurdle or problem they're bumping up against. I like to think of our customers' pain points as:

- the things they toss and turn about at night—what's keeping them awake?;
- the very specific moments in their day where they run up against this problem (and how it presents itself);
- the thoughts, fears, and feelings they have in their head, some of which they might be too fearful to share or discuss; and
- the "Oh my goodness, you too?!" moments you share with a friend—the stuff you think that only you think or feel, but that once you share with a friend you realize you're not alone (or crazy!).

At the same time, you also want to know what your ideal customers' desires are—what do they wish things were like instead? To get some good responses, you can ask your ideal client:

- In your dream world or ideal situation, how would life/business/family, and so on be different?
- What would be possible for you if things were this way instead of how they are now? What types of things could you do or focus on instead?

At the end of the day, people purchase products because they help them solve a problem (avoid pain), bring them closer to their desired result (gain pleasure), or some combination of the two. Taking the time to truly understand your ideal customers' pain points and desires will yield dividends many times over. If you don't know what your ideal customers struggle with, you won't be able to speak directly to them (which is necessary to make them feel seen, heard, and understood) in your copy and marketing. You also won't be able to create products that fully resolve their problems or bring them closer to their desired outcomes. No matter how successful you are already, or how many years you are into your business, I encourage you to continually revisit these principles and engage with your customers. You always want to know what they're struggling with, what they want instead, and to meet them where they are.

Transformation

Last, but certainly not least, I want you to begin to paint the picture of the transformation you create, or what you provide the opportunity for, for your ideal customers. What does the "before" and "after" for your clients look like? For some, this transformation might be more visual and apparent on the surface, like a *Queer Eye*–style makeover. But for others, the ideal customer's "transformation" is more of a shift in energy, anxiety level, and confidence. If you sell products, you may be able to tell a visual story of a "before-and-after" type impact your product has had on a customer's life.

In your research phase, you want to begin to formulate what you think this transformation will look, feel, and sound like for your customers. As you read further through this chapter and the book, you will begin to actually see the transformation happen in real time. Not only are these transformative moments gold nuggets for your marketing, they are also a real sign of product efficacy and success. The ultimate key to a $1 million product is that it actually works and creates replicable results for others.

If you are creating a new product within your existing business, you can utilize the transformational experiences and testimonials you have received already to create a product that works for others, too. Spend time interviewing your customers to really get to know why this transformation has been so positive and important to them. Ask them:

- What has it allowed you to do that you couldn't do before? Why does that matter?
- Why did you believe it wasn't possible for you to achieve this transformation (if you did) and what about my product or service actually allowed you to achieve it instead?

Just like keeping up with your customers' pain points and desires on a rolling basis, knowing the transformational experiences of your customers is equally as important.

During this phase, it's important to keep an open mind and see what the market really demands. Through learning your ideal customers' pain points, desires, and potential transformations, you will be able to speak more and more of their "language" and less of what is in your heart and mind. A good $1 million product solves others' problems, not just yours.

PHASE #2: "LET'S JUST GET IT OUT"

When launching a business or a new product, there's a tendency to want to have everything perfect before it goes out to the world. When I started my podcast *On Your Terms®* in 2021, I couldn't wait to hit "publish." A podcast had long been on my marketing mind, but I had been too busy building my business to actually start one. When you enter the podcasting world—similar to the YouTube world or TikTok world or really any other marketing medium—it's tempting to want to do everything at once. *Should I learn how to mix audio? And edit the podcast myself? What about the equipment—do I need an incredible mic, and my own editing software? Should I learn more about how to title the show, turn it into YouTube videos, and write my own show notes before I go live?*

At nearly every turn when I started, it seemed there were a million new things I could learn. One of the downsides to really loving what you do is that it all seems fun to learn! But it's not exactly good for your business to be so tied up in a podcast, or a product, that hasn't even proved itself as a concept yet.

That's when I remembered the same mantra I'd applied many times over to launching nearly anything in my business: "Let's just get it out, and we'll go from there." Did I sloppily approach launching my podcast without a hope, care, or loose plan in place? Absolutely not! But luckily, I didn't wait for everything to be perfect or to learn all of the things before launching either. I had a title, invested in a designer for some attractive cover art, and had my editing team lined up. In terms of figuring out how to actually research, plan, structure and market a podcast episode…well, that took time. And a lot of practice. Honestly, more than 230 episodes later, I'm still figuring it out. But my "product" has improved and performed better over time. And as it has, I've optimized it and poured more resources into it, too. Let's apply this "Let's just get it out" approach to your product, shall we?

Minimum Viable Product

Ditching the all-or-nothing mindset is crucial to your overall business success, let alone your product's success. While it's possible to either research our potential product's viability to death or just wing it and throw spaghetti at the wall, the right approach is actually somewhere in between. Yes, we need to do the research we just talked about in phase #1, but we also need to push our digital product baby out of the nest at some point, too.

The minimum viable product (MVP) theory is essentially the grown-up version of my "Let's just get it out" approach. The idea behind MVP is to get a basic version of your product into the market quickly, instead of spending and possibly wasting lots of time, money, and energy to make it look pretty or create every feature before you even know if it's viable. In order to MVP-test your product, you would release your product to a small group of buyers. Doing so will reveal three things:

1. If people will purchase your product—whether it's in demand, if the copy speaks to them, your messaging is clear, and your pricing is within the right range.
2. How they like using your product—you can use their feedback to improve upon or create new features or improve the back-end experience in the future.
3. Whether it works/delivers on the promised results— which is what tells you whether your product will continue to sell and build momentum, and also gives you the marketing verbiage you need to create hype and demand for it moving forward.

So as you prepare your product for beta testing, keep MVP in mind. You don't need the fanciest design or software at this point. You need to build the product just enough—in other words, what's minimally viable—to test selling it. In order to do this without seed money or lots of start-up funding, we turn to beta testing.

Beta Testing

MVP is a theory or idea of how far to build a potential product before taking the action of beta testing in the field. When I first created the Ultimate Bundle®, I had an idea of what I thought the product should look like and include. But after putting the MVP theory into practice, I beta tested the product to a small subset of my email list before I put too much time, money, or effort into designing and building it out further. I knew it was a careful balance between investing too much time in an unknown product versus investing just enough time to get it off the ground for beta testing. Ultimately, my final product ended up looking very different (for reasons I explained earlier) than what I had created at the outset. Although I sustained a little bruise to my ego, the product ultimately ended up being much more successful because of the feedback I received from my beta test launch.

There are many ways to beta test your product. You could

- promote it on social media, letting your audience know what your product is, how it will help them, and the result you're hoping to help them achieve;
- send an email newsletter to your list, letting them know the same thing; or
- personally reach out and contact however many beta testers you're looking for.

There's really no right or wrong way to beta test your product, but there are a few things you can do to get the most juice for your squeeze. One of the biggest, most impactful, factors to running a helpful beta test is to make sure you target your ideal customer. Getting your friend or a colleague from work to "buy" or test your product for free may or may not yield the most helpful feedback if that person is not the type of buyer you're hoping to attract. You also want to know that your ideal customer is willing to pay something for this product.

When beta testing your product using one of the strategies or promotional tools listed above, cap the number of beta testers at a reasonable amount. You can also restrict how long beta testers have to sign up for it and advertise it as a "one time only" opportunity (if it is). For one, you'll create urgency among those to whom you advertise your product. If there are only ten slots available, for example, that will motivate potential beta testers to take action versus allowing an unlimited number of people to test it out. And if you tell them they only have until Friday to get in on this deal, they can't mull it over for six months. Remember, you're just looking to get people to use your product and report their results so you can optimize and improve. You want to beta test your product to enough people to actually get a sample size of data, but not to so many people that you're overwhelmed or can't make sense of all the feedback. When I beta launched the Ultimate Bundle®, I sold it to fifteen people at a significantly reduced price in exchange for their feedback, which brings me to my last beta testing tip.

The benefit to your beta customer is that they get to beta test your product at a discount in exchange for their participation in helping you to make this product better and offering feedback. You can ask for all different types of feedback. I have asked beta testers to offer a video testimonial at the end of their product use, hop on a video call with me to talk through their experience, or provide me with a written testimonial. I would also recommend, regardless of which type of feedback you select, sending out regular surveys (or at least a final survey) to collect data from beta participants in a more systematic way. Between a won't-see-this-again discount, expiring access, and a limited number of slots available, you should be able to create enough urgency to get your desired number of beta testers to take action.

A final suggestion here: When you beta test your product is also a great time to practice your customer onboarding process. Set up your contract and checkout software so that when your beta testers purchase your product (at a reduced rate) you can also iron out any details with your systems and tools.

When someone purchases your program or product, do they receive confirmation emails? If you sell a digital product, is it delivered smoothly? Can customers access it easily? If you sell a physical product, is everything triggered for your receipt, shipping notification, and eventual shipping to go off smoothly? Did your return process work? These are all things to test out now so that when your sales volume increases later on, you're able to handle the influx.

Since beta testers get the discounted product in exchange for offering their feedback, make sure you add a provision to your contract about exactly what you expect in exchange. Be specific about what kind of feedback or participation you're looking for: Do they need to do a sixty-minute Zoom call with you at the end? Complete a Google form each week? Provide you with a one-minute video testimonial? When is their feedback due? No detail should be left to chance.

Customer Interviews

Whether you want to launch a new product or you have an existing one you would like to improve, customer interviews are crucial to growing your $1 million product. My company conducts customer interviews a few times per year, even for products I have sold for many years.

One to two times per year, reach out to your customers and ask for five to ten volunteers to participate in an interview with you (or a member of your team or your copywriter, if you have one). The purpose of customer interviews is to get to know your customer and their "customer journey"—basically, what their life was like before they found you, once they found you, and now. You want to learn as much as you can about the aspects we discussed earlier in this chapter:

- What their pain points were/are
- What their desired outcomes were
- How they found your product
- What your product did for them or how it resolved their pain points

- What specific aspects of your teaching, or your product's features, helped them to resolve their pain points
- What they are able to do (or not do) now versus before working with you and purchasing your product

Record your calls or video chats (with their permission, of course) so you can review them as needed. You can also provide the recordings to your copywriter so they can really get to know your customers, their pain points, and their desired outcomes. The best copywriters will even integrate and use your customers' exact language in their copy. I pay special attention to patterns I see and hear in my customers' pain points, desires, and results. Those are the phrases and experiences I use most often to create content and write my emails. The more you rely on your existing customers' words to market to potential customers, the more those potential customers will "see themselves" in your marketing—and feel like your product is made for them. Hello, new customers.

Results

Last but not least, as you test your product either in a beta launch or through normal means of selling it, pay attention to the results people get. Are they getting the results you alluded to in your marketing? Are they seeing any unexpected results? Here are some key questions to explore as you analyze results:

- What tangible data can I use to advertise to future customers (e.g., "More than 55 percent of my students gained at least 500 subscribers within 30 days of completing my email list building course!")?
- What did your customers say your product helped them with specifically to achieve that result (e.g.,

"After watching Sam's training on how to write better sales page copy and implementing her tips, my sales increased by 12 percent!")?

- What are your customers saying about how the product has made them feel, compared to when they started (e.g., "After taking Sam's course, I can finally breathe a sigh of relief knowing I'm legally protected!")?

- What are your customers able to do now that they could not do before they got your product? In other words, what problems has your product solved and what possibilities has it opened up for them?

Get Organized

This is a good time to create an organized system to collect testimonials from your customers. You could use many of my question prompts above to create a survey using programs like Google Forms or TypeForm so their answers stay organized. Be sure to ask for permission to share their words, feedback, and photograph or video, if you collect one. That way, you won't have to reach out later to ask for permission. Last but not least, ask them to upload a photo headshot as part of their survey so you can use it to create great testimonial content.

PHASE #3: THE OLIVE GARDEN EFFECT

I belong to the best gym in the world. From the warm greeting I get each morning, to the card I received from the entire staff after my mom died last year, I feel a little silly saying it, but my gym makes me feel like I matter. I'm not just "another member" or a number to them; I'm part of their lovely community that truly cares about one another. It's not only made me stay a member for three-plus years now (and go to the gym consistently five or more times per week, for the first time in my life), but it's made me tell everyone I know to go there, too. Every time I'm at the gym, I see people I've referred there and think, "*This*. This is how it works. You create something really good that people love, and they naturally want to tell other people about it." Let's walk through how my gym puts this into practice as an example, and then chat about how you can adapt this strategy for your business.

My gym provides a great service and creates a great environment → which makes me a really happy customer → which makes me go to the gym consistently → which gives me better results → which makes other people ask me, "What's this gym you go to that you can't stop talking about? And how did you get those triceps?!" → which leads me to referring them to the gym → And then they become happy members and refer their own friends and family. The cycle continues.

Treating your customers like they're the most special part of your business community is crucial to long-term business success. It is so easy to get trapped in a cycle of thinking about how to get new or more clients. But in my experience, nurturing the heck out of your current customers is a strategy that reaps a higher return on investment that will ultimately lead to less work on your part, too. There are two reasons it's a great idea to invest your time and energy into making your customers happy, repeat, referral-makers.

One, it takes a lot of work to get someone to the point where they feel comfortable and confident enough to purchase your product from you. And research shows that once someone becomes a customer, it's easier, and cheaper, to get them to purchase from you again (customer retention) than it is to acquire a new customer. This is especially important if you sell recurring revenue items—like a monthly membership or service fee—because you essentially have to work each month (or payment cycle) to get them to say yes again.

Two, happy customers refer and attract new customers. If your customers have a great experience, it's only natural they will share it with others. And if they experience great results, people will ask them how they got those results, and your customer will refer them to you (e.g., me and my gym). This is exactly why I've spent so much time discussing building out a product after truly getting to know your customers' problems (and desires), and focusing on getting them great results. A product that gives people results is fine—but if it's not marketed directly to the people who need it most (or not designed to solve the problems they see as most important) in their own language—it might never get discovered.

The easiest way to create happy customers is to create a great product that works. If you give someone more time, energy, and happiness or ease their stress, confusion, or heartache, they will love you (and your product). But in order to optimize their experience and maximize the chances your customer will achieve the results your product offers, there are a lot of things you can do on the user experience end to help facilitate that.

After you're out of the MVP and beta testing phases, you can invest more into your product to make it easier to use, have fancier features, nicer to look at, and simpler to complete or digest. I've found the following factors to be most crucial to a customer's enjoyment of a product:

- **Ease of use.** Try to streamline people's initial access to your product, your onboarding process, and any instructions. I recently purchased a podcast growth membership from Jeremy Enns that allowed me to access only the first module of the membership on Day 1. Jeremy said he aims to help you complete one step at a time, and he doesn't want you to feel overwhelmed by the entirety of the membership on the first day. He gave me one simple task upon signing in, and once that was completed, I was able to gain access to the next module and task. What a great way to ease my way in! And very organized, too.

- If you sell an online course, digital product, or service, for example, you can add a "welcome" video that lays out your customers' first steps once they purchase. You can also use the same email marketing software you used to set up your email broadcasts and sequences to create a new customer onboarding sequence. In it, you can drip out emails at whatever interval would be best for your customer to help keep them on track. I have found that offering customers some sort of sample schedule or "to-do list" is helpful for when they first purchase and might feel overwhelmed. It helps to ease buyer's remorse, too.

- **Completion rate.** People like to feel that they've completed something, and they will obviously get better results if they do. It's really important for you to focus on doing whatever you can, design- and content-wise, to get your customers to complete your course or use your product. Think about how many times you've canceled a gym membership because you weren't using it. What are some things you can do to get them to use your product more often? You want your product to become a valuable part of your customers' lives.

- **Customer support.** In today's world, people expect to have access to reliable customer service. Create a support or help email address for your company, and make sure it is posted in several places for your customers to easily find. You can also create an FAQ section on your website or inside your digital product to answer questions that come up most often.

- **Dependability.** I like to underpromise and overdeliver. The fastest way to lose a customer's trust is to promise more than what you can actually deliver, or to not be available consistently. With digital products, people often offer live calls or a certain level of support that they can't keep up with long term. Make sure you're clear about what you're offering and how long it will reliably be available.

- **Cost per use.** One of the things people love most about my products is that they're reusable. This makes the cost feel worth it! It's like your favorite pair of jeans. They might have felt a little too expensive at first—but when you factor in how often you wear them, the cost per wear makes the spend worthwhile. Do what you can to make your product one your customers come back to and use often, so they are continually reminded of how valuable and worthwhile your product is.

- **Feedback.** How will you know how to improve your product if you never hear from the people using it? Build surveys into your product in order to get regular feedback from customers. You can include a survey with the delivery of your product, send a survey out a certain number of days or weeks after the purchase, or send out a survey at some regular interval (e.g., two times per year to all customers) to get feedback. I include a link to a survey inside my digital product. I also include a link to submit a feature request or recommendation, which we track and regularly integrate and use to improve the user experience. People love knowing they have an opportunity to participate in making something better, too.

DO WHAT YOU CAN AND LET THE REST GO

There needs to be a careful balance between taking really good care of your customers and not making yourself too responsible for their happiness or results, giving too much to current customers to the detriment of your bottom line, and focusing too much on retention over acquisition, or vice versa. I want to help you navigate this delicate balance and avoid the common "happy customers" pitfalls. Let's start with the most common and delicate thing to balance—wanting your customers to be happy, but not being able to control how other people feel or how they implement your product.

The Happy Trap

As much as I'm here to encourage you to take really good care of your customers and focus on their happiness, I also want to be careful to tell you that at the same time...

You are not responsible for their happiness.

As my mindset coach, Jennifer Diaz, once told me, "You are responsible *to* people, not *for* them." As an ever-recovering people pleaser and part-time perfectionist, it was easy for me to become obsessed with wanting to make sure people liked me, my business, and my products. If someone was unhappy, I thought it was my job to make them feel better. But over the years I've learned that even if I jump through every hoop, and make every accommodation, someone will still be unhappy. And that does not necessarily mean I did something wrong.

Of course you want the majority of your customers to be satisfied with the product and experience. However, the goal here isn't for everyone to be happy with you, love your product, or sing your praises from the rooftops. You cannot control how someone experiences your product because you cannot control how someone uses or implements it. And as a general life rule, we cannot control other people or how they feel. Period.

Once, a prospective customer contacted me to ask if I would guarantee her satisfaction, ahead of time, before she purchased a product from me. She explained how she had recently paid a business coach a lot of money and left the experience sorely disappointed with her results. She felt the coaching package was an epic failure because she did not get the results she maintained were promised to her. Old me would have responded to tell her, "Yes! My product is amazing! I have thousands of very happy customers, so I'm sure you will love it, too!" But I didn't because I know now what I didn't then: I am not responsible for her happiness or her results. If you've ever waited in line for a Starbucks order, you know that you can't make everyone happy all of the time. All I can do is create a great product, not make overly dramatic, unrealistic, or fraudulent promises about results, and do what I said I would do. After that, there are a lot of factors at play. *Will you show up and do the work? Will you implement it in the way I suggested? Will you be consistent and take responsibility for your own actions and part in this? Are you the kind of person who asks for their latte extra hot, only to send it back for being too hot?*

Your customer is ultimately responsible for how well they do. You should stand by your product all day long. But you're not responsible for—nor can you control—how satisfied people are. You're responsible only for providing the product and experience you promised. *What if someone purchases your product and never opens it? What if they don't follow your directions at all?* That's not a knock against your product. And it's not your fault if it doesn't work for them, either. The reverse is also true. If your customer achieves incredible results using your product, that is not entirely because of you. It's because of the hard work they put in! It was also their (smart) decision to invest in a product that would help them get closer to their goals. This is a crucial takeaway if you want to healthfully separate from your business (which we'll talk about later on) and survive in the long haul of business ownership.

She's (Over)Giving

As you set out to create your $1 million product, you might worry about what to charge for it. Many entrepreneurs struggle with feeling that their product is worth what they charge—especially when they sell high-ticket products and services. As a result, entrepreneurs will give endlessly to current customers. Instead of charging for upgrades or new content, some throw everything in at no additional charge. At times that comes from a deeper internal worry that what we have already created is not enough. If we don't truly believe our product is worth what we charge for it, we may find ourselves giving more, all in the name of hoping that will make it "worth it."

What has made the most difference for me in the giving department (which I'm still guilty of overdoing) is working on stepping into my worth, value, and time. After you sell some of your product, and especially as you start to see the impact it makes on people, you need to practice taking that all in as a sign of its value. People are paying for your product and getting results. That's all the proof you need.

Overgiving to your customers might be hurting your bottom line, too. You can generate a lot of new product ideas, and therefore revenue, from your current customers' needs. Instead of giving the new product to them for free, though, consider offering it to them with a loyalty discount or some other bonus. Remember: Lean into customer retention ideology. These are your people—your Olive Garden family. Don't know what they want? Try surveying them to find out! Or better yet, ask them in one of your voice-of-customer interviews.

Acquisition Versus Retention Balance

Although it's cheaper to retain a current customer than to attain a new one, I like to take more of a "both" approach rather than an "either/or." Yes, you should take good care of your customers and learn what else they need or want from you in order to retain them. At the same time, your business needs to have new leads coming in (otherwise known as lead generation) and additions being made to your email list steadily and consistently. If you only focus on your current customers, you're missing out on broadening your customer pool. And if you only focus on acquiring new customers, you're missing out on relatively easier, cheaper ways of generating revenue with your current customers. We'll talk about lead generation and email/social media marketing in our next chapter.

WHAT WE LEARNED

- How to properly research your product's viability, demand, and supply so you are able to create a product that people actually want to buy and that works.
- Leaning in to your and your product's unique differentiators can help you stand out among a crowded product field.
- By focusing on creating a minimum viable product (MVP) and getting it out there, you can more quickly beta test your product, get customer feedback, and integrate that feedback for a better product and customer experience.
- Focus on creating a product that delivers good results to your customers, and thus a good experience with the

product itself, so you have customer testimonials to use as social proof to boost additional, new customer sales.

WHAT'S TO COME

- You'll learn an organized marketing ecosystem method to attract, nurture, convert, and celebrate customers so you have consistent leads pouring into your business at all times.

CHAPTER 8

Creating Your $1 Million Product Marketing Ecosystem

As a kid, I'd sometimes fake being sick so I could stay home from school and watch *Law & Order* reruns. I have to be honest: *Law & Order* wasn't the only reason I wanted to skip school. I was addicted to *The Price Is Right*, too.

My seven-year-old self couldn't get enough of the custom T-shirts, product placements, or Bob Barker's skinny little microphone. I especially loved the game Plinko. In case you don't remember (or weren't addicted to the show like I was), Plinko is a game where contestants drop a flat disc, called a Plinko chip, into the top of an upright wooden board filled with pins set in a triangular shape. As the player dropped the Plinko chip at the top of the board, it would bounce and bop its way between and through the pins, taking a random path before it made its way to the bottom of the board.

Unfortunately, most entrepreneurs build their marketing system more like a game of Plinko and less like the organized, intentional flywheel it should be. You could drop a hundred Plinko chips at the top of the board and never be able to predict where they would end up. Even if you dropped a chip into the same slot at the top, it wouldn't always end up in the same spot at the bottom. That sort of unpredictability and chaos won't work for your business or marketing system.

I'm assuming you've picked up this book because you have one goal: to grow your business. In order for it to grow, you have to do two things: grow your audience and make more sales. In order for you to sell more of the product you researched, built, and beta tested in the last chapter, you need to have a consistent flow of qualified leads—potential customers—coming into your business at all times. Leads can opt in to your email list, follow you on social media, listen to your podcast, or subscribe to your YouTube channel. More than anything, you need to attract the *right* leads and get them added to your business's orbit in order to nurture them enough to want and be ready to buy from you.

In this chapter, you will learn how to create an intentional, methodical marketing ecosystem—a flywheel, as it's sometimes referred to—that attracts qualified leads, nurtures them, and converts them to happy, results-seeing, referral-giving customers. Like an actual flywheel, the more traction you gain over time, the more energy gets stored, and the more self-propelling your flywheel will become.

Before we get into the first step of your marketing ecosystem—the attract phase—I want to note how a traditional marketing funnel treats customers like the "end of the road." For example:

ATTRACT LEADS → SELL TO THEM → THEY BECOME
CUSTOMERS → GO OUT AND GET MORE LEADS →
START THE PROCESS ALL OVER AGAIN

When it comes to marketing your business and getting *more* sales, the way you treat your current and former customers is just as important as what you do to attract new ones. By taking really good care of your current and former customers, you won't have to rely on an entirely fresh batch of new customers that you had to go out and find on your own. Over time, you will rack up more and more customers. They will become fans of you and your product—"foot soldiers," as I like to call them—and start marketing for you. Plus, if you ever have a time in your business where you can't be as forward-facing or marketing-driven as you would like to be (you had a baby, are sick, become a caretaker, want to take an extended trip or vacation, etc.), this will be one of the strategies you can rely upon to continue to bring new leads into your business.

But just because you focus intensely on your current and past customers does not mean you do not need to simultaneously attract new ones. Lead generation is a both/and thing, not and/or. In order to be successful in today's online business world, you have to attract and retain customers, work on getting them to be repeat buyers, and simultaneously seek out new leads—all at the same time. In this chapter, we'll explore how to strategically strike that balance through the attract, nurture, convert, and family phases of your marketing flywheel. Let's jump in.

ATTRACT

In this phase, your goal is to attract new qualified leads to your business. You're not interested in just any ol' leads. You're after the people who, generally speaking, fit the profile of the person who wants or needs to work with you—someone who could end up becoming a customer. In other words, people who have the pain points, problems, questions, concerns, hopes, and desires your business addresses. Although there are dozens of ways to generate leads for your business, I'm going to focus on the top four, and dedicate the entire next chapter to one of them (content). Ultimately, no matter how you initially attract leads to your business, do what you can to get those leads onto your email list. We will discuss several strategies throughout this chapter and the next.

Freebies

Freebies, as we discussed in chapter 6, are free downloadable resources people are required to opt in to access. Freebies are a great attraction tool and email list builder. If you make your freebies valuable (those "no-brainer" freebies we discussed), your freebies will consistently attract new leads. Your freebie may be the thing that attracts a person to your business in the first place, or it might move someone from following you on social media to taking the next step and getting on your email list.

To me, freebies are the epicenter of any lead generation strategy. Even if I'm creating content for social media or in digital ads to attract leads, my ultimate goal is to drive people to my email list. Once the new leads are on my email list, my job is to nurture them—which we'll discuss in the next section.

Social Media and Content Platforms

It probably comes as no surprise that one of the best places to get leads for your online business is…online! Where do your potential customers hang out? Sure, they might be at your gym, in your dance class, or sipping lattes at your local coffee shop. But you can reach way more people, in a more targeted, time-efficient way, online through social media and other content platforms like YouTube or podcasts.

In the beginning, I recommend picking one social media platform and starting to experiment there. At the time of this writing, the primary platforms are Facebook, Instagram, TikTok,

X (formerly Twitter), Threads, Pinterest, YouTube, Substack, and LinkedIn (whether some of these platforms qualify as social media or something broader is something we will discuss in the next chapter). Your first goal is to learn the ropes of the platform. What kind of content do you see performing well there? What do you like consuming there? What is it about that content you enjoy? Practice creating content for your ideal customer. Turn the focus away from yourself and your journey to speaking directly to them and the journey you believe they're on.

By focusing on one platform and learning how to create content specifically *for* that platform, you can start to gain traction there—this is better than trying to use multiple platforms at once; it's important to master one before moving on to others. Plus, most social media platforms reward creators who keep that platform's features and consumption goals in mind. And not all platforms or their content are the same—an Instagram Reel (a one-to-ninety-second video clip) won't necessarily perform well on TikTok, where people also post similar types of videos. The way people consume content on TikTok and why they spend time there versus other platforms is very unique to TikTok.

Since the purpose of posting content for your business on social media is to attract qualified new leads, you'll also want to consider what phase of the buying process they might be in. Perhaps they are already aware of their problem, but don't know a solution exists for it. They may be aware of the solution to a problem they're experiencing, but not know you or your solution-driven product exist. Or they may not be quite sure what their specific problem is, but coming across you and your business on social media might be the thing that helps them identify it.

The time between someone becoming a lead and becoming a customer will lengthen depending on where your lead is at on the awareness scale. The more problem- and solution-aware they are, the sooner they may be ready to buy. If they're totally unaware of their problem, your content can carry them along the awareness journey and nurture them until they are ready to purchase.

Most social media content does not consider a lead's awareness level. In fact, most content assumes the person consuming your information has way more knowledge than they actually do about you, your product, and even your area of expertise. I routinely hear entrepreneurs use acronyms to describe their product (*I'm completely unaware of who you are, what you do, and why I should trust you yet—how will I know what you're talking about when you refer to your "UB" program without explaining it?*), or talk more about what they have for dinner each night (guilty as charged!) than what they sell or do for a living. At any time, someone can stumble across your social media pages wondering if you're the solution to their problems. Make sure you have content available to them that at least provides some clues.

Years ago, my social media mentor, Natasha Samuel, taught me about content pillars. Your content pillars are the categories you'll focus on when creating content for social media. You might have pillars that are educational, consist of testimonials and social proof, feature user-generated content, give behind-the-scenes information, or are entertainment-based. Your pillars keep you organized, intentional, and on-theme to hit many of the different touch points that are necessary for someone to go from lead to customer. If you ever feel that you don't know what to post on social media or that you're not getting traction from what you post now, it might be a good time to hash out a content-pillar strategy. With this type of intentional strategy, you will become known for what you do online.

Ideally, you would have three to five content pillars and post at least one piece of content from each pillar every week. In order to create your content pillars, think about the broader categories or topics you teach and that relate to your products. You want your pillars to be broad enough to post a variety of content, while also being focused enough to relate to your core business values and topics. As my business has evolved over the years, so have my pillars. You can easily mix up the type of content (like video, B-roll with text overlay, static post, carousel, long-form video, voice-over, etc.) you create, as long as it falls into one of your content pillars.

Let's review an example of what content pillars might look like for a fitness coach with an online business:

- **Educational workout tips:** Sharing form cues, sample workouts, workout schedule (split) examples, and the like.
- **Fueling for performance:** Content about how to fuel for pre- and post-workout performance, self-care tips for better workouts, and so on.
- **Customer content:** Sharing stories, wins, and behind-the-scenes details of how your customers are implementing what you're teaching them to help your future customers see themselves in this content.
- **Hero content:** What I call "how you walk the walk" content, in which you show your audience how you personally implement all the things you teach. Show how you set your clothes out the night before, meal prep on Sundays, or plan your weekly workouts each Monday.
- **Personal:** Share your gardening hobby, books you're reading, travel adventures, examples of behind-the-scenes activities in running your business, family content, or something else that makes you unique and personable. Ideally, you'd bring it back to how each of these ultimately makes you a better athlete, coach,

and fueled-fitness pro. But overall these are personal touchpoints to create more connection with your audience.

In the next chapter, we will explore exactly how to create content on social media that builds a community and attracts, engages, nurtures, and converts them into customers. So, let's put a pin in social media for a moment, and shift to one of my favorite, most successful strategies to date: SEO.

Search Engine Optimization (SEO)

When it comes to social media, there is only so much you can do to ensure that people see the content you post. But there is a better way. There are people out there looking for you, or someone who offers what you do, at all times. Sure, you can go on social media and try your darndest to go viral (the chances of which rely primarily on luck), but why try so hard to win the lottery when you have a proven strategy sitting right in front of you?

Search engine optimization (SEO) can be applied across many different areas of your business—but the idea behind it is the same. By optimizing your content and website with proper keywords, good blog post titles, and optimized images, among other pieces, you will have a higher probability of landing in search results on your given topic.

Here are some examples of how you can optimize and integrate SEO across your entire business:

- **Your website:** SEO-ify your entire website, including all of the main and sub-pages, such as home, blog, about, et cetera. I did this myself in the beginning and then hired an SEO expert to further optimize my website once I had the budget.

- **Your blog posts:** To start, use tools like Keywords Everywhere and Answer the Public to discover what terms, phrases, and questions your ideal customers are searching for. Write ten blog posts for your website using those topics and keywords, ideally including a link to a freebie (an opt-in to your email list). Moving forward, post at least one SEO-optimized blog post per week, being sure to stick to your content topic area (Google loves consistency!) and write high-quality content (Google loves high quality!). Learning how to write blog posts for SEO is an entirely different skill than the general copywriting you will use elsewhere in your business. But it's a skill I highly recommend investing some time into learning. As you grow, this is a great thing to outsource. In my case, it was one of the easiest, most effective tools I implemented early on when I had very little budget.

- **Your social media posts:** Current platforms like Pinterest, Instagram, YouTube, and TikTok are highly productive search engines within their own right. You can utilize a lot of the same keyword strategies on those platforms to get discovered as you would for SEO blog posts, but instead of using the same tools, you utilize the platforms themselves. Each of those platforms has their own hashtags, search features, and ways of discovering what's popular or trending. Instead of driving yourself crazy trying to implement these strategies in all the places at once, pick one and dedicate yourself to learning it really well.

- **Content platforms:** If you have a YouTube channel, Substack, or a podcast, you can integrate SEO strategies into your content planning there, too. For my podcast, we research what keywords or phrases people search for on the topic my episode will be about. That keyword then becomes part of the episode title. We integrate those keywords several times throughout the show notes, which are then posted on my website blog. For YouTube, I use Keywords Everywhere and TubeBuddy in order to optimize my video titles. I also title the video file I upload, as well as the thumbnail image, using the keyword. For Substack, you can SEO-optimize your individual posts to try to show up in a Google search on your topic (this is a great tool if you don't have a website, and even if you do!). Again, if you have decided YouTube or a podcast is going to be *your thing*, I'd highly recommend investing time into learning how to utilize the tools those platforms offer that ultimately make your job easier.

Like any of the strategies we're discussing in this section, SEO is one part of a larger, overall integrative marketing plan. Think of SEO as the compounding interest you earn on a bank account. It's working even when you're not and keeps adding up, no matter how small those growth increments may be. Eight years later, I'm glad I invested so much time and energy into SEO. I see how it snowballed and gathered energy over the years—resulting in consistent leads flowing into my business.

Ads

Once you have a lead-generation system that works—utilizing the SEO and social media strategies we've discussed so far—it's time to turn up the heat. Once I consistently attracted new leads onto my email list using the organic marketing strategies discussed so far, and converted many of them to customers, I decided to invest in Facebook and Instagram ads. Hear me loud and clear: You want to have a well-functioning funnel set up before you invest in ads. Ads are not a way to cure a poorly converting funnel. When done right, ads will send more leads through your business than you could ever attract organically. It's like turning a faucet from a drip to full blast. Of course, not all of those leads will be the right fit or convert. But other than ads, there's no organic way to get in front of that many people so quickly.

Know this: You don't have to run Facebook ads to be successful. For one, there are lots of kinds of ads you can run (Google ads, Pinterest ads, print ads, newsletter ads, more targeted in-person opportunities like sponsoring a conference or retreat, etc.). My business was very successful for many years without them. However, once I had built a well-functioning sales funnel, ads made my life easier. Running ads allowed me to pull back from social media a bit, which I think we can all agree isn't the healthiest place to spend the majority of our time. I could create less organic content (I'm a content machine, what can I say!), which allowed me to focus on bigger-picture goals in my business.

I didn't invest in ads until two to three years into my business. You shouldn't run ads until you have the capital to afford to do so as an experiment. If investing in ads will put you in a difficult financial position, it's not time yet. If you can afford to invest as an experiment to see how they go—and stick to running ads for several months to allow them to gain traction—then it may be a good idea. When considering ads, remember to budget for both the ad spend (it's like the amount you "feed the meter," except in this case the meter is Facebook, Google, or wherever you choose to advertise) and ad management fees if you hire an ad agency to run them for you (which I highly recommend—ads are complicated and can become very expensive if mismanaged!).

Though we now have our attraction methods in place—freebies, content, SEO, and ads—our job doesn't stop there. We need to keep engaging with, and nurturing, those leads to help them continue on their path to becoming our customers.

NURTURE

The nurture phase is really a continuation of the attract phase. You're still "courting" someone to one day become a customer. Now that you've attracted them into your business's ecosystem, your job is to continue to nurture them around your topic. Remember, you don't know where your lead is on their "awareness" journey. They may require many touch points and pieces of information before they feel comfortable in taking action. So, your job is to keep showing up, be consistent, and never assume people know who you are, what you do, and how you can help them. During this phase, you have one main goal: Become top-of-mind in your topic area to your leads.

Top-of-Mind

You know when you search for a product online and then start seeing that product everywhere? Well, some of that is due to the Baader-Meinhof phenomenon, otherwise known as the frequency illusion, in which once you become aware of something, you start to see it everywhere, therefore overestimating its popularity and how new it is. Paired with the mere exposure effect, the idea that we prefer something the more we're repeatedly exposed to it, and confirmation bias, which says we look for information to confirm our instincts and that aligns with our preconceived desires and values—it's important to stay top-of-mind in an attention-demanding world.

If you stay focused and consistent with social media content, sending emails to your email list, and with your content channel, your leads will start to feel the effects of the frequency illusion. Think of it this way: There are lots of other businesses out there, and lots of things going on in your leads' lives. Their attention is very difficult to get. How are you going to set yourself apart? *By being everywhere.* I don't mean on every platform, all the time. But by consistently showing up on the platforms you're dedicated to and that you know matter most—email, Instagram, blog, podcasts, and so on. That's likely where your leads are consuming content anyway.

But you don't become top-of-mind just by posting all over the internet. You stay top-of-mind by consistently showing up and reminding people who you are and what you do. Don't underestimate the value of repeating yourself. You might feel like you've told your story a thousand times, and explained what your products are even more times, but that just means you're doing it right. Remember, you're bringing in new leads all the time. They may or may not know what you're talking about. Maybe someone sent your Instagram account to a friend, or your email was forwarded to them by a classmate.

As your business grows, there will be new eyeballs on you at all times. You have to put your own ego aside and remember that you're actually not that important to them. (I don't mean that in a bad way! People are people—they're busy and have lives of their own. It's just important to remember you're not the center of their universe.) I like to keep in perspective that I'm constantly fighting for a piece of their limited attention and time—like trying to keep a balloon from hitting the ground. That's the idea behind top-of-mind marketing. Each time the balloon falls or begins to float away, you swoop in and bump it back up in the air.

Since our attention spans are so limited these days (and there are so many distractions), it's equally important to move your leads to a place in your business where it's a bit easier to actually get their attention, like email. With social media, the apps are designed to encourage doom scrolls and lots of engagement with various accounts. Right after they see your social post, the algorithm might serve up competitors' content or someone else's ad. But when you get someone onto your email list, you (technically speaking) have their undivided attention.

At the end of a long, hard day, I like to watch *The Bachelor* or *The Bachelorette* to unwind. It requires zero brain effort on my part and makes me appreciate that I'm not in my twenties anymore, worrying about what I look like or what I'm wearing. If you've ever watched the show, you know how the "lead" (aka, the bachelor or the bachelorette) takes the contestants out on either group dates or one-on-one dates. In the group dates, the contestants have to literally and figuratively shove each other aside to get the lead's attention. But on the one-on-one dates, one contestant gets the lead's undivided attention—a hot commodity in an otherwise overstimulating and time-cramped situation. When looking at your attraction marketing strategy, make sure you're not just on a bunch of group dates. You need to move your leads to a one-on-one place like email so you have more of their attention.

CONVERT

You can't just create and post educational content all day. Well, not if you actually need to make some money in your business, that is. A few years ago, I moved out of my hometown of Philadelphia to New York. I had never been to the North Shore of Long Island before, nor did I know anyone who lived as far out on the island as I did. A few months after living there I thought, "Why hasn't anyone asked me to do anything with them? Why haven't I met anyone here?"

That's when I realized I had to make the first move. I couldn't wait for people to come to me—I was the newbie who didn't know anyone and needed new friends. Many of them had lived here for decades and had families and plenty of friends.

Getting customers is really no different than making friends. You're going to have to put yourself out there—you're going to have to ask. Except instead of a coffee date, you're going to have to ask for a sale. Terrifying, I know! But I swear it gets easier with time and some automation.

What does automation look like when it comes to sales and is there really such a thing as those "passive" sales you've heard of? The key to automation and, at the very least, simplifying your sales and making them *more* passive, is a sales funnel.

A Well-Oiled Machine (aka Your Sales Funnel)

A sales funnel is the journey on which you methodically take a lead to convert them to a customer. It's really not that different from the marketing funnel we've already explored, but this time the main focus of the funnel is to get them to purchase something from you in the end.

Someone who enters your sales funnel with no prior exposure to you or your brand is called a "cold lead." Someone who has been through your funnel or has been a part of your community who has more familiarity with you and your products is a "warm lead." Practically speaking, you'll have both warm and cold leads go through your sales funnel all the time. But historically, warm leads convert at a higher, faster rate, since they're already more familiar with you, your company, and your product.

Using the attraction strategies we discussed in the previous section, a sales funnel typically starts with something free that pulls people in. Let's use a webinar as an example throughout this section. If your webinar and sales funnel are up and running at all times (and therefore someone can purchase your product at any time), that is called an "evergreen funnel." With evergreen funnels, someone can sign up for your webinar at any time, watch it, go through your sales sequence, and purchase. An evergreen funnel is a great way to create consistent sales in your business without having to live-launch or run sales all the time, which we'll talk about in the next section. But since your evergreen funnel is available all the time, you have to work a little harder—or be a little more creative marketing-wise—to give leads the incentive to take action now.

Leads enter your evergreen funnel through what we call the "top of funnel." Top of funnel entry points typically include digital ads, freebies, and social media posts that lead to your free webinar. The action you're asking viewers to take from that post or ad is to sign up for and watch your webinar. Once they do, your lead has entered your funnel.

From there, the goal is to get your lead to watch the webinar—preferably all the way through. After they sign up for your webinar, you want to deepen the "top-of-mind" marketing we discussed previously, if you haven't already. Following your webinar, you want them to start getting your sales sequence emails, see you on social media, and check out your podcast or whatever marketing channel you use to nurture leads. People in my sales funnel will write to me after they buy saying, "All of a sudden I just started seeing you everywhere!" That's not because I didn't exist before they entered my funnel; the frequency illusion and a little bit of tech magic on the back end, thanks to Facebook ads that start to appear wherever they hang online, have a real effect. Remember, your sales sequence emails should follow a very specific structure (see chapter 6) in order to properly nurture and convert them into buyers.

As we discussed earlier, your sales sequence needs the right level of urgency to get your lead to take action. Try using things like…

- automated timers;
- expiring discounts;
- disappearing bonuses that aren't available outside of the sale; and
- live elements, like a free live Q&A call with you on a certain date which they miss out on if they don't purchase now.

With urgency, you incentivize leads to take action now (buy) versus six months from now. But sales funnels and webinars aren't the only way to make more sales and convert leads to customers. A good old-fashioned sale works great, too.

Promotions and Sales (aka, Live Launches)

If my sales system was an ice cream sundae, my evergreen sales funnel would be the ice cream base, while my promotions and live launches would be all the fun toppings you get to add on top. And just like any good sundae, I like to have a nice balance of toppings and ice cream (what kind of sundae would be all toppings and no ice cream, or vice versa?!) when it comes to my evergreen funnel versus live-launch ratio.

A live launch is when you run a sale in your business in real time, with a start date and an end date. For example, maybe your products are on sale over a long holiday weekend or to celebrate your company's birthday. Or you could, like I do, run a live version of your evergreen webinar, with a live sale afterward. Once the end date passes, the sale and all of the associated discounts, bonuses, or live elements associated with it are over. How long you run a live launch depends on the price of your product, the amount of nurturing you think needs to be done to properly warm up and convert leads, and the type of product you sell. For a digital product valued around $2,000, I typically run a seven-to-ten-day sale, but the entire promotion period lasts well over a month once you account for a teaser and invite period. Here's what a sample timeline could look like for your live launch with a live webinar component:

- **SEVEN TO THIRTY DAYS PRIOR TO INVITE OR SALE: TEASER / HYPE TIME**—Start to tease your audience that a sale is coming (and a live webinar, if you're hosting one) at least two weeks prior to the sale/invite to the live event. Ideally, I start dropping subtle hints at least one month prior, and progressively get more specific and repetitive the closer it gets.
- **SEVEN TO TEN DAYS PRIOR TO WEBINAR: INVITE**—If you're hosting a live event like a webinar or challenge to lead up to your sale, you should invite your audience to sign up for that webinar or challenge daily for at least ten days before the live webinar. Once they sign up, they should receive a "show up" sequence of emails reminding them of the date/time, stressing the importance of the class, and warming them up to what you'll teach.
- **LIVE EVENT (e.g., live webinar)**—This is the anchor date I choose first and use to engineer the rest of my

timeline. Pick the date you would like to hold your live event, and then work backward to give yourself enough time to tease/hype that it's coming and invite people to sign up. The day of the live event is typically the "kickoff" day for your sale to begin, too.

- **SEVEN TO TEN DAYS AFTER WEBINAR: SALE—** Your sale period can vary based on the type of product you sell and how expensive it is. For a more expensive product, give buyers more time to decide. It's a delicate balance between enough time and creating enough urgency. For a longer sales period, I suggest having a "fast action" period (typically the first one to three days of a sale) in which buyers get the biggest discount or most bonuses. The rest of the sales period is called "closed cart" and runs until the sale ends.

- **ONE TO THREE DAYS AFTER SALE: DOWN-SELL—**This is an optional period of three to five days that begins after your sale ends to run a promotion to a smaller, typically more affordable product. The hope is to capture any additional sales you might have missed from those who didn't buy your original product on sale.

- **ONE WEEK AFTER SALE: SURVEY—**After a sale, I like to send a survey to everyone who didn't purchase to find out why. Even if it's just a one-question survey, you can ask, "Other than the price, what's the reason you didn't buy [name of your product] while it was on sale?" Use that feedback to help plan a better sale next time.

Here's a sample schedule for how I would structure a live launch with a live webinar happening on October 28th:

- Teaser: October 1–16
- Invite to Webinar: October 17–27 (with show up reminders once they sign up)
- Live Webinar: October 28
- Fast Action Sale: October 28–31
- Closed Cart Sale: November 1–4

If a live launch isn't something you want to do, or if it all feels like a bit too much for you right now, run a simple promotion to sell more of your product. With promotions, you can run a sale on your product, but without the live event and all of the associated steps that go along with it, like the sign-up period. In my business, I run longer live launches (with a live webinar) about twice per year, and I have an annual five-day promotion with no live event once per year.

How Many Sales Are Too Many Sales?

Too much of a good thing can be...not so great! If you run too many sales in your business, your audience may get a bit fatigued. A good way to spot fatigue is if you see a large unsubscribe rate from your email list over time (higher unsubscribes during a sale are completely normal, but if they go really high or stay high after a sale, that is concerning), have declining sales, or get less engagement from your email list.

I've had years where I've run too many sales and others where I didn't run enough. It's taken time and testing to find what works for me and my unique audience. Be patient and experiment with what works best for you, your audience, and your product.

Sales, funnels, and promotions aren't the only ways to actually sell your product. There are more subtle and smaller, yet still effective, strategies we've yet to explore.

(Not So) Subtle Sales

I like to think of social media as the waiting area, while email is like the main dining room. We want to attract people into our waiting area, entertain them and make them comfortable and excited to eat, but then welcome them into the dining room to "place their order."

You don't have to wait for a big sale period to pitch your product. Each week, you can "soft-sell" your product or service by writing about it, pitching it, and sharing a call to action for your subscribers to purchase it. You may or may not get the most sales using this method, but you can at least consistently make sales. Even if this steady mentioning of your product doesn't result in immediate sales, this is the kind of priming we discussed earlier that will help boost your sales down the line. Your leads need to hear about your product, what it is, and why it will help them many times before they will purchase. If someone asks about the Ultimate Bundle® outside of its sale period, I usually reply back with a special link and a limited-time discount code. It's a great way to ensure consistent sales year-round.

FAMILY

The final step to coming up with our million-dollar product is creating the family-like customer experience we discussed in chapter 7. Here are the three R's to remember in regard to your customers that help grow your business:

- **Retention:** If you sell a product that has a recurring cancellable fee, like a membership, or you offer refunds and returns, you want to treat your customers like family so you can retain them as customers. The most important factors to retaining customers are getting your customers to actually use your product, showing them the value inside, and providing friendly personal touches, like a handwritten thank-you note or a quick email or DM to say "Thanks!"

- **Recurrence:** Once a customer purchases something from you, they are more likely to purchase from you again (assuming, of course, they're satisfied with their purchase and experience). As we discussed, the cost of finding new customers is much higher than the cost of getting a current customer to purchase another item from us. That means you may have to dream up another product, a recurring support service (like a membership), or create a "VIP" level of your service or product in order to make additional sales to your current customers. You can also add small additional products or services to your checkout pages, which we call "order bumps." Think of them like the candy at the supermarket checkout line—they're little, no-brainer items you might add to your cart because they're there.

- **Referral:** Happy customers let other people know about you. If you treat your customers well, they will have a positive experience they won't be able to wait to tell others about. Your happy customers' kind words will naturally attract new customers just like them, all without you spending a dime on advertising. You could let this happen organically, or create a referral program to reward them.

WHAT WE LEARNED

- How to attract new leads into your business using tools like social media, SEO, and freebies so you build up a solid pipeline of future, qualified customers.
- The various ways to nurture those leads and to become top-of-mind in your space so you're the first person (and product) your potential customers think of when they're ready to purchase.
- How to use various sales and promotions to convert leads to buyers.
- The three R's of retention, recurrence, and referral are key to helping your business attract qualified leads that you don't pay for or seek out.

WHAT'S TO COME

- The Big 3 approach and how it helps you create less content with more impact.
- Whether you really need social media to build a successful online business.
- Why evergreen content will help you attract, nurture, and convert in a way that "toilet content" never will (in less time!).

CHAPTER 9

Building Your Content Community with the Big 3

The really important kind of freedom involves attention, and awareness, and discipline, and effort, and being able truly to care about other people and to sacrifice for them, over and over, in myriad petty little unsexy ways, every day.

—David Foster Wallace

After finishing second in four of the last five Ironman World Championships, British triathlete Lucy Charles-Barclay won the world title in 2023. She ran 26.2 miles, biked 112 miles, and swam 2.4 miles—*in eight hours*—to win! I recently fell into a Lucy Charles-Barclay rabbit hole on YouTube. Cozied up in my sweats, I watched her training videos, mindset chats, and day-in-the-life vlogs documenting how she trains for her competitions.

Besides being a gifted and talented athlete, there is a common thread in Lucy's training: consistency. Although it may sound boring to others to do the same bike, run, or swim routine day after day, Lucy shows how important her consistent training routine is to her overall success. She shares about the small tweaks she's making to her run, swim, and biking habits—and how those tiny changes stack up over time to equal more noticeable shifts. Lucy did not give up after finishing as a runner-up so many times in a row. I imagine her consistency and dedication had something to do with her finishing first in 2023.

While we may not be training for an Ironman competition anytime soon, running a business of any kind—online or otherwise—can feel like running a marathon. Although it's advertised as more of a sprint with a fast payoff, the reality is that building your own business takes time, patience, consistency, and repetition. If you're working to build an online community, email list, or a long line of customers, consistency and repetition are your new best friends. If you were training for an Ironman competition, you wouldn't bike 112 miles on Day 1. You would start slowly, practice consistently, add on, and work your way up.

But working your way up can feel overwhelming. Unless you're a personal trainer, you've probably walked into a gym or an exercise class and felt a terrible sense of overwhelm. *So many weights, strange-looking pieces of equipment, and things that look like torture devices...where to start?* When I first started going to the gym, I didn't have a plan and would wander around for over an hour, hopping from one machine to another, with little to nothing to show for it later. Without a plan, I was overwhelmed with the number of available options. I'd stop going to the gym entirely for months on end. Until one day when I would restart the cycle, again and again.

The online space is also filled with overwhelming choices. Unfortunately, as business owners, we often make the "wrong" choice when it comes to deciding where to spend the majority of our marketing time online. Or we hop from platform to platform, spinning our wheels with little progress to show for it. There are so many platforms to choose from: YouTube, Pinterest, Instagram, TikTok, Facebook, X (formerly Twitter), Substack, Threads, LinkedIn, blogs and podcasts.

Each of these has gone through up-and-down phases of popularity; it's easy to get sucked into the app du jour. Several apps and platforms have come and gone in the eight years since I started my business. I have seen creators' entire communities disappear overnight because an app lost favor or was sold to another company.

We might bounce from app to popular app or make a feeble attempt at posting everywhere, all the time, in the hopes that something sticks. Between false hope, switching platforms, and algorithmic changes, at times it feels impossible to figure out how to build an audience online. I think we can all relate to one (or several!) of these scenarios:

- You start a TikTok account, thinking that if you post a few videos that look like ones you've seen do well, your account will quickly blow up. (But they only get a few views, so you stop posting.)
- You reach out to your email list with a link to your offer, thinking that just sending it will make the sales roll in. (But no one buys, so you ghost your list for a month.)
- You make your website live, thinking once it's up the visitors and sales will start pouring in. (But you barely have visitors, so no one buys. You think your site is a flop.)
- You post a few videos on YouTube, thinking they will rack up views and loads of new subscribers. (But hardly anyone watches, so you stop posting and try a different platform.)

While there are many platforms and tools to choose from, there are even more opinions about which one is "the best." Many experts shout TikTok's praises from the rooftops, while others swear they'll never use it because they can't stand the way it makes them feel like they're on sensory steroids. All of these creators are doing well in their businesses. So, is one platform, or even one strategy on any given platform, the "right" one? Or are there many ways to build a community?

There are multiple wild-card factors when it comes to social platforms. What if a law passes that takes away a social platform? What if that platform becomes more heavily regulated? Or what if Instagram goes down for a day, but you've built your entire business's existence on it? It's not that social media doesn't have its place of importance in your business. It's about making sure you pour the right amount of energy into the right platforms so you get the most business bang for your buck.

Or could it be that the platform you choose doesn't necessarily matter, but rather how you treat each platform, and how you show up on it? Are some apps better for growing your business than others? If so, why? First, we'll start by creating two platform categories: discovery and nurture. I want you to think of which platforms you're going to dedicate yourself to that will lead to your being discovered by new people, and which you'll nurture your audience on. Let's discuss each platform category in more detail.

DISCOVERY PLATFORMS

Some platforms lend themselves to discovery better than others. The primary focus of discovery platforms is getting you in front of new people, who then become leads. You primarily post evergreen content there. In that content, as we've learned, you use a call to action to get someone to opt in to your email list or take some other promising action.

As we'll discuss later in this chapter, the Big 3 platforms tend to be better discovery platforms because they have greater searchability, SEO-capabilities, and longevity than some of the more traditional social media platforms (e.g., Instagram, TikTok, X/Twitter). As you read this chapter and do your own research on which platforms you want to make use of, create a list of which platforms you'll focus on as your "discovery" platforms and which you'll designate to be more of your nurture platforms so you ensure you're properly balancing your marketing time.

In my business, I focus on one or two discovery platforms instead of spreading myself thin across several platforms. Some examples of discovery platforms, which should all be optimized for SEO purposes, are:

- YouTube
- Podcast
- Substack
- Pinterest
- Website, including freebies/lead magnets you optimize to drive traffic to your site and email list
- Blog
- Instagram and TikTok (although I would consider these your secondary discovery platforms, not primary, for reasons we'll discuss later)

Discovery platforms tend to favor longer-form content, which allows you to establish yourself as a subject-area expert, unlike the quick clips or stand-alone images typically posted on social media. They also allow you to build a dedicated audience who get to know you on a deeper level. The long-term goal is that those audience members will become your customers. Once they've discovered you on one or more of your discovery platforms, you then nurture them on those same platforms, as well as your nurture platforms.

At the same time, I will admit that social media is also an important discovery tool. Your potential customers may spend a lot of time on social media. It's also possible that's where they go to look for new clothes, recipes, and workout tips. I don't believe social media is all good or all bad. I integrate it into my marketing strategy and use it as a discovery tool (both through my content and the digital ads I run on platforms like Instagram), but I'm not building my house (my business) on rented land (social media). I see the other discovery platforms, especially those we'll discuss in detail coming up, as more of a marketing foundation and social media as a secondary concern. It has its place in a business's marketing strategy, just make sure it's the right place for you.

NURTURE PLATFORMS

Once someone has discovered you online, your job is to deepen your relationship with them through your nurture platforms. You'll want to familiarize them with what you do, what you sell, and how you work. This deeper connection will hopefully lead your potential customers to know, like, and trust you enough to take action (i.e., buy). As you've probably already guessed, I consider an email list to be the absolute best nurture platform for an online business. With email, we capture more of our customers' one-on-one attention. Unlike with social media, your customers won't have loads of ads or competitors' content showing up at the same time as yours. Email allows you to control how and when you get content into your subscribers' hands. As we discussed in chapter 6, your weekly emails sent to your audience should deliver high-value content.

Social media is, however, a fantastic nurture tool, too. Apps like TikTok and Instagram are so visual that they allow you to connect with your audience in a different way than email. Your customers get to actually see and hear you in action, which allows them to get to know you better and decide whether they want to work with you or purchase from you. You can show more personal sides of yourself, too. On platforms like Instagram, you can utilize Instagram stories to show more of your life and your day-to-day behind the scenes. For example, in my Instagram stories, I often share about my love for cooking, videos of delicious meals I've whipped up, and the love of my life—my dog. I get more messages about the dog than almost anything else I share! Yes, you run a business. But people are more likely to purchase from someone they see themselves in and feel a connection with. You just have to give them something to connect to.

Now that you know you need both discovery and nurture platforms in your marketing plan, it's time to choose your discovery platforms first. The Big 3, as we'll discuss, are the most popular discovery platforms available to you. As the self-appointed Goldilocks of content platforms and feeling somewhat like a bubbe figure in the online space (or at the very least, an aunt), I can tell you that dedicating yourself to a Big 3 platform will help you gain traction, build an audience you connect with, and make sales...for the long haul. What are the Big 3 discovery platforms? Let's dive in.

INTRODUCING: THE BIG 3 (DISCOVERY PLATFORMS)

In 2018, I paid five figures for a VIP day with Janelle,[1] an online business expert, to get feedback on my business. Besides purchasing

---

1. Name changed.

my favorite Bombas socks, it was the best money I ever spent. During the time when I had the VIP day, I spent the majority of my marketing time on Instagram; I'd spend hours each day creating original content for Instagram stories, which expired twenty-four hours after I posted them. I would also post daily on my Instagram feed, developing content and writing captions. I wrote weekly blog posts on topics unrelated to what I sold in my business (my time living in France was fun to write about, but it wasn't exactly training Google to understand that I sold legal templates). I posted on nearly all of the other popular social media apps, too. I didn't realize it then, but I was massively wasting my time and barely gaining any traction for it. I couldn't figure out why my business wasn't growing as much as I thought it should be, given the amount of effort I put in. I promptly responded to comments at all hours of the day and regularly showed my face. (*Note: Showing your actual face on social media routinely improves your engagement and statistics.*) Why didn't I have more to show for it? Clearly, I needed Janelle's help.

Janelle and I sat together for hours unpacking all the different pieces of my business. "So how often do you post on Instagram?" she asked. I told her about my intricate, daily, and disappearing Instagram stories, five-times-per-week posts, and hours spent engaging with my audience.

"But wait," she asked me, confused. "You create a brand-new training *every single day* on Instagram stories…and in twenty-four hours it just goes away?"

"Yep, even on weekends!" I proudly exclaimed. By the time the words had left my mouth, I'd realized my mistake.

"What the heck am I doing?!" I thought. Wasting a whole lot of time, that's what. I thought I was doing the "right thing" by posting so much on social media. That's what "they" all said to do. I just hadn't realized that all that time could have been better spent elsewhere—or maybe not at all.

Janelle called me out for just how much content I was creating across the board. "It's entirely too much," she told me. "You need to let the evergreen pieces you create—the really good ones that have lasting power—marinate. They need more time to get out there. But you're so busy pumping out new content, the content you've already created never has a chance to shine. Plus, if you're creating evergreen content, you don't need to push out so much stuff day-to-day. Slow down. Create less. But make it more worthwhile by focusing on one of the Big 3: YouTube, a podcast, or a blog."

I needed to hear Janelle's advice in order to grow my audience, let alone my business. From that day forward, I snapped to and spent my marketing time more wisely. Instead of focusing on disappearing Instagram stories, I slowed down and created (less) evergreen content on one of the Big 3 platforms.

Unlike most social media apps, the Big 3 platforms—YouTube, podcasts, and blogs (all optimized for SEO purposes)—offer the opportunity to create longer-lasting, searchable content. The Big 3 are "discovery" platforms—places where you can continuously be discovered through the kind of content you post there and the attraction strategies these platforms allow.

Social media can also be a "discovery" platform, but because of its ever-changing algorithm, less-than-stellar searchability, high volume of content posted each second, and preference for short-form content, it's not as ideal as the Big 3. What you post on TikTok or Instagram has only a short window of opportunity to do well and be seen. Sure, people can technically see or find your content later on if they somehow stumble onto your page. But in terms of your content getting in front of new people or people already searching for your topic, posting on social media is essentially like throwing a piece of confetti into the air and watching it fall. It has a short, fast trip down, and by the time it hits the floor, there are already millions of pieces of confetti from other creators. The process never ends.

If you're frustrated by how much time you spend on social media, or how little traction your really good content is getting there, it's time to reevaluate where you're spending your time. When used properly, social media can act as both a discovery tool and a nurture tool. Of course it plays an important role for online businesses. Next time you stand in line at Chipotle, see if you can find one person who's not on their phone. Even if you focus on building your YouTube or podcast presence as your primary discovery platform, people will look to connect with you on social media, too. It's a great way to offer behind-the-scenes, personal access to you. However, it's my view that on the whole, social platforms should be in the backseat (or, at the very least, passenger) of your marketing strategy rather than letting them drive.

For now, the goal is to pick one Big 3 platform (YouTube, podcast, or blog) as your primary discovery platform. It doesn't have to be your only focus or the only place you post content in your business now or forever. As we learned in chapter 8, your Big 3 platform of choice will be the top, or entry point, of your content ecosystem. It's how you're going to attract new leads into your business. It should be the place where you create original content, and the place to which you adapt your original content. It should also be a platform you can see yourself using consistently for at least three but ideally six months.

For example, if YouTube is your primary platform, your main objective is to create great videos to attract new leads. Should you decide to podcast, you'd focus on producing great audio-based content (unless, of course, you choose to produce a video podcast. In that case, you'd focus on creating a great podcast that's also visually appealing), and with blogging, you'd focus on producing great written content. Whichever you choose, you want to aim to create great content *specifically for that platform*. Instead of creating a random video and then squeezing it onto YouTube, Instagram, TikTok, or Pinterest, each of which has different demands and consumption preferences in order to perform well, you focus on creating for your chosen platform.

By picking one platform and dedicating yourself to it, you will actually be able to build an audience and eventually gain traction on the platform. You will also be able to become known on the platform and build a pipeline of clients to your products. If you keep bopping around from platform to platform, though, you won't have enough time or experience to gain traction or build your audience. You gain traction on any given platform only with time, dedication, and a whole lot of reps.

You might doubt whether it's a good idea to dedicate yourself to one of the Big 3 platforms. You might be thinking of someone you know who went viral on TikTok and relies on all of their leads from it. Or you may listen to a podcast that focuses only on succeeding on X. Social media can be alluring. Don't get me wrong, it's a powerful tool for growing your business. We're not done with discussing social media—it has its place in your business. But it's better to not rely on it entirely for your business's survival, that's all. We're not throwing a bunch of confetti in the air each day, hoping one piece of it floats longer than others. We're tired of the changing algorithms, the way social media makes us feel, and how little we get out of it versus the amount of energy it takes to be on it. Some of my colleagues have left social media entirely. And their businesses have lived to tell the tale!

Some of the benefits of the Big 3 over traditional social media apps include the following:

- **Discoverability:** Yes, you can be discovered on social media, too. But with the Big 3, you can be discovered more consistently over time. People are looking *for* you on these platforms, versus your trying to find them on social media. Posting on social media is sort of like walking into a crowded warehouse and screaming through a megaphone while thousands of other people are screaming through theirs. With the Big 3, particularly with blogging and YouTube (which is owned by Google and prioritized in Google searches), you can put your content directly in front of the people already searching online for "money tips for teachers."

- **Searchability with longevity:** Sure, social media apps like Instagram, TikTok, or Pinterest (which falls somewhere in between a search engine and a social media app) have search features, hashtags, and topics. But try finding a piece of content you posted on any given topic. How many other completely unrelated pieces of content does it compete with? Can you find it a week after you post it? How about a month?
- **Stability:** Yes, the Big 3 have their own algorithms and their features change, too. But these three platforms as ways of posting content have been around in more or less the same form for a long time. However, as of this writing, Google has begun to integrate AI Overviews into its search results. AI Overviews offer summaries of creators' content without users having to click through to the creators' websites any longer. Many creators, myself included, have been negatively impacted by this. Whether it sticks and its long-term impact are to be determined.
- **Focus:** Picking one platform that doesn't change as often as social media does will help to keep you focused

and dedicated to something long enough to actually gain traction from it.

- **Long form:** All the Big 3 platforms allow you to create long(er) form content than what's allowed on social media. On social media, it's hard to squeeze your topic into a seven-second clip. Try talking about the nuances of contracts in seven seconds! *While dancing!* But with things like podcasts, blog posts, or YouTube videos, you're able to have longer, more nuanced, and therefore fuller conversations with your audience. This type of content not only helps to establish you as an expert in your field, but it also allows your audience to get to know, like, and trust you.

Which of the Big 3 Is the One for You?

Over the years, I've tried all of the Big 3 platforms one at a time, as I suggest doing here. At the start, it's hard to know which one you will like, or which will work best for you, especially if you don't have any prior experience with that platform. If you don't know where to start, let's talk about how to select a Big 3 platform.

Once you decide to shift away from solely or primarily focusing on social media as your marketing platform, it is difficult to know what the best alternative is. The fact is, no particular one of the Big 3 is going to make or break your path to success. You don't necessarily have to pick a platform based on what you believe will help you grow the most, make you the most money, or gain you the most followers. Or you can! It's truly up to you. All that to say, there are many different reasons why you would choose any one of the Big 3 platforms. No one platform is objectively better than another. What works for you might not work for me, and vice versa. In this section, we'll focus on some of the factors to consider so you can choose one that's best for you (or *best for you right now,* you can always change your mind later).

Factor #1: What Sounds Like Fun?

Sometimes the best platform to start with is the one you are already a fan of. You'll be familiar with how the platform works and what the trends and features are, which we'll talk about in more detail in the next section. If you absolutely love podcasts and already understand how podcasts work, you're going to have a leg up on someone starting one without any prior knowledge or experience.

If I've learned anything over the past eight years through creating content online, it's that you cannot underestimate the value of having fun. If you force yourself to create content on a platform you don't like—or to create a type of content you can't stand—it shows. If you get excited about writing, start a blog! If you can't wait to pick up your mic each week to record new podcast episodes, it's a good sign that you picked the right thing. As we've talked about many times throughout this book, consistency is key. And just like your favorite workout or other healthy habit, you'll stick with what you enjoy doing. So, make sure whatever you pick is the type of thing you can see yourself doing consistently for at least six months. Can you imagine sticking to it, even if you're not getting engagement or gaining followers? If you're already dreading the thought of it, it's probably not the right medium for you.

Factor #2: Where Are Your Customers?

It's also important to consider where your customers hang out and consume their content. We want to make it easy for you to find new customers. If you know from your research we talked about in chapter 3 that your ideal customers are active on YouTube, that may be a good place to start building a presence.

Factor #3: How Will You Present Your Content?

What makes the most sense based on the type of content you'll create? Does your content require video, like a cooking demonstration would? Or do you rely heavily on the written word and telling a beautiful story? Then blogging might be best for you. No matter what type of content you talk about, you can get creative with how you present it. For example, if you teach about exercise, you might maintain a YouTube channel featuring sample workouts or form demonstrations. But you could also start a podcast with weekly episodes on the latest fitness trends, dive deep into relevant fitness topics or hurdles your clients face, and bring on guests who will supplement and support your valuable content.

Factor #4: What Is Your "It" Factor?

You can also pick a platform based on where your talent lies. Are you a natural on camera? Can you write a story better than you could tell it on film? Or are you a pro at public speaking, especially when you're behind a mic and there's no camera on you? Given how crowded all of these spaces are, it's important that you're good at the medium you choose. If you're new to all of these, don't worry if you're not good at any of them yet! You can practice and get better. But you might be surprised to find that one of them comes to you more naturally than the others.

Factor #5: Experiment

My dad was rarely angry with me. But nothing annoyed him more when I was a child than when I would get really, really into something, only to quit it almost as quickly as I started. When I was eight, all I wanted in the world was a Razor Scooter. I swore to him up and down that I'd use the scooter every day. But after riding the scooter around his cul-de-sac just a few times, I decided it was boring and tossed it to the side. Even though this trait drove Dad nuts, I see now I was just (a) being a child; and (b) experimenting. Sometimes you've got to try something in order to know if you'll like it.

If no one platform jumps out at you, and you don't know what you love or what you're good at, experiment! Pick something, keep an open mind, and get started. The only "rule" is that, unlike my Razor Scooter, you have to try the platform long enough that you can actually gain some insights as to whether or not it's working. Don't expect to post once or twice and be an overnight success. It's extremely rare. Since this is your business and not a scooter, you're putting too much time, money, and energy into this to be hopping around (or should I say, scooting around?) to other platforms every five minutes.

———

Considering all five factors, which platform makes sense for you (YouTube, podcast, or blog)?

FACTOR 1: _____

FACTOR 2: _____

FACTOR 3: _____

FACTOR 4: _____

FACTOR 5: _____

———

The best platform for you and your business (right now):

_____

Try, Try Again

One of my favorite YouTubers, Makari Espe, had been on YouTube—off and on and in various forms—since she was a teenager. Within weeks of each other in 2023, she was part of a group layoff from her job and her dad, Larry, suffered a massive heart attack, and she decided to give it another go. Makari started posting YouTube videos that were well produced, narrated, and thought out. A few months in, she made a video where she "Queer Eyed" herself—giving herself the same life makeover the show *Queer Eye* gives its guests—that took off.

She then made a video where she did the daily amount of recommended cardio for thirty days straight. Originally, Makari posted this video with a personal introduction about why she chose to focus on this challenge—her dad's heart attack had inspired her to take her heart health more seriously. Although the video did well, Makari thought it could do better if she changed the introduction to be more about her viewer. She swapped out the intro to be one more focused about how cardio could benefit them. The video went viral.

Makari is a fantastic example of tenacity, learning how to master the platform you choose, and keeping an open, research-like mind. Her videos are unique and well tailored to a specific YouTube audience. After making several attempts at YouTube in the past, Makari has now been able to go full-time with her channel.

Getting Started on the Big 3

Before embarking on any new business adventure, it's important to first check your mindset. As you enter new or intimidating territory, put on your curiosity hat. You're here to experiment and see what works for you. It will take time and effort. And it may take some adjustment along the way! Remain open and curious to how it will go, adjust as needed, and you will ultimately have success.

Step #1: Research

When you choose your primary Big 3 platform, you don't have to know everything about it to start. However, since you've narrowed down where you'll spend your marketing time, you'll need to get to know this platform better than you know others. Over time, you'll need to become an expert at it.

One of the best ways to learn about a platform is to become its fan. Whether you've chosen blogging, podcasting, or YouTube, you should check out different types of creators on that platform. Not only will you learn what's popular, what's trending, and what commonly used features on the platform you can take advantage of, but you'll also learn what you do and don't like about those features. You can create great content when you know what gap you're trying to fill. If you're a YouTube fan, for example, but you wish there was a type of content, or a way of presenting content, out there that doesn't exist, you can create it.

There's a fine line between doomscrolling, overconsumption, and "research." You should spend more time creating content than consuming it. Before I started my podcast, I listened to a variety of podcasts in my free time. Anytime I had a long drive or was cooking or gardening, I'd pop in my AirPods and listen. I didn't pick legal or business podcasts. Instead, I learned from shows in a different arena about storytelling, how podcasts were produced, and trending features. Once I started my own podcast, however, I made sure to spend more time creating my own than listening to others', and to always create before I consumed.

When you see other creators on your platform, ask yourself:

- What do I like about this creator's content? Why?

- What don't I like about this creator's content? Why?
- What elements of what that creator does would translate to what I do? How can I put my unique spin on it?
- What's missing from similar creators in my space on this platform? As a consumer, what do I wish I could find?

As part of your research, you should also discover what SEO tools are available to you based on the platform you chose. For example, if you've chosen YouTube, you'll be able to

- optimize the title and description of the episode to be found in search results;
- upload your video file and thumbnail with the keyword you've chosen in your SEO research as the file name; and
- use your keyword and related keywords several times in your description.

Each of the Big 3 platforms has a multitude of SEO features. And each one deserves its own research to ensure you're using them all to the best of your ability. The optimization tools on these platforms are like free marketing help. Utilizing them can push your content out to the people looking for what you're offering. After almost a decade in business, I'm still learning optimization strategies. It's an ongoing part of my business that continues to change, especially with new AI features being integrated into search engines. Keeping up with and implementing SEO and optimization strategies is one of the best return-on-investment strategies you can adopt.

Remember: As an entrepreneur, doing research and learning will always be a part of your to-do list. You don't want to stay in research mode too long because with content, there's often no way to really know whether it will work until you try. It's normal to want to delay something new and seemingly scary, but for your business's sake don't.

Step #2: Create a Content Plan

You already know how important it is to be consistent with creating and posting content, whether it's to your email list, on social media, or on your Big 3 platform. With consistency in mind, create a realistic content plan, which should include a schedule of the content you're going to post, when you're going to post it, and what the content will be about. With this plan, you'll not only be able to stay consistent, but you'll be able to see the up-high view of what you want to post, too. Your goal is to develop a nice, balanced cadence to your content schedule so you're not always posting the same type of content or ignoring any important content pillar types.

As we learned in chapter 8, content pillars are key to your content plan (see page 204 for a refresher). If you have four content pillars, cover each of those in your content at some point in your plan.

Not all content pillars deserve equal attention. For example, one of my content pillars is educational content about contracts, LLCs, and other legal issues that impact online entrepreneurs. The majority of the content I create falls in that pillar since it's core to my business. I'm still sure to regularly post content that falls into other pillars; they just don't get as much "airtime" as my main content pillar.

Focus: Your Audience

A common pitfall is to start delivering content that's more about you than your business. While I do advocate for having one of your content pillars be something more personal, it's important to remember that you're running a business. Just like the lesson I shared from YouTuber Makari Espe, the point of your content should be to help those who are watching it. The majority of your content should be about your chosen core topic, customers, and products.

To create a content plan you can stick to and that yields results, mix up your approach between being strategic and having fun. I've watched countless creators on YouTube announcing their departures from the platform. One of the most common reasons? They're sick of creating content they feel like they're supposed to create, and they want to get back to creating content from the heart. You can get so focused on outcome, results, and the algorithm that the joy of what you do goes away. When starting out, you want to build an audience first. And you don't want to build an audience about just any ol' topic—you want an audience full of people who want to hear more about your topic area and who ultimately need what you sell.

In the beginning, one of the best ways to build an audience is to think of every piece of content you create through the lens of "What's in it for them?" Why should my audience watch this video or listen to this podcast? What are they taking away from it? How does this benefit them in any way? When I feel like creating more personal content, I force myself to answer these questions. It usually directs my content in a more helpful-for-my-audience direction, and therefore builds trust, loyalty, and numbers.

But that doesn't mean you can't balance or combine fun content with the pieces of content you know your audience is looking for. In other words, don't get so methodical that you dread posting or only create content to satisfy the algorithm gods. Not only does that not typically work, but it might lead to content burnout on your end, too. It's sort of like getting to go out to play after you've gotten all of your homework done. If you create your main content, go play with some types of content that feel really fun. As with so many things we've talked about thus far, it's all about finding a balance. If you post all "strategic" content, that won't go well, and if you post all personal-focused content, that likely won't go well either (unless you're an influencer or lifestyle vlogger). Remember: Your business doesn't have to provide you with all of the happiness, creativity, or joy you seek. You can cultivate that elsewhere in your life, and let your business be your business. If you're feeling unfulfilled, your business doesn't have to be the thing that turns that around for you.

Step #3: Creator Mode—Activated

Building an audience is like building muscle. You need many reps, consistently over time, in order to strengthen it. While I do recommend posting consistently, it's important to focus on quality over quantity. If that means one great podcast, YouTube, or blog post per week, so be it. There is utility, however, in some temporary or up-front quantity over quality when you're starting out. You will get more comfortable creating content, work out the kinks in your filming and uploading process, and even learn more about what your audience wants. By creating lots of content consistently, you'll give yourself enough data to offer your audience more of what they want and less (or none!) of what they don't.

Step #4: Create Community

Think of your audience like a community—instead of racking up followers and likes, know that people want to feel that they're part of something. They want to feel connected to you and the work you're doing. By sharing a few types of content consistently, people will know what to expect. They know that on your podcast, YouTube channel, or blog you always talk about a few topics that are important to them. The more they can see themselves in you, the more connected to you they'll feel. The goal here isn't to get people to like you or for you to act differently from normal. It's to open up enough to show certain parts of you or your hobbies in order for people to be able to connect with you.

Even though I sell legal templates, my love of food and cooking, as I've mentioned, is one of my personal content pillars. Through that, I've built a community of foodies who love talking about food and cooking—and they also just so happen to need legal templates for their online businesses. People are more likely to keep up with you and your content if there are other aspects of your content that draw them in. This in turn makes them more likely to engage with your business when they need to buy what you sell.

Step #5: What Does the Data Tell You?

Regardless of which platform you choose, you will have access to an overwhelming amount of data tools, all of which will tell you how many people watch/listen, how long they watch/listen for, what else they watch/listen to, and more. As someone who's trying to figure out what their audience wants and likes most, pay attention to the trends in the data available to you. Ask yourself:

- Does one content type tend to perform better than another? Which one?
- Regardless of how well it performs on the platform itself, does any type of content bring more email leads?
- Regardless of how well it performs on the platform itself, does any type of content make more sales?
- Are there any trends I'm noticing when it comes to titling, cover art, copy, or any other visual elements?

- Am I using SEO or optimization principles wherever possible? If not, where can I easily add in an optimization step in my uploading or content creation process?

PUTTING IT ALL TOGETHER

We've talked about a lot of marketing strategies throughout this book. Let's pull them all together and learn how to organize a flowing marketing system that consistently generates new leads, then nurtures and converts them to customers when the time is right.

Phase #1: Pick Your Platforms

You'll start your marketing system by picking your Big 3 platform, the foundation from which you'll create your original content. You should also choose one or two social media platforms, like Instagram, TikTok, Facebook, X, or Threads, as your discovery and nurture platforms to focus on.

Phase #2: Create (Mostly) Evergreen Content With a Single Call to Action (CTA)

On both the Big 3 and the social media platforms you chose, create mostly evergreen content. Remember, evergreen content is content that drives traffic to your business for the long haul. Maybe it has a CTA that leads people to a freebie (which puts them on your email list), or is on an always-relevant topic. Either way, try to create the majority of your content with an evergreen CTA in mind. That way, over time your content will stack up and bring in a steady flow of traffic. Only using one CTA per piece of content will help clearly direct your community to the next step you want them to take toward purchasing from your business.

Phase #3: Build Your Email List

You'll create one or two irresistible freebies to attract people to your email list. Now that you're driving all that traffic to your email list from your evergreen content, your main focus is nurturing and building your email list. As I often tell my team, "All roads lead to the email list." Nearly every piece of content we create, or marketing campaign we launch, has the goal of building our email list. Every time I'm asked to speak or give a training in someone's community, I think, "How can I get the attendees on my list?" Your email list, no matter its size now, should be a main priority in your business.

Phase #4: Email List Camaraderie

Speaking of prioritizing your email list, you want to consistently email relevant, helpful content to your subscribers. Since they have taken the extra step to commit to your business on a deeper level, you should give them your best or more-exclusive content. Unlike with social media and its finicky and ever-changing algorithms, you'll know your content is guaranteed to actually be delivered. Giving your email list your focus and attention is worth it. If you're not emailing your list consistently, you shouldn't be posting two Instagram Reels per day.

Phase #5: Sell to and Nurture Your List

The benefit to giving your email list consistent, valuable content is that you've earned the right to sell to them. Remember: You have a business. You're allowed to sell things and make money for what you do. Target never feels badly for asking you to buy a blanket or for putting up a highway billboard. Let people have agency—they can buy, stick around, or leave whenever they like. The key is to find your Goldilocks pace—not selling too often, but not selling too infrequently either.

Phase #6: Do It All Over Again

If you like repetition and consistency, you're going to love building your online business. There's a reason we call this a marketing ecosystem. It continuously flows and requires that you revisit and revise various phases at different times. Never stop creating new, irresistible freebies to drive traffic to your email list. And continue to innovate and evolve as content platforms evolve alongside you; I'm always looking for new opportunities to send traffic to my email list. No matter the number of social media followers or email subscribers, growth never stops being a priority.

You aren't creating a "set it and forget it" marketing system. This is a living, breathing thing. As things have changed and evolved in the online business world, my Phase #1 Big 3 focus has shifted from time to time, too. I'm always rethinking and revisiting Phase #2, creating new pathways of evergreen content that feed leads to my funnel. I consistently come up with new ideas for Phase #3, introducing new pathways to my email list and tinkering with my strategy based on the results I see. Things in the online business and content creation industry are always changing. That's a good thing. It keeps us on our toes and makes us lifelong learners. Tap into that curious, investigative mindset and you'll love the endless possibilities this industry has to offer you.

BUT CAN'T I JUST USE SOCIAL MEDIA?

I'm just going to say it: Creating long-form content on platforms like YouTube or podcasting platforms is harder than creating social media content. It takes more thought to plan and prepare for, it's harder to edit, and there's a longer, more difficult learning curve. Getting the results you want can take longer, too. As we've discussed, the Big 3 can require a long-term, consistent approach to see a bigger payoff.

Social media promises something that the Big 3 cannot: the potential for a quick win. Maybe you've posted something on Instagram and it went viral. But I've never known anyone (besides a well-known celebrity) to see overnight success after posting their first podcast episode. I know the prospect of building your entire marketing ecosystem on social media is alluring. The Big 3 might not seem as sexy or fun as social media. But it would be irresponsible of me if I didn't talk about social media and its personal impact on us as individuals, on our society, and on our health. As you have likely already noticed, there are lots of social media marketers telling you to post here, there, and everywhere. You'll see endless content about new tricks and trends that seemingly change every day. Everyone thinks they have *the answer* for how to "crack the code" of social media's powerful, elusive, and ever-changing algorithms. In reality, no one—except the developers at the helm of the codes themselves—know how they work or when they will change again.

Although social media is a powerful and arguably necessary tool for growing our businesses, it doesn't do so without a cost to us. Nearly all of my colleagues in the online business space have at one point or another complained about the toll social media has taken on them. For every person I know who has done well on social media, I know twice as many who say that social media doesn't work for their businesses at all or like it used to. I know even more who personally resent the apps but feel like they're chained to them for the sake of their businesses' success. Several creators have had to take a long-term or sometimes even permanent break from social media for mental health or burnout reasons. Sure, there are loads of upsides (e.g., discovery, nurture, free advertising, engagement with your audience, powerful reach, friendships, etc.), but there are many downsides, too. Even if you are one of the lucky ones who crack the algorithm and create viral content or build a large audience, it nearly always reaches a breaking point. You also have to ask yourself, "At what cost?" It's a place where we waste precious time in our businesses on the apps and not enough time actually moving our businesses forward.

Social media has its place in your business. It just doesn't have to be the foundation of it. My dedication and obsession with building and nurturing my email list, as well as focusing on evergreen content on Big 3 platforms, has saved my business and my mental health. When my parents died, I was able to significantly reduce or stop posting on social media for lengthy periods of time and instead rely heavily on my email list. If I hadn't spent years building up and nurturing my list, I wouldn't have been able to keep my business afloat while I grieved.

If you sense a mama-bear, protective approach in the marketing strategies I've taught you thus far, it is because I'm worried about all of us. I've seen what happens to people who spend lots of time on social media, build their identities around it, or become dependent on an app. Heck, I've even seen what happens to myself when I just spend too much time scrolling. It leaves my brain feeling fried and my attention span and ability to be present flies out the window. When I spend even a little bit of time each day on social apps, I don't feel my best.

Can We Find a Balance?

I know it's easy for me to sit here and say, "Don't go on social media!" I've built a following, a healthy-sized email list, and a long customer list on social media. Since my business is more established, it's not as consequential for me to pull back from social media. But I'm still on it. Just not the way I used to be. I don't think being on social requires an all-or-nothing approach.

Is there a healthier way we can build our businesses on social, while also balancing our health and well-being? Can we be both driven and conscientious that we're truly living our lives offline, not living to be online?

For me, this approach and mindset take a lot of careful planning and consideration. I plan content with my team, batch-record my videos for an entire month in one sitting, and practice healthy boundaries with my screen time. I relapse sometimes. But I always come back to my intention: to be more present and live my life to the fullest. No matter what stage of business you're in, I'd recommend treating social media, and the time you spend there, as just another part of your job. Get in, and get out. Post what you need to post, share something to your Instagram stories or wherever you like to post, and get off the app. Do what you need to do to not be tempted to spend more time than necessary there. For me, I delete the app each day and the entire weekend. Yes, it's a pain to re-download it when I need it. But the benefits far outweigh the annoyances.

I'll leave the social media mental health analysis and the impact it is having on us to the experts, but I do advocate for a "Spread your chips around; don't put them all in the social media basket" approach. Not only is it better overall for our businesses, but it's better for our hearts and minds, too.

WHAT WE LEARNED

- Trying to post on all the platforms and apps, or switching which ones you're focusing on, leads to inconsistency and prevents you from building an audience on any platform at all.

- The Big 3 platforms—YouTube, podcasting, and blogging—are more sustainable and longer lasting than most social media platforms.
- The Big 3 require consistency and long-term dedication since they may not have as quick of a payoff as social media (promises to do, but may not in reality).
- Choosing a Big 3 platform can require some experimentation, but picking something you enjoy creating content for is a great way to ensure you'll do so consistently.
- While social media still has a place in our businesses, it may not be the best idea to solely focus on it, both for our businesses' sake, due to its unpredictability, and for the sake of our mental health.

WHAT'S TO COME

- Building your own business online comes with its own set of challenges and growth opportunities.
- How being more visible online may bring out some insecurities, mean comments, and judgment (from both yourself and others).
- We will discuss how to build your sense of self and self-confidence, and how to separate yourself from your business and create healthy boundaries to protect your sanity.

CHAPTER 10

Growing Pains

If you live by the good numbers, then you must die by the bad numbers.

—Trevor Noah

My mom wasn't born in Paris in the 1920s, she just had the attitude of someone who was. "It wouldn't kill you to wear a little lip rouge, Sammy," she would say. From the time I was a young child she told me, "Brassieres are meant to be seen." While she proudly paraded around with a lacy red bra peeking through her completely sheer top, I hid behind oversized clothing and my practical, butter-soft nude T-shirt bras. She couldn't stand the fact that none of my dresses had rhinestones or thigh-high slits in them. Although she expressed displeasure at how often I wore my hair in a ponytail, she noted that I "could pull it off, even though having it down would be nicer." She crowned me a "carb queen" before my tenth birthday, and told me I'd spend the rest of my life trying to work off the belly fat I was developing if I "didn't cut back soon." I was terrified to gain weight, get dressed, or simply just be myself.

The list goes on, and I would prefer not to share most of it here. Despite all she did, I'm so protective of her that it hurts to say these things about her. But the longer I was treated this way, the more I retreated and hid myself behind her gigantic shadow. The only way to be accepted or loved in my household was to be like her. But I couldn't have been more different if I tried. Or perhaps I tried to be different to see if I was still worth loving.

This isn't a story about how awful my mom was (she could be), or how terrible and deeply rooted in misogyny and sexism the things she said to me were (they were). I've done enough therapy to understand why my mom was the way she was. I love and forgive her, and I know she did the best she could with what she had. It is also true, however, that her comments left a deep, ugly impact on me. If you're an adult living on this earth, then by now you are probably aware of how much impact your childhood experiences, especially those involving your parents, had on you.

And that never became more apparent to me than when I left the law and started my own business. Every insecurity I had, every wound hiding just beneath the surface, reared its ugly head. If you have difficulty taking up space, or lean toward being perfectionistic, a people pleaser, anxious, or insecure, these tendencies may come to light as you build your business. While that might sound like something you would want to avoid, in reality, it can lead to a journey of self-discovery with incredible growth opportunities.

TEAR IT DOWN

My dad thought splashing cold water on your face cured all difficult emotions. I was (am!) a sensitive kid who cried more than the women sent home on *The Bachelor*. Every time I'd cry, my dad would say, "Splash some cold water on your face!" Although I don't agree with his parenting choice to not allow me to express and process emotions, I have adopted his cold-water tactic as a lighter reset moment when I need to move forward from something. And let's just say, I've had to splash a lot of cold water on my face since I started my business.

It takes courage to be the recognized face of an online business. It is like stepping out onto an empty stage naked while staring into a crowd of strangers. It is one thing to work in an office or have a job where you only meet customers face-to-face. It's an entirely different thing to do the bulk of your job online, using platforms that cater to people around the world. If you weren't afraid of being seen before, you will be now.

Let's discuss some of the things you may experience, or are already experiencing, as an entrepreneur, and how to navigate through and turn those moments of vulnerability into growth lessons. Hearing about all of these obstacles might make you want to go back to a time when you didn't have your own business. That's certainly not my intention. In my experience, and in the experiences of those around me, many of the things we'll discuss in this chapter are common; they're part of the process of putting yourself out there on the internet. If there's a good chance something might happen, it's best to address it head-on. We don't need to run away from these things. We can proudly hold our heads up high, knowing we're not alone in this thing called entrepreneurship. If you don't ever experience any of the feelings I'm talking about here, phew! I'm glad you're coming out unscathed.

As I'm sure you know, people on the internet have lots of thoughts about things. Keyboard warriors comment on how you look, what you say, and how you say it. Unkind comments can range anywhere from being mean-spirited, judgmental, and bullying, to racist, sexist, homophobic, xenophobic, transphobic, anti-Semitic, or other hate speech. Nearly all businesses also deal with actual or threatened vitriolic reviews from disgruntled customers, regardless of the veracity of their claims. Several of my customers have struggled to remove mean, dishonest, or hate-filled reviews about them or their businesses online after they wouldn't refund a customer's money (despite a clear "no refunds" policy) or otherwise comply with their demands.

You may also experience judgment from your own community. One of the most common complaints I hear is from people starting a coaching, course, or creator business in a more traditional profession who have received hateful messages for trying to be part of their industry. For example, money coaches sometimes report that they receive negative comments and judgment from some colleagues in the financial community, like accountants, CPAs, and financial planners.

Maybe one of the most hurtful or surprising places from which you might receive pushback is your own family and friends. Change isn't just difficult for you to make. It's difficult for those around you to see, too. Sometimes they want to keep you safe, to protect you from what they see as the "risky" path you're taking with entrepreneurship. Other times people project their own fears and insecurities onto you. If something would be scary for them, they think it must feel and be the same for you, too. If you leave your job to start your own business, you may be judged by your coworkers or boss. As you know, I certainly heard my fair share of opinions from my colleagues and bosses as I made my way out of the law firm.

I don't know about you, but the judgment I got from colleagues, family, friends, and my peers was way easier to deal with than the negative self-talk I put myself through. There was nothing they could say to or about me that I likely hadn't thought myself. As we discussed throughout chapter 5, it is common to deal with things like impostor syndrome, comparison trap, and a scarcity mindset as you're working to build your business. Although those emotions and feelings are sometimes triggered by things other people say about us or to us, they ultimately hit a sore spot only we knew we had. As adults and entrepreneurs, it is ultimately our job to deal with our own stuff and not make it the rest of the world's problem.

Even though entrepreneurship helps you to confront difficult things head-on, things you may have otherwise avoided in life, this stuff can get in your head. As entrepreneurs, we spend so much of our time alone. We often don't have many people around us who do the same work, or really anyone who even understands it. So when someone leaves you a hateful comment on a piece of content, or you get a nasty reply to one of your emails, it can leave you feeling like you're the only person in the world dealing with these types of things. I bring this up not to scare you; rather, I want you to feel less alone, and realize that what feels like, and is, a really painful moment might actually turn out to be a beautiful growth opportunity.

If you're obsessively checking your numbers (like revenue, followers, and subscribers), tossing and turning in bed at night, worrying you're not doing things right or enough, or dreaming in Instagram Reels, you might be too closely intertwined with your business. Whether it's actual burnout or you're just dancing awfully close to the edge of it, you know something's wrong when you want to go live out in the woods and not speak to another human again. You might even feel like you're working day and night on your business, and you can't remember the last time you got through a conversation without wondering how your email list subscriber count was doing. For me, when I dreaded doing things I once loved (and kept putting my keys in the freezer), I knew I'd pushed myself too hard. I hadn't taken care of the actual me, just the CEO me.

So now that we see what might be in store for us and how we might feel if we're too closely intertwined with our businesses, how do we navigate it? What do you do to not just pick yourself up from the difficult times, but actually come out better on the other side? Let's talk.

BUILD IT BACK UP

One of the best ways to combat feedback and criticism is to have a strong sense of self. One of my favorite mentors, Jamie Mendell, once equated that with how a tree improves its chances of surviving a storm as it deepens its roots and widens its trunk. The deeper you dig into who you really are, the stronger your foundation becomes. Not only will you be able to withstand whatever strong winds come your way, but some won't even move you.

Who Are You?

I came into entrepreneurship without a clear sense of who I really was or who I wanted to be. I couldn't make a decision about anything. This wasn't because I was extremely flexible or open-minded. I truly didn't know what I wanted. As my business grew, so did the criticism I received. At the time, I didn't have strong enough roots to stand in my power and let it wash over me. Instead, it knocked me over entirely. I thought every mean comment or criticism about me was true. I hesitated to create, say, or write anything out of fear of what people would say. Each hurtful comment brought my productivity to a screeching halt. As the comments increased,

I knew I couldn't go on in that way. By then I had learned putting yourself out there, especially online, opens you and your work up to feedback. And that usually, the harshest feedback has more to do with the person saying it than who they're saying it to. I needed to grow stronger roots and build a stronger foundation so I could be more stable as I received it. But how?

In order for you to discover what you truly want, you first have to stop listening to what everyone else wants. It is easy to accidentally consume too much content. By having such constant access to everyone's opinions and day-to-day lives online, we lose touch with our own intuitions and feelings and start honoring others' instead. When it comes to creators' opinions on business strategies, it's easy to turn what you see online from being examples of *ways* to do things to the only or best option. There's a difference between learning from experts and endlessly searching for other people's opinions without ever forming your own.

Maybe it's the number of decisions you're forced to make on a nearly daily basis as an entrepreneur, or how much of your true self your business will require, but the act of building your business day-to-day will help you plant deeper roots. Like Goldilocks, you realize what you don't like before you know what you do like. For example, whether you try one of the Big 3 platforms, a new-to-you social media app, or a new style of content, you might not like something you thought you would or that your friend likes. This is where your roots begin to take hold: If you find something you enjoy and it's working for you, listen to the internal feedback you're getting about *why* this works for you instead of the external feedback you hear about why it shouldn't. Remember what we discussed in chapter 6: We're interested in what makes you unique. In order to stand out, you have to actually be unique and show it, too.

Like most things in life, in business you learn by doing. The more you work with people or sell products, you may realize you enjoy certain ways of doing it. For example, many of my customers start out offering one-on-one coaching services because they heard they "had to" from someone online. But once they start their coaching practice, they might not love coaching clients that way, or how much of a time-for-money trade it is. Some of them have gone on to discover that they like selling online courses, digital products, or group programs better. Others love coaching clients one-on-one, and vehemently reject the idea that they "have to" offer online courses or digital products. Luckily there's something for everyone and no right way to build a business.

Absolute statements, like "You have to be on TikTok!" or "All businesses who don't use AI are going to fail!" are not helpful. Whether it's luck, the algorithm lottery, or that intangible special something, people's performance on various platforms seems somewhat random.

There's something about putting yourself out there in your business and getting more comfortable with taking up space that encourages you to take on more risks or try new things in other areas of your life. Here are a few examples of others who have been inspired to create after becoming entrepreneurs:

- Online tech expert and business strategist Louise Henry started the nonprofit organization Tim's Club in honor of her brother, Tim, and others with autism and intellectual disabilities. Since Louise knows how to build an email list, design a marketing strategy, and ask for what she needs (sales in her business's case and donations in her charity's case), she's successfully translated her business skills into a successful personal passion project.
- Copywriter Katelyn Collins finds inspiration in her clients' work and hobbies. From learning more about finances to van life, Katelyn feels that her clients' work has inspired her to explore areas she might not have otherwise.

- Registered dietitian and business coach Jaime Mass was inspired by her clients to learn more about money, investing, and real estate. Her business has allowed her more time and location flexibility, which she's taken advantage of to travel the world with her husband. She now intentionally spends more time in nature, because she's conscious of how much time we spend indoors, behind a desk, on our computers.

Finding Confidence

Personally, finding entrepreneurship has been like the satisfying click of a seat belt being fastened. While my business has directly sparked professional interests, it has also inspired me personally. To start, my business has made me more confident. Not because I've always done everything well or things have always gone smoothly. But through running my business I've learned I can always figure things out. Thanks to a love for what I do, I can adjust and pivot when things aren't going well. I don't give up; rather, I'm excited to learn how to turn things around. Knowing I can navigate whatever comes my way has made me more open to trying new things, putting myself out there, and being a beginner. Recently, I climbed a glacier nearly two-thousand feet in Norway. Pre-entrepreneur me wouldn't have even signed up for such a crazy (and cold) adventure. But I know I can do hard things. Whether your business has a direct or indirect impact on your personal life, the opportunity for growth is incredible.

Your self-confidence will also grow through your dedication to your business, even through hard times. Whether you're not seeing the results you want, or you're in the phase of entrepreneurship where you're doing a whole lot more building than selling, you will feel more than proud when you come out on the other side. You know what builds character?

- Emailing your seven-person email list like there are a thousand people on it.
- Showing up on social media, even when only one person watches your video.
- Running your group program with two people in it, even though you hoped to sell it to ten.

With every single sale you run, promo you design, or marketing strategy you execute, you'll learn from your wins and mistakes. Over time, you'll start to recognize *why* things are going well or not going well. This is absolutely key to your long-term business success. You have to learn the pathways to making things tick. You will be able to self-diagnose and adjust, sometimes even on the fly in the middle of a launch. You will surprise yourself with how you showed up, despite things not going smoothly or the way you'd hoped. And one day you'll look back and realize you're a lot more confident than you were when you started. Plus, if you can't stand up and speak before two people, or go live on Instagram with three people watching, what makes you think you'll be ready when there are a hundred or five hundred? Now's the time to practice and build that muscle.

Let Them Be Wrong

There was a time, long before I'd set healthy boundaries with my phone, when I'd open social media first thing each morning to see yet another mean comment. Whether it was someone calling me (or my dog!) ugly or trying to poke holes in the veracity of what I had said, it was all painful to see. It is hard not to defend yourself (and especially my dog Hudson). You want to reply back to every person, especially those whose comments are incorrect, and teach them a lesson. It's only natural to want to set the record straight, defend your education and knowledge, and fight back against a bully. It is also incredibly exhausting and distracting. I felt like I was constantly putting out fires, only for another to ignite right before my eyes.

Within your own space, there are likely many different opinions about what you do. Although creating some content around how you differ from other approaches in your space is good, it's never helpful to make all of your content about it. I followed a fitness account, for example, that spent so much of their time tearing down a competing approach that I forgot what they did and why I even followed them in the first place. Balance your unique differentiators with an even greater amount of content about what you actually do, what you believe, and why. If a trainer preaches the importance of practicing slow, gentle daily movement instead of high-intensity training, I want to hear about how the benefits of gentler movement over high-intensity interval training will help me. Some people may push back, but there's enough room for everyone's various fitness needs online.

Every once in a while, I receive comments on my social media content from nonlawyers challenging me on my legal knowledge. Recently, someone repeatedly and angrily commented on my content claiming I was "ripping everyone off" because "everyone knows you can mail yourself a document for copyright protection." From a legal perspective, this comment was dead wrong. The myth of a "poor man's copyright" has taken on a life of its own. Because I didn't want people to see this person's incorrect comment and mistake it as true, I felt I had to reply. But when the person continued to harass me about the same issue, I knew it was time to let it go. Not only do you have to let it go in practice, but mentally, as well. In the early days, I spent too much time fuming about how rude and ridiculous the person was being. But over time, I saw all that did was negatively impact me and my business. It took me away from what I should have been focusing on: growing my business and moving forward. It's not worth my time to fight the one or two keyboard warriors who feel greater in number than they really are. My time should go toward attracting more of the people actually looking for and appreciating my help.

If you fight every injustice you see on social media, you will burn out faster than a sparkler on a birthday cake. As your business and audience grow, you will get more feedback and more of people's projected issues thrown onto you. But it's not always your job or responsibility to set the record straight. The more you can let them be wrong, or even just have a difference of opinion, the better you will be able to stay in the game.

You Are Not Your Revenue

In online entrepreneurship, you become the face of your business. Not only are you the person likely servicing clients or creating the products you sell, but you also appear in all of the ads, social media content, and emails. If you're not careful, you can easily become enmeshed with your business. It becomes harder and harder to tell where you end and your business begins. I can't tell you how many eyeroll-inducing dinners I've sat through with online business owners who had nothing to talk about except how many followers they, or someone else in the industry, had. Just like someone's weight, I find your follower count to be the least interesting thing about you.

Early on, it's very easy to become one with your business. You eat, sleep, and breathe all parts of it. Eventually, though, the goal is to separate you as a person from your business so you don't take the ups and downs of entrepreneurship personally. You are the same person regardless of whether your business makes $1 or $1 million in revenue. Either way, you are not your revenue.

You are you, no matter how your business does. No one can take that away from you. You aren't defined by how many followers you have or how big your email list is. Having a higher follower count doesn't make you a better person, let alone a better coach, creator, or maker.

Honestly, outside of a very small group of people, no one really cares or even knows what most of that means. I can count on one hand how many people in my life care about the size of my email list. Even then, they know that doesn't mean anything *about* me as a person. It means my business has a big email list. My email list is the size it is because I have consistently emailed my list for over eight years. My emails provide a lot of value and I've created thousands of pieces of content with calls to action in them. The size of my email list doesn't define me or how good my business is. It means I have executed what turned out to be a successful business strategy after a lot of trial and error.

What you do in your business doesn't have to be synonymous with you as a person, it can just be what you do for a living. Although it is improving, the hustle culture will make you believe that you need to eat, sleep, and breathe entrepreneurship in order to be successful. It's almost treated like an initiation into entrepreneurship. While I do think an initial hustle period is not only common but possibly necessary to get your business off the ground, it's not something you should or can sustain forever. There are a lot of parts of my life, and hobbies I do, that I keep completely private and separate from my business. While I don't share about my marriage or friends as often, I'm happy to share my workouts or what I'm reading. Those are connection points I tend to have in common with my audience. Choosing what I do and do not share allows me to retain a healthier boundary and remember that I am not my business.

Boundaries Within Yourself

Change starts within. If you feel like you've lost yourself in the process of building your business, it's time to set some boundaries.

To start, pay attention to your mindset and attitude around how you identify as an entrepreneur. For example, do you catch yourself admiring other people who have lots of followers on social media simply because of their follower count? Or do you often judge someone's business as being "good" or "bad" because of those numbers? If you're not defining yourself by it, you have to stop defining others by it, too. Pay attention to your self-talk. Notice what comes up. Do you put a lot of judgment, harsh criticism, or unnecessary pressure on yourself? Are you focusing only on growing bigger, faster, and stronger without ever questioning why or whether it's necessary? Be curious and stay open to whatever comes up for you. But maintain healthy boundaries even within yourself.

While it's incredible that we can create businesses through social media or even from a smartphone, that ability has consequentially blurred the lines of where work and personal lives begin and end. I'm often checking myself to see whether I'm working to live or living to work. The apps you use to grow your business are the same ones you use to find a quinoa salad recipe for dinner. But you don't want the relative ease and flexibility of growing an online business to overtake your personal life.

During my dad's illness, I realized how attached I was to my business and that pushed me to want to change. I have empathy for my past self, who was so scared and in so much pain that she numbed herself out by scrolling mindlessly on social media. I'm thankful that I pivoted and started setting boundaries with myself and my work, too.

One of the things that helped me shift was starting to treat my business like work. That might seem obvious to you, but when you love what you do (and subconsciously love distracting yourself with work to avoid difficult feelings), it's easy to work all the time and not even realize it. Here are a few ways that helped me to healthfully separate from my work:

- Shutting down my computer/devices at the end of a workday so I couldn't easily access them.
- Accessing certain platforms on my desktop/laptop only, and deleting the apps from my phone (e.g., Pinterest, YouTube, Instagram).
- Not having work email on my phone unless I was traveling (not on vacation).
- Cleaning up my workspace at the end of each day and resetting for the following day.
- Shifting my mindset about how much I admired some people online simply for having large followings.
- Choosing carefully who I spend my time with, and seek friendships with, to ensure they're people with values similar to mine.
- Seeking out and nurturing personal hobbies that have nothing to do with my business, and many of which I never share publicly.
- Getting dressed for work, or at least changing out of athleisure or pajamas.
- Planning something for the end of the day, like a family walk, a tennis match, or a visit to the beach to help transition out of work mode.
- Turning off nearly all notifications on my phone so I'm able to do focused work and be present when I'm not at work.
- Allowing myself to be fully off when I take time away or go on vacation, instead of half-assing it and as a result not feeling rejuvenated.
- And my favorite tip of all: showering and changing into comfortable clothes at the end of the day to signal to my brain and body that work is over, and it's now time to begin to relax.

To Hustle or Not to Hustle

Did that list have you rolling your eyes? I understand. You might be in the thick of it right now, whether with your life or your business. If it's life, I get it and I was right where you are. These tips aren't always an option or practical, given your circumstances. I wasn't setting these types of boundaries at the outset. I do believe there's somewhat of a "healthy" hustle period required to build a successful business. There's no way around it: Starting a business is difficult and requires you to wear many hats. If you're in this stage, this might be a chapter you come back to when your business is up and running. For me, that took a few years. It was only then I began to feel that I might have an unhealthy relationship with both social media and my business in general. When or if the time is right for you, this chapter will be here to support you.

While so much of your relationship with your business will come from within, there are also boundaries that need to be set with others to maintain a healthy lifestyle, too.

Boundaries with Others

When it comes to setting business boundaries with others, you have two primary groups of people to deal with: customers and your audience/the general public. The majority of your customers are likely lovely people. I've had positive experiences with 99 percent of the people who have ever purchased from me. But thanks to a little something psychologists call negativity bias, the ones you will remember are the other 1 percent.

Here are the two best tips I can give you about setting boundaries with customers:

1. It is absolutely impossible to make everyone happy all the time. Whatever you do, it will piss someone off.
2. You can't control, nor are you responsible for, other people's emotions or reactions.

With that in mind, we have to stop ourselves from getting sucked down every rabbit hole a disgruntled customer tries to drag us down. There's a difference between providing great customer service, which I like to think my company does, and running myself ragged trying to make difficult people happy. This is one of the biggest perks to getting legal protection in place for your business. By having clearly communicated rules and policies in place, you will avoid awkward conversations and boundary pushers trying to get more than they're owed. This isn't important just for your sanity and energy; it's also important for your bottom line. Time costs money. And as a small business owner, you can't afford to spend time on one-off issues over and over again.

With the understanding that you and your business are separate entities, you won't have to waste as much energy feeling guilty or badly about disgruntled customers. It's not *you* saying no to the refund request; it is your business's policy. You are not a bad person for having rules and sticking to them. You're a business owner who is doing what you need to do to protect your business at all costs. Sometimes, as a business owner, it's worth it to bend the rules just to resolve an issue and no longer expend precious energy on it. The point is, the choice is always yours. Stand strong in your decision and don't apologize or fret over it any longer.

Your customers might also demand a lot of your time and attention. It's important for you to have time and communication boundaries at the outset of working with someone. For example:

- How can your clients contact you? Via email, phone, text?
- What if one of your clients direct-messages you through social media? Is this allowed?
- How often do you check your messages?
- How quickly can your client expect a response?
- What are your working or "office" hours when your clients can typically reach you?
- How often are your clients able to check in with you or ask questions? (For example, some coaches who use Voxer, a walkie-talkie-like messaging app, set daily time limits for voice memos.)
- How long does your support last? When does your contract end?

For example, customers who purchase my online legal program get access to a private community for support. I ask all customers to post their questions there, so that my answers can help the entire community. From time to time, I get Instagram DMs from someone saying, "Hi! I'm a customer. Can you tell me X, Y, and Z about how to legally protect my business?" I politely ask them to post the same question in our private community or to email it if they're uncomfortable posting it for other people to see.

You might think that your business doesn't have the volume or demand for this type of strict boundary yet, but I'm thankful that I created this boundary when my business was tiny and my customers were few and far between. All of these small boundaries you set add up to allow you to be a more focused and productive entrepreneur. One day, you will look back and realize they are part of what allowed you to actually grow your business. You need enough white space to be able to execute your dreams.

Your Business, Your Way

Thanksgiving is my Super Bowl. Not because I agree with the origins of the holiday (I don't!), but because it's the only holiday that solely focuses on food and togetherness instead of gifts. When I started my online business, I hadn't ever thought about the fact that Thanksgiving is a prime-time sale period. For years I'd cursed under my breath as I heard stories of big-box stores opening earlier and earlier, with reports of people skipping their family dinners to stand in line for a gigantic TV. I didn't want to turn my own business into a digital version of that. I didn't want it for myself, or for my team either. So even though it went against what everyone told me I "had to" do, and even though my competitors often ran their biggest sales of the year on Black Friday, I decided to skip it. Could we generate loads more sales if we ran a great Black Friday sale? I'm sure! But I wouldn't know because in eight years, I've never run one. Instead, I spend Black Friday in my pj's, lapping up another helping of my infamous cranberry sauce, and unplugging. I hope my team does, too.

You get to build your business according to your values and priorities. If money isn't always your top priority, you get to choose whether you'd rather run another sale or not. Make sure you don't miss the opportunity to do things your way because you're too busy doing things someone else's way. The more you confidently embody doing things your way, the less you'll feel controlled or influenced by what's going on around you.

Your Evergreen Machine

I don't want to paint a false dichotomy here. With a lot of the strategies you've learned so far, it's not really a choice between "making money" in your business and taking time off. If you set up your business correctly, use evergreen content strategies, and build out the funnel we've discussed, your business could be making sales while you're eating Thanksgiving leftovers. Mine does!

The idea here is to give yourself a break and permission to do things your way, even if one of the alternatives could be "better" than what you choose.

Support

I was one of those people who liked to do things myself, because if I didn't, they'd surely be done incorrectly. Then I started a business.

Allowing yourself to get both internal and external support will help you to scale your business. You can't do this alone, especially if you have a service-based business (since there's only one you and only twenty-four hours in a day). So, let's look at why support is crucial to your business's long-term health. First, we'll start with internal support from within your own business.

Internal support comes from your team—contractors and employees you hire to not just take things off your plate but to execute tasks better than you could. Hiring support will free you up to focus on bigger-picture issues in your business, like marketing strategies, product development, client work, PR/collaboration opportunities, and evergreen content creation. Many solo entrepreneurs get stuck doing admin tasks, managing projects, onboarding clients, handling contracts and payments, and other tasks that keep them from moving their businesses forward. Here are a few ways to think through the kinds of support you may need for your business:

- What types of tasks in your business don't require you (e.g., graphic design, creating your website, etc.)?

- What tasks or processes can be automated (e.g., payments and contracts)?
- What tasks or processes can be organized into a standard operating procedure (SOP) document, so someone on your team can handle it instead (e.g., requests for refunds, booking you on a podcast, etc.)?
- What are things you catch yourself doing each day or week, thinking, "If only I could get rid of doing _____, I could finally get to ___!" (e.g., bookkeeping, writing sales copy, designing your website, etc.)?
- What are some things you enjoy doing in your business that someone else could do better? These are typically things you don't *have to* do, but that you might enjoy doing (e.g., website management, graphic design, podcast or YouTube editing, etc.).

The more you can focus on money-generating or needle-moving activities in your business, the better. That's hard, though, when you're stuck on tedious, time-consuming tasks that you don't have to be doing. The other big benefit to having internal support in your business is the opportunity to create some white space for you. When I first started hiring, I thought I had to fill every now-free moment with big-picture CEO tasks. But over time I also recognized the value in having white space—downtime to simply just be, unwind, or do something creative. That's often when I get my best ideas and have breakthrough moments.

Not only is it more fun to work as a team, but hiring team members is another contributing factor to personally separating yourself from your business. It's easier to feel one with your business when you're the owner, manager, assistant, and tech support guru. There was something about not having to do everything myself, and feeling supported by others who truly wanted to work for my company, that made me feel like my business was something bigger than just me.

Hiring team members will certainly be necessary as your business grows—and it's important to do this legally. There's a big legal difference between hiring contractors and employees. The US and state governments heavily regulate how a worker is classified. You can't hire someone and then choose to designate them as an employee or a contractor. Instead, it matters the manner in which the person works for you, when, and where. I recommend reading the free resources on irs.gov/businesses to familiarize yourself with the factors used to designate someone as either a contractor or an employee. If you misclassify someone, the fines and penalties can be significant. Talk to your local small business attorney or CPA for further guidance.

We also need external support from people in our lives who don't work for us. Whether it is family, friends, or your peers, you need people around you who will be there to listen, cheer you on, and offer you support in whatever way you need it. On one hand, I enjoy having friends who don't have anything to do with online business. There are many days when I only want to talk to someone who doesn't care about social media or email lists. But on the other hand, over time I've learned how helpful it is to have people in my life who understand exactly what I'm going through. The key is to surround yourself with people who are also on a journey of not self-identifying with their business or social stats. For a while, I spent time with people who talked about people being good or bad based on their social following. You can't help but absorb that type of energy when it's all you know. But as I set out to shift my mindset and personally separate myself from my business to protect my sanity, I surrounded myself more with people who were on the same path.

If you're making a career change or a big life move, there may be some people who don't agree with or understand your decision.

This seems to only get worse when those same people don't understand what online business is. I'm not advocating that you cut off every person who doesn't understand or love what you're doing. But they may not be the people to look to for support. Find people who want to cheer you on, people who have walked in your shoes and tend to get it. As the brilliant Brené Brown says, "If you are not in the arena getting your ass kicked on occasion, I am not interested in or open to your feedback."

WHAT WE LEARNED

- Building your own business online comes with its own set of challenges, but in fact they are opportunities for growth.
- Being so visible may bring out insecurities, negativity, and judgment (from both yourself and others).
- Separating yourself from your business is healthy. It will help you to take feedback and criticism less personally.
- Hiring support in your business is not only a great way to grow it, but a healthy way to separate from your business, too.
- Seek support from within and from people in your life who offer you encouragement and positive energy. If people who aren't "in the arena with you" don't get it or support you, let them be.

WHAT'S TO COME

- Action plans on how to integrate what you've learned here moving forward.
- A letter to read before you go.

CHAPTER 11

You've Got This

On a sticky, hot July day in 2012, I walked into the Philadelphia Convention Center for the first of my five-day bar exam with a big smile on my face. I was so excited to see my law school classmates, many of whom I hadn't seen since we'd graduated months earlier. They asked me, "What's wrong with you? Why are you smiling? Aren't you freaking out?!" I wasn't smiling because I thought I'd ace the bar (in fact, I was convinced I was going to fail) or because I had a cocky attitude, but I felt completely at ease knowing I'd given my all in studying for it. If that wasn't good enough, then honestly nothing would be. My back pain from studying twelve-plus hours per day for months told me I'd left it all on the line.

We can't always control what happens to us in life or how things go. All we can control is how we show up and how we respond. As you leave this book behind, I want you to feel confident in growing your business, knowing you're putting your best foot forward. And putting your best foot forward might look different for you than for everyone else around you, and that's okay.

Whether it was years ago or when you first opened this book, you likely started your entrepreneurial journey feeling scared, overwhelmed, or worried whether you could make this whole business thing work. No matter how long you've had your business, you've probably experienced several moments when you've felt discouraged and frustrated. Maybe you weren't sure you could or even wanted to keep running your business. And if you're anything like me or thousands of my clients, you even had moments you were pretty sure you wanted to quit and call the whole thing off.

My hope is that you now feel less alone and more understood. I hope you know now that what you felt and are feeling is normal. Those of us in the arena with you, building a business on our own, feel it, too. These feelings don't always go away for good. They may come and go and peek their heads through at the most random or inconvenient times. But now you've got a plan.

Your business journey may feel unpredictable because businesses, especially the online sort, aren't stagnant. We're in an ever-changing environment, relying on apps and technology outside of our control that can change in an instant. But that's a good thing. You're at the forefront of a very exciting time in digital marketing, online entrepreneurship, and social media. You're part of something as it is changing. You can even be part of the change if you want to.

If you take only one thing away from what you've read here, let it be this: You can build a successful online business using a chill marketing system that doesn't require you to permanently attach yourself to your business, your phone, or ruin your personal life. Your business may not be the thing that makes you happy, but I hope it provides you the space and opportunity to seek it from within. With this book in your back pocket, you have the opportunity to craft a business plan and marketing strategy that suit you and the way you want to build your business. I hope I've shown you that there's no one way to build a business, show up online, or market your products. Not only are there countless ways to build a business, but you might create your own way that no one has seen before.

Before I send you off to conquer the online world, let's revisit what we've learned and put together an action plan.

ACTION PLAN #1: If you haven't started your business yet, but want to:

- Review chapter 3 on how to do the proper research on your business idea. You need to know whether there is demand, supply, and how you will uniquely differentiate yourself and your products.
- Review chapter 4 on how to budget to start your business so there's not too much financial pressure when it starts.
- Research business names, register your business, get business insurance, and start a business bank account.
- Review chapter 6 on how to create your first freebie, start creating social media content that has a call to action to your freebie (which will put them on your email list), and focus on nurturing your email list through consistent weekly emails.
- Review chapter 7 on how to create a product from the ground up that has long-lasting sales potential.

ACTION PLAN #2: If your business is up and running, but you want to have a more chill, effective marketing strategy that consistently brings in leads and clients:

- Audit your current content strategy. Where do you spend most of your time? Revisit chapter 9. Is most of your content searchable? How much of it is evergreen?

- Depending on what you find in your audit, revisit and pare down your content marketing strategy to focus on a solid discovery platform (one of the Big 3) and an effective nurture strategy (e.g., your email list, evergreen content on social).
- Review chapter 7 to see if there are any steps you missed in creating your signature product or create your first signature product.
- Review chapter 8 to create a marketing flywheel and funnel to drive leads toward purchasing your signature product.

Along this journey, you'll be tempted to deviate from what your intuition tells you. Don't squander this opportunity to choose your own path by walking down someone else's. You get to define your goals, values, and dreams. They don't have to look like someone else's to be valid. You don't owe anyone an explanation or justification for why you choose to do business the way you do. Depending on your goals, you can choose to do or not do things that everyone says are "required" (other than the legal stuff, of course.)

As artificial intelligence (AI) apps and tools creep further into our world and further saturate an already saturated social media space, remember that uniqueness always wins the day. No bot or AI tool will ever be able to sound, look, act, or react exactly like you. It can't take all of your experiences, knowledge, and unique perspectives and integrate them into copy without sounding like it was written by a robot.

You will experience all sorts of trends and external pressures as you build your business. Keep coming back to your home base. If you want to build a chill, yet still successful business, you can do so. You've just got to tune out the potentially AI-generated noise and tune into what you want.

As we come to the end, I'd like to share this letter I wrote to inspire you as you move forward in entrepreneurship:

Dear Friend,

You're embarking on the greatest journey. I know you might be worried about things now, but I'm here to tell you that things might go better than you could have imagined. Yes, you'll feel pulled and stretched along the way. But one day you'll look back and realize how much you've grown. You'll hear about how hard it is to build a business, and scary stories about times it didn't work out for others. Their story isn't your story. Put your head down and get back to work. Do what you must to block out the noise. Don't squander this opportunity, because it's a good one.

As someone walking this path alongside you, more than anything, I want to encourage you to remain curious. Get curious about strategies, opportunities, and ways of doing things. Be open to not knowing the answer. You don't need to know everything to be an expert in your space. Let your curiosity and openness lead your love for learning. You don't need to know how everything might turn out. There might be hidden lessons in that uncertainty. When things feel scary or uncertain, ask yourself, "What if this goes better than I can imagine right now? What if I remain open to the possibilities this may bring? What might I learn if I take this chance?"

I know you're an independent, strong, hardworking person. Please let your independence shine. The world needs to see you for who you are, not as a carbon copy of someone else. The world needs to get to know you and what makes you unique. Watching you live out your life's purpose as you confidently stand within who you are will inspire many others to find their own uniqueness.

Last but certainly not least, when things feel hard—which I know they will at times—do something to make yourself laugh. Life is so much bigger than social stats, subscriber counts, and the amount of revenue you make each month. Get out in nature. Put your bare feet in the grass. Don't lose sight of what's important to you and why you're doing this. When you send out an email without a subject line, giggle. When you forget a link in one of your most important email sequences, laugh. It's not that serious.

While building your business might not fix everything in your life, chances are that it will help you to become a stronger, more confident, and empowered person who can better handle life's challenges. You have support now, through an incredible community of peers and colleagues. You've surrounded yourself with like-minded, motivated people who see you for who you are and love you even more. Entrepreneurship has shown you that you're in the driver's seat. Life doesn't run you; you run your life.

From one entrepreneur who's just trying to figure it out to another: You've got this. Now go splash some cold water on your face.

xo,
Sam

Acknowledgments

I'm one of those people who always read the acknowledgments section in every single book. I love seeing the names of all the people who contributed to making a book come to life. But until I wrote my own, I truly had no idea just how much effort, by so many people, it really took to make a book happen. I know authors always say they couldn't have done it alone, but I truly would not be here without many of you.

I'm so grateful to Jenn Racioppi for connecting me to Richelle Fredson, my wonderful book coach and friend. Thank you, Richelle, for your patience and dedication during such a tough period in my life. I wouldn't have been able to write a proposal, or get this book published, without you. Anyone who wants to write a nonfiction book should contact Richelle, take her course, and listen to her podcast.

In March 2023, I went to a business retreat in Mexico. I had the hope and dream to write a book, but I wasn't sure how I would make it happen. I told all of the women at the retreat that my next step was to finish my proposal and get an agent. "I'm going to try to get Wendy Sherman!" I told them all. I wanted to shoot for the stars. I am so incredibly grateful Wendy took me on. Wendy, you have patiently answered all of my questions and held my hand along this journey. You believed in me and my dream to get this type of book deal, and with this incredible publisher. I'm so grateful for all of your guidance and support throughout this process. We did it!

To my editor, Nana K. Twumasi—thank you for believing in this project. You have been incredibly generous with your time and expertise to make this book the best it could be. It's been an incredible privilege to work with you. Thank you to Natalie Bautista and all the teams at Hachette Book Group and Balance.

To my incredible Sam Vander Wielen LLC team—thank you so much for everything you have all done to help support me in the pursuit of this dream. Lindsey, I wouldn't be able to function without you. You are an incredible teammate and an even better friend. I am beyond grateful for you every day. Thank you for all the times you encouraged me to keep going.

Leanne, my first hire! I can't believe how far we've come together and how much things have changed. Without you, I wouldn't be able to do any of this. Thank you for taking such good care of our customers all these years.

Michelle, you've been there for me on both the business and the personal side throughout this entire journey. I'm endlessly grateful for our bond and friendship. You inspire me every day with your creativity, sense of humor, and commitment to your creative endeavors. You are the best friend I could ask for, even if you are a miserable childless cat lady. I'm so grateful to you and Ant for adopting me and Ryan as your on-Long-Island family.

I'm so fortunate to be surrounded by a group of hardworking, talented women like Katelyn Collins (thank you for being such a supportive friend and writing such amazing copy!), Christina Roberts, Natasha Samuel, Jessica Sciuva, and Megha Khosla.

My incredible mindset coach and dear friend, Jennifer Diaz, has been an integral part of this book. So much of what I have taught you here was filtered through Jen's teachings. Jen helped me to feel confident enough to finish my proposal and to even go out and get my dream agent (hi, Wendy!) and publisher. She patiently listened to all of my "what if…" voice memos and encouraged me when I needed it most. More than anything, Jen always champions my need to rest, even when I resist it. As much as Jen has helped me as a coach, I cherish our friendship even more. Jen, you are an incredible person and I love you to pieces. I can't wait to read your book one day.

I don't know that my neck or nervous system would have been able to handle writing a book without the help of my weekly wellness crew—Ashley for taking such good care of me each Friday; Lorraine, Peter, and Karina for always kicking my butt at the gym; and the entire Energy family for giving me the best fitness community. You make me feel so strong, confident, and refreshed every week. Thank you to my therapist, Suzanna, for helping me through the hardest time in my life. Without you, I wouldn't have been able to stop crying long enough to write this book.

One of the best and most unexpected benefits of starting my own business was the incredible group of friends I have been able to make. I've met the best people in my life through online businesses and Instagram (see, I told you social media isn't all bad!). Jaime Mass, you've become like a sister to me (which is good, because Norm would have loved you like his daughter). I can't thank you enough for all you've done to support me and see me in my grief. I love and appreciate Simi Botic, Jamie Mendell, Louise Henry, Christina Castillo, Athena Concannon, Shila Griffith, Bonnie Galam, Danielle Swimm, and Margo Carroll.

I also have to thank Dr. Shannon McCurdy and the entire University of Pennsylvania hematology/oncology floor of nurses and med techs for giving me so much time with my dad, Norm. You took the absolute best care of him and for that, I am forever grateful.

Thank you to the thousands who have joined the Ultimate Bundle® over the years, purchased a template, followed me on social media, listened to my podcast On Your Terms®, or responded to an email of mine. I have the smartest cookies as customers and subscribers. I love having you as part of my community, and I'm forever grateful for your support.

Thank you to the thousands who have responded so positively and encouragingly over the years when I shared I was writing a book. I hope this book turned out to be everything you hoped for and more. If you finished reading it, email me "I LOVE PENGUINS" so I know.

Reading has played such a special part in my life. From our librarians, to every independent bookstore owner and employee, to book reviewers—thank you for all you do to get our stories in people's hands. There is no algorithm that can replace your expertise and spot-on recommendations.

I feel so lucky to live in the best neighborhood. I am especially grateful for our wonderful neighbors and friends-turned-family, Marty and Jackie, for adopting me, Ryan, and Huddy into your family. We love you both. Thank you to Rose, Janet, Jen, Jennifer, and everyone else in our storybook neighborhood for all of your love, support, and encouragement.

Mom, I miss you so much. Thank you for showing me what it was like to be a book-obsessed woman. All I ever wanted to do was read so that I could hang out with you while you were studying for med school. You inspired me to go after my dreams, especially after seeing all that you overcame to chase yours. I love you and I forgive you. I'm glad I grew in your belly, too.

Acknowledgments

NORM! Dad, I printed out all of my emails and made them into a book! Well, sort of. You were the first one to tell me that you thought my weekly emails were so good that they could become a book. I wrote this entire book with you at the forefront of my mind. You'll be happy to know (and not surprised) that I also wrote it with lots of snacks on hand, usually from Trader Joe's. I couldn't have done this without your constant encouragement and enthusiasm to share what I had to say. I'm not going to lie, I miss you so badly that it physically hurts. Knowing that this dream we both shared is now out into the world is bittersweet. I wish you could have been here to celebrate its release, but please know that you are a part of each and every one of these pages. I love you so much.

To my sister, Cara; brother-in-law, Steve; and two adorable nephews, Sebastian and Oliver, thank you for all of your love and support. I don't know of many siblings who could have navigated what we have gone through together so well. Sebby and Ollie make me so hopeful for a brighter future. I love them to pieces and am so proud to call myself their Aunt Sammy. I love you all so much.

Hudson, my baby Bernedoodle, I wouldn't have been able to write this book without you forcing me to take breaks and peel my eyes away from the screen. You came into my life just days after my dad's worst diagnosis, and for that, I am grateful. You kept me moving, laughing, and smiling through a period I otherwise wouldn't have. I mean it when I tell you every day that you're my best friend. You are the best little guy I could ask for. Thank you so much for all of the joy you bring to me, Ryan, and everyone you meet. You are the light of my life.

And last but certainly not least, to my husband and best friend, Ryan. You know how much I hate it when people publicly profess things to their spouse when they could just tell them when they're sitting next to them. So when you read this, just look at me and let me tell you what I really feel: I love you so much, even though everyone always tells you that you look like Ryan Reynolds. If that makes me Blake Lively, I'll take it.

To you, for reading this book and taking a chance on yourself. Thank you so much for including me on your business journey. You've got this.

Index

Index

Index

Index

About the Author

SAM VANDER WIELEN is an attorney-turned-entrepreneur and the founder of Sam Vander Wielen LLC, a leading contract template shop for online business owners that generates multi-seven-figures in revenue annually. Since 2017, Sam has helped over 350,000 online entrepreneurs legally protect their online businesses, all while navigating the devastating back-to-back loss of her parents, her own brain surgery, and becoming a caretaker. Sam's content focuses on legal protection, email list building strategies, and evergreen funnels. Sam lives in New York, on Long Island, with her husband, Ryan, Bernedoodle, Hudson, too many coffee mugs, and a towering stack of TBR fiction.